"A major contribution to feminist criminology, Evelyn Rose's book shifts the debate about domestic violence law and policy to an international plane. By implicating the structures, institutions and agencies of the state in a spectrum of harms to women and children separate from the original domestic violence victimization, she identifies a 'state crime' of domestic violence susceptible to management by increments of justice and equity. A game-changer."

— *Evan Stark, Professor Emeritus, School of Public Affairs and Administration, Rutgers University, New Jersey, United States. Author of Coercive Control: How Men Entrap Women in Personal Life (Oxford, 2007).*

"Evelyn Rose's valuable new book joins those of MacKinnon, Pateman and Tickner in deepening our analyses of how and why patriarchal states and their officials are complicit in, and perpetrators of, violence against women. *Domestic Violence as State Crime* has sharpened my feminist understandings."

— *Cynthia Enloe, Research Professor of Political Science, Clark University, Massachusetts, United States.*

"This searing and necessary book provides a new conceptual architecture for addressing domestic violence and holding states accountable for male violence against women. In a vital paradigm shift, Rose brings into focus the failure and complicity of states in the ongoing epidemic of domestic violence, re-invigorating radical feminist critiques of state power."

— *Michael Salter, Associate Professor of Criminology, School of Social Sciences, University of New South Wales, Sydney, Australia.*

"Eloquent, passionate and ambitious, this book examines the role of the state in the perpetration of domestic violence. Evelyn Rose cogently argues that there has been a failure to recognise and address domestic violence as a systemic, institutional and structural problem. She argues that the state is often presented as a neutral arbiter of harm, but in practice is implicated in domestic violence as an initiator, contributor and participant. This book is original, refreshing and compelling, and a must read for scholars, activists, policymakers and practitioners."

— *Nicola Henry, Professor of Social and Legal Studies, Social and Global Studies Centre, RMIT University, Melbourne, Australia.*

"This innovative and transformative book names domestic violence as state crime and will change the way we think about violence against women. Identifying state complicity in domestic violence from passive bystander to active agent, Rose's original and compelling intervention shows why new approaches are needed to this most devastating of crimes."

— *Jennifer Balint, Associate Professor in Socio-Legal Studies and Head of School of Social and Political Sciences, University of Melbourne, Australia.*

Domestic Violence as State Crime

Domestic Violence as State Crime presents a provocative challenge to the way that domestic violence is understood and addressed. Underpinned by a radical feminist perspective, the central argument of this book is that domestic violence against women constitutes a patriarchal state crime. By analysing the international, collective, structural, and institutional dimensions of this harm, the author outlines a spectrum of state complicity ranging from passive bystander to active producer, participant, and perpetrator.

The wide-ranging analysis in this book draws on data from comparable liberal-democratic contexts including Australia, the United States, and the United Kingdom, in order to comprehensively show how domestic violence state criminality functions in practice – even in the present and in supposedly progressive contexts. This analysis provides valuable insight into why this epidemic-scale crime is ever resistant to a diversity of contemporary interventions. Drawing its concepts into a cohesive whole, the book then posits an overarching feminist typological theory of domestic violence as state crime. It also considers how domestic violence might be addressed if we confront its state crime dimensions and adopt a more holistic and transformative approach to remedy, redress, prevention, and justice.

An accessible and compelling read, *Domestic Violence as State Crime* offers an innovative scholarly and activist contribution to the study of violence against women, feminism, criminology, and the broader critical study of law, politics, and society. It will appeal to anyone who is interested in thinking differently about domestic violence and the state.

Evelyn Rose is an Honorary Fellow in Criminology in the School of Social and Political Sciences at the University of Melbourne, Australia.

Crimes of the Powerful

Crimes of the Powerful encompasses the harmful, injurious, and victimising behaviours perpetrated by powerful groups, privately or publicly operated businesses, corporations, and organisations, as well as the state-mediated administrative, legalistic, and political responses to these crimes.

The series draws attention to the commonalities of the theories, practices, and controls of the crimes of the powerful. It focuses on the overlapping spheres and inter-related worlds of a wide array of existing and recently developing areas of social, historical, and behavioural inquiry into the wrongdoings of multinational organisations, nation-states, stateless regimes, illegal networks, financialisation, globalisation, and securitisation.

These examinations of the crimes of the powerful straddle a variety of related disciplines and areas of academic interest, including studies in criminology and criminal justice; law and human rights; conflict, peace, and security; and economic change, environmental decay, and global sustainability.

Gregg Barak, Eastern Michigan University, USA
Penny Green, Queen Mary University of London, UK
Tony Ward, Northumbria University, UK

Most recent titles in series:

Corrupt Capital
Alcohol, Nightlife, and Crimes of the Powerful
Kenneth Sebastian León

Domestic Violence as State Crime
A Feminist Framework for Challenge and Change
Evelyn Rose

For more information about this series, please visit: *https://www.routledge.com/ Crimes-of-the-Powerful/book-series/COTP*

Domestic Violence as State Crime

A Feminist Framework for Challenge and Change

Evelyn Rose

Routledge
Taylor & Francis Group

LONDON AND NEW YORK

First published 2022
by Routledge
2 Park Square, Milton Park, Abingdon, Oxon OX14 4RN

and by Routledge
605 Third Avenue, New York, NY 10158

Routledge is an imprint of the Taylor & Francis Group, an informa business

© 2022 Evelyn Rose

British Library Cataloguing-in-Publication Data
A catalogue record for this book is available from the British Library

Library of Congress Cataloging-in-Publication Data
A catalog record has been requested for this book

ISBN: 978-0-367-67689-6 (hbk)
ISBN: 978-0-367-67691-9 (pbk)
ISBN: 978-1-003-13237-0 (ebk)

DOI: 10.4324/9781003132370

Typeset in Bembo
by codeMantra

MIX
Paper from
responsible sources
FSC™ C013985

Printed in the United Kingdom
by Henry Ling Limited

For Tasha. I love you more than anything and wish I could have protected you. May the horrors of the past fade as your future brightens, my precious.

Contents

Acknowledgements

Many wonderful people have helped me see through this research and book project. To colleagues and friends at the University of Melbourne – thank you for your intellectual and professional support, and to Jennifer Balint and Sara Meger in particular. Outside of Melbourne University, Ben Moffitt and Nicola Henry also deserve thanks for their generosity. The amazing international online co-working community I belong to also deserves special mention, as do the many people in everyday life who've shown an interest in my work. From my dentist and osteopath to the local grocer and electrician, I've found that individuals from every walk of life are genuinely concerned about domestic and family violence and want to hear new ideas for understanding and addressing it. All of these people and the opportunities they've provided to discuss my work have bolstered my commitment to getting innovative feminist ideas out there. On that note, I want to mention my indebtedness to generations of courageous feminist pioneers and to Catharine MacKinnon in particular, whose intelligent, creative, and intuitive work on violence against women is the epitome of what I think feminist academic and activist work should be.

Last, but far from least, I have special individuals from my personal life to thank. Dear friends of my inner circle: the source of deep honesty, sharing, and comfort. And those at the centre of my life: my ever-supportive Nigel and my bright, beautiful, precious Tasha, who I love infinity times around the Universe.

Part I

Domestic violence, feminism, and state crime

Chapter 1

The need to radically rethink domestic violence

The shadow pandemic of the Covid era

> *It's 8:30am on an ordinary Wednesday morning in February 2020. On a peaceful, leafy suburban street in Brisbane, Australia, Hannah Clarke and her three children, Aaaliyah, six, Laianah, four, and Trey, three, are in their car, about to leave for the regular school run. Rowan Baxter, Hannah's ex-husband and the children's father, is hiding in the bushes, waiting. Once mother and children are all strapped into their car seats, he enters the front passenger side, douses his ex-wife and children with petrol, and sets them and the car alight. The car explodes in a ball of flames. All three children are stuck in the car and burned alive. Hannah escapes the car but cannot get her children out; she dies later that night in hospital of burns to 97 per cent of her body.[1]*

These horrific murders are a mere glimpse into an urgent global problem without compare. Domestic violence is a harm of such epidemic scale that at least a third of women worldwide have experienced victimisation, and high-income developed countries of the supposedly peaceful liberal-democratic West are no exception (WHO 2013; Bradel et al. 2019). In the United States, over ten million women have experienced intimate partner rape, and every fourteen hours a woman is fatally shot by her partner or ex-partner (NCADV 2017; 2020). In England and Wales, two women every week become intimate partner homicide victims (ONS 2019) and despite Australia's tiny population, an average of one woman every week is killed in similar circumstances (Walklate et al. 2019). The United Nations Office on Drugs and Crime (2019) recently confirmed that the most dangerous place for women is the home, and that this situation is not improving.

Since the onset of the global Covid-19 pandemic, domestic violence has only increased in prevalence and diversified in form. Government restrictions and lockdowns have forced couples and families into closer proximity with one another, providing new opportunities for unique and expanded repertoires of abuse and severely constraining victims' ability to seek help.

DOI: 10.4324/9781003132370-2

Research from the United Kingdom and Australia reveals that many perpetrators are using the pandemic and government restrictions as tools of abuse, including to justify enhanced micro-monitoring and surveillance, increase victims' isolation, and restrict access to food, medication, and other essentials (e.g. Boxall et al. 2020; Pfitzner et al. 2020; Women's Aid 2020). As well as escalating harms for those already living with domestic violence, newly abusive relationships are emerging. Across several global contexts, Boserup et al. (2020) report that domestic violence has increased by a third since the introduction of various lockdown measures. Domestic violence had already been widely described as an epidemic and a pandemic (e.g. Price 2018; Moreira & Pinto da Costa 2020), but the Executive Director of United Nations Women recently named it the "shadow pandemic" of Covid-19 (Mlambo-Ngcuka 2020: n.p.).

Sex, gender, domestic violence, and coercive control

The data tell us, loud and clear, that domestic violence is a gendered problem. Women do use violence in the family and it is also unacceptable, but the most prevalent and harmful domestic violence is used by men against women (Flood 2012; Kimmel 2013; Garcia-Moreno et al. 2015; Bradel et al. 2019).[2] The term 'domestic violence'[3] is now widely understood to encompass an array of controlling, abusive, and violent tactics which perpetrators use to dominate and control their partner, the relationship, and the family. Stark (2007) famously identified this as coercive control: a deliberate, instrumental harm which is contingent upon sexual inequality and which is overwhelmingly perpetrated by men against women. Common coercive control tactics include micro-monitoring, surveillance, stalking, isolation, psychological manipulation, financial abuse, derogatory sexual treatment, and a spectrum of intimidation and threats. Notably, physical violence is not always used if the perpetrator can maintain control without it, and because many tactics are invisible to outsiders, perpetrators can maintain a positive public image whilst waging a reign of terror at home. This type of domestic violence is often obscured, misunderstood, unreported, and undocumented, yet exceedingly harmful and dangerous (Breiding et al. 2014; Meyer & Frost 2019).

Coercive controlling domestic violence can become murder if the victim[4] dares to assert her autonomy and leave the relationship, which is precisely what happened for Hannah Clarke. Following these murders, a clear picture of Rowan Baxter's controlling and violent regime emerged (see Brook & Foster 2020; Gleeson 2020; Jepsen 2020; McGowan 2020). Friends and relatives attested to Rowan's constant manipulative and abusive treatment of his wife. Hannah's mother revealed that Rowan had monitored and stalked her daughter through her phone and social media, forced her to have sex with him every night, regularly made serious threats, and prohibited her from wearing revealing clothing including shorts, even though they lived in the subtropics and Hannah worked in the fitness industry. A victim support worker confirmed Hannah's disclosure of a spectrum of financial, verbal, emotional, physical, and sexual abuse. Police also reported that Hannah had sought their assistance several times during the marriage. When Hannah decided to leave her husband, he did not accept this new reality and tried to reassert control in numerous ways, leading Hannah to obtain a protective order. At the time he murdered his ex-wife and children, Rowan Baxter was due to appear in court for breaching this order and assaulting Hannah just a few weeks prior.

Crimes like this are a daily media feature and top priority social, cultural, political, and policy issue across the Western world. A diversity of victim protection, offender accountability and rehabilitation, and broader prevention measures are in place. We have respectful relationship education, couples counselling, helplines for victims and offenders, anger management and behaviour change programs, safety apps, risk assessment tools, protective orders, mandatory arrest policies, specialist law enforcement units and courts, and more. Yet domestic violence continues at epidemic levels. With all the attention, awareness, education, specific programs, and money being thrown at this problem, why have we not seen major improvements? Are we misunderstanding or mispresenting it in some way? Are we overlooking something vital?

What's the problem? Bad men, bad attitudes, and broken systems?

Since the 1990s and over the past decade in particular, there have been positive global shifts towards acknowledging the prevalence, severity, and urgency of addressing domestic violence. The problem is now widely recognised as the most pervasive gender-based harm worldwide, a pressing human rights concern, and critical social and political issue (Garcia-Moreno et al. 2015). Cross-contextually, it has been identified as stemming from sexual inequality, prescriptive gender roles, and problematic masculinity (e.g. UNGA 1993, 2003; Fulu et al. 2013). But despite acknowledging that domestic and other violence against women stems from structural inequality, international prevention initiatives often conceptually disconnect it from material political, economic, and social conditions (Salter 2016). It tends to be attributed to problematic individuals and abstract cultural ideas rather than substantive, institutional, structural, and state-level policies and practices. There is also limited recognition that the very same institutions, agencies, systems, and states that purportedly prohibit, prevent, and punish domestic violence actively contribute to its exacerbation and extension. This narrative production process is not neutral; rather, it is highly political. It enables institutional, structural, and state responsibility for the problem to be avoided and creates a limiting filter through which responses are imagined and designed.

In Australia, the recent Victorian Royal Commission into Family Violence exemplified this kind of progressive yet partial account. The Commission adopted a positive and reformist agenda yet persisted with conceptualising domestic violence as an individual, interpersonal, and cultural problem.[5,6] It officially undertook to investigate "systemic" issues and consider all levels of society including government and institutions in its investigations (RCFV 2015: 2,3). The final report progressively names domestic violence as a distinctly gendered problem that is "deeply rooted in power imbalances" and has causes that "are complex and include gender inequality" (RCFV 2016: 2). But despite frequent reiteration of inequality as the root of domestic violence, the Commission's account is largely individualistic: centring ill, addicted, poorly educated, or defectively acculturated men who require treatment, education, condemnation, or punishment (also see Yates 2020). Sexual inequality receives no serious attention and is not considered a substantive problem; rather, it is an unfortunate fact and is discursively equated with "community attitudes" (RCFV 2016: 2). Like inequality, attitudes have no apparent origin, and there is no serious consideration of responsibility for these issues. Although, notably, the report does acknowledge widespread problems with domestic violence response systems – and even notes discriminatory patterns in the way that violence and victims are treated – it avoids genuine critique of these deeply flawed systems and persists with the narrative of the state as a neutral authority.

But the truth is that the state is not simply a neutral arbiter of harm that occasionally neglects its duties due to unfortunate practical realities and bureaucratic bungling. It is not the oft-cited economic constraints, policy oversights, or lack of service integration (see e.g. Groves & Thomas 2014; RCFV 2016; DHHS 2018) that have made domestic violence a problem of epidemic proportions across the developed world. The uncomfortable reality is that domestic violence is so prevalent because it has been and continues to be created, legitimated, perpetuated, and even endorsed by the very same state structures, institutions, and systems that purport to prevent and address it. For Hannah Clarke, the origins of her abuse were historically and institutionally established. Rowan Clarke's controlling, possessive, jealous, and sexually abusive behaviour clearly aligned with a classic, legally defensible notion of ownership over his wife. He dictated what she wore, where she went, what she did, who she saw, how she behaved, and this was widely perceived as legitimate. As Hannah herself had told a friend, she did not think she was in an abusive relationship because her husband did not "hit" her during their marriage (see Jepsen 2020: n.p.). Even Hannah's own mother Suzanne admitted that she did not recognise her son-in-law's controlling behaviour as abusive or dangerous, since it came across as relatively unremarkable – albeit "prudish" – husband behaviour (Clarke in Jepsen 2020: n.p.). Hannah was clearly failed by society and its officially and institutionally entrenched cultural beliefs about marriage and the perceived legitimacy of male control over women.

Once Hannah did decide to leave her husband and sought help and protection, contemporary state institutions also failed her and her children. These victims were murdered *after* Hannah had pursued recommended help-seeking avenues, *when* a protective order was in place, and *whilst* they awaited court adjudication of an order breach. Further, in a blatant expression of official victim-blaming and justification of men's violence, a police detective heading the murder investigation urged the media and the public to keep an "open mind", to "not take sides", and to consider that this might be "an instance of a husband being driven too far by issues he's suffered" (Thompson in McGowan & Smee 2020: n.p.). Along with the numerous examples I analyse throughout this book, this evidence clearly points to the state not as neutral arbiter of domestic violence but as a central part of the problem. It points to domestic violence being so prevalent and intractable not *despite*, but precisely *because of* the state.

Throughout this book, I argue that domestic violence should not just be understood as an individual interpersonal crime, a symptom of problematic attitudes, or a problem exacerbated by state failures, limitations, and oversights. Rather, I argue that domestic violence should be understood as a state crime: a state-created problem founded upon, enshrined in, generated through, modelled by, mirrored in, and systematically supported by structures, institutions, and agencies of the state. This is because the state functions not only as a complicit bystander to domestic violence; it is also an active participant in and contributor to the problem. It plays a demonstrable historic, contemporary, passive, and active role by obscuring, allowing, enabling, endorsing, exacerbating, extending, and even co-perpetrating and perpetrating domestic violence. The state is very much an active producer and reproducer of this harm, and as I demonstrate throughout this book, its role can be identified as state criminality.

Uniting feminist and state crime thinking

Reflecting shifts in the international political and policy arena, academic attention to domestic violence has increased exponentially over the past decade, transforming it from a marginal feminist sub-field to a mainstream area of study. Along the lines of the official narratives I outlined earlier, a significant body of social science works broadly reiterate the gendered and inequality dimensions of domestic violence yet focus on individuals, attitudes, behaviour change, and technical system reform (e.g. Hegarty et al. 2015; Babcock et al. 2016; Radcliffe & Gilchrist 2016; Haggard et al. 2017; Liel 2017). The more critical literature delves into the substantive connections between inequality and domestic violence, looking beneath individuals and attitudes to socio-economic inequality, problematic sexist culture itself, and the specific conditions that exacerbate domestic violence (e.g. DeKeseredy & Schwartz 2013; Flood 2015; Salter 2016). Critical works also illuminate systemic problems with responses to domestic violence. They document ill-conceived, ineffectual, counterproductive, negligent, and even directly harmful state action and inaction which entrenches and exacerbates the problem and causes "secondary victimisation" (Laing 2017: 1314; also see Guggisberg & Fisher 2010; Elizabeth et al. 2012; Meyer 2016; Goodmark 2018; Douglas 2019; Reeves 2020). Mills (1999: 585) even identifies that domestic violence-related interactions with the state can "replicate the very violence [it] seeks to eradicate".

Looking at the deeper origins of domestic violence, generations of radical feminist scholars have analysed the relationship between sexual inequality and domestic violence, as well as the role of the state, structures, and institutions in producing and perpetuating it. The patriarchal state has been clearly named as underpinning all violence against women, and men's violence against partners and children identified as a state-condoned method of maintaining patriarchal power in the family and the wider society (e.g. Taylor Mill 1869; Brownmiller 1975; Barry 1979; MacKinnon 1989; Russell & Radford 1992; Stark 2007; DeKeseredy 2016). Feminist legal scholars have shown how state legal institutions systematically subjugate women, dismiss their victim claims, and both tacitly and explicitly endorse men's violence (e.g. Romany 1993; Copelon 1994; MacKinnon 1994; Charlesworth & Chinkin 2000; Meyersfeld 2010). Indeed, state failure and neglect to adequately respond to domestic violence has been named sex-based discrimination and a human rights violation. Domestic violence has also been conceptualised through innovative frames suggestive of international crimes, crimes against humanity, and group-based atrocity (e.g. Russell 1982; Caulfield & Wonders 1993; MacKinnon 1993; 1994; Copelon 1994; Johnson 1995; Stark 2007; Pain 2012).

Critical and feminist work on domestic violence therefore clearly points towards conceptualising it as a state crime. Authors acknowledge that domestic violence emanates from sexual inequality, they trace the state's creation and maintenance of these sexual inequalities that underpin domestic violence, and they document entrenched and institutionalised state failures, discrimination, and additional harms to victim-survivors. But institutions, structures, and the state itself are not adequately conceptualised as part of the perpetration and perpetuation of domestic violence, and these works fall short of clearly or comprehensively identifying, conceptualising, or theorising domestic violence in state crime terms. This is why integrating frames of thinking from state crime criminology is necessary.

The state crime literature identifies, analyses, conceptualises, and theorises mass harms with group, organised, and state dimensions. Alongside widely recognised state crimes like the Holocaust atrocities of World War II and South

African apartheid, state criminality is also identified in developed contemporary Western democracies: societies which are supposedly built upon equality and the rule of law. In these contexts, researchers identify rampant capitalist state crimes including state-facilitated corporate crime, industrial-scale environmental destruction, and the criminalisation and over-policing of the poor (Quinney 1980; Chambliss 1989; Barak 2008; Bernat & Whyte 2017). Liberal-democratic societies have also been named as the site of state crimes through the enduring racist violence of colonial and imperial projects (Tatz 1985; Cunneen 2008; Henry 2015; Curthoys et al. 2018).

But this field has not adequately attended to harms against women. When these have been recognised, it has largely reflected the official recognition of organised sexual violence in armed conflict (Henry 2011; Simm 2018). Outside of war, state crimes are most often discussed without nuanced attention to sex or gender and overlooking the fact that women's victimisation manifests through distinct contexts, locations, forms, and experiences. In liberal democracies, the irony is that despite interrogating the inherently paternalistic – and thus patriarchy-derived – harms of racist imperial and colonial projects, state crime scholars have not comprehensively addressed systematic violence against women through the same lenses. Women in these societies experience unique types of historical and contemporary victimisation based on their biological sex, gender identity, and their symbolic and substantive structural position in society. Structural and institutionalised sexual inequalities, which directly underpin domestic and other violence against women, surely warrant attention. In relation to systematically discriminatory and negligent state responses to domestic violence, state crime frameworks are also eminently applicable. Where direct state endorsement and exacerbation of domestic violence has been documented, state criminality is staring us in the face. These dimensions of domestic violence need to be explicitly named, comprehensively theorised, and firmly located in the state crime domain. Then, with a more holistic understanding of the problem, we gain a more holistic platform from which to imagine and design our responses.

Throughout this book and when asserting my case for domestic violence to be understood in this way, I adopt and advocate a broad, inclusive, and evolving conceptualisation of state crime. Following interdisciplinary scholars who identify a diversity of state criminality across various contexts and sites (Barak 1994; Tatz 1999; Green & Ward 2000; Kauzlarich et al. 2003; Balint 2012), my definition of state crime includes violations of international criminal law, human rights law, and constitutional law. I also include state criminality via acts of commission and omission, thereby acknowledging direct, indirect, active, and passive state roles. I identify both state and non-state institutions as key sites of state crime and consider that state criminality can emanate not just from official state agents but also from non-state actors who operate with state authorisation. Crucially, my definition also incorporates state criminality in the form of historical and structural violence, oppression, and micro-oppression. Consistently, I consider victim-survivor individuals and collectives as important contributors to the process of defining state crime. It is from this comprehensive definitional base that my multi-faceted feminist theory of domestic violence as state crime emerges.

Overview and contributions

The central contributions of this book are to explicitly and comprehensively identify, conceptualise, theorise, and propose addressing domestic violence as a state crime. This multi-dimensional argument unfolds over three parts and nine chapters.

Part I comprises the present introductory chapter and Chapter 2, 'Reasserting radical feminism: Being, feeling, knowing, thinking, doing'. In the second chapter, I relate the personal experiences that locate me within my work before linking these to the feminist knowledges and ethical principles that guided the research. I then outline the structural and radical feminist perspective on domestic violence and the state which underpins my conceptual and theoretical arguments, and explain the transdisciplinary feminist problem-driven approach I term *upcycled appliqué,* which facilitated the insights of this book.

Part II consists of five chapters, each representing a standalone lens for understanding the state crime dimensions of domestic violence. In each, I explain the layered upcycled and appliquéd lens through which I nominate a type of *domestic violence state crime.* After outlining each hybrid theoretical type, I then identify and analyse how it functions in practice. Drawing on data from my local context of Australia and comparable Western liberal democracies including the United States, the United Kingdom, and New Zealand, I focus on the workings of state institutions with direct domestic violence interface: the criminal and civil legal apparatus and state-based social services. Across the chapters of Part II, there is some necessary overlap: at times, I draw on the same data and case examples but analyse them from different angles and through different lenses; arguments also intersect as I map the complementary and mutually supportive patriarchal state crime dimensions of domestic violence. This process highlights how different forms of patriarchal power and violence function in coherent and synchronous ways. It also underscores that domestic violence is not just an interpersonal crime, nor just a set of distinct forms of state criminality, but also a holistic state crime phenomenon.

In Chapter 3, I nominate domestic violence as a *state crime against humanity*: demonstrating how, both empirically and conceptually, it can be understood via key international criminal legal principles. I identify how it constitutes an international crime of extreme gravity and global significance, and also how it has distinguishing features that demarcate crimes against humanity. With distinctive and repeated patterns of harm and clear dynamics of perpetration and victimisation, domestic violence is not only an individual interpersonal crime but a collective harm against women. It is also an important part of the wider systematic group-based subjugation and violation of women and it operates in accordance with state-level ideological and political support.

Chapter 4 details how domestic violence constitutes what I term a *micro-state crime*. Based on a feminist reconceptualisation of the state as a patriarchal microcosm of the nation-state, I challenge key state crime concepts of sovereignty, territory, state actors, and state violence, enabling state crime theory to be advanced into the private sphere. I also put forward new ways of understanding domestic violence as a system, method, and tool of state crime ideology and governance which further demonstrate the value in understanding it as a type of state crime.

In Chapter 5, I discuss domestic violence as a *structural state crime*. This involves identifying state-created socio-economic, industrial, cultural, ideological, and epistemic structures which in themselves constitute structural violence state crime against women and which also have direct links with the production, perpetuation, normalisation, minimisation, and justification of men's domestic violence against women. These create the structural foundations upon which domestic violence is produced and reproduced on an epidemic scale.

Chapter 6 explains how domestic violence constitutes an *omissive institutional state crime*. This is because liberal-democratic states have mandated obligations to uphold principles of equality and human rights and actively prevent and protect against domestic violence. Therefore, when they fail these obligations and instead function as passive bystanders and negligent enablers, they become omissive criminal actors in domestic violence. I identify a range of systematic institutional, agency, and bureaucratic omissions, oversights, and failures that illustrate how this form of state criminality operates in practice.

In Chapter 7, I identify domestic violence as an *agentic institutional state crime*. This is because states, through their institutions, agencies, and officials, are not just complicit via omissions in men's domestic violence - they also play a direct and active role in its production and reproduction. I nominate and discuss in detail three forms of agentic institutional state crime: productive, where individual perpetrators are provided specific state-sanctioned opportunities for new domestic offending; reconstructive, where domestic violence is officially re-framed in a manner that effectively decriminalises perpetrators' violence; and abusive, where the state actively participates in abusing victims, constructs and enacts intimate abusive relationships with them, and in some cases perpetrates direct state violence against them as it enforces perpetrators' interests.

In Part III, Chapter 8 unites Part II's frames of theorising domestic violence as a state crime into a wider cohesive whole and explains how these constitute an overarching feminist typological theory of domestic violence as state crime. With a diagram of the typology to help illustrate its component parts and their relationships, I explain the set of mutually supportive harms

and how they fit together to create a comprehensive phenomenon and experience of domestic violence as a state crime. To illustrate and elaborate on
these connections, I revisit the Hannah Clarke case, along with another case
example, and analyse them through this typological lens. In both, I identify the existence of all five types of *domestic violence state crime*, explain their
inter-connectedness and mutually amplifying impact, and explore how
they function as a cohesive machine of patriarchal state crime. To conclude,
I further explore the notion of domestic violence not just as an experience of
interpersonal victimisation but as a holistic experience of harm across time
and space and emanating from multiple sources and sites.

In the final chapter, I consider the implications of conceptualising domestic
violence as a state crime. A state crime lens highlights the need to diversify
beyond the individualistic and attitude-focussed approaches which presently
dominate theory, policy, and practice, and to consider a broader range of
response options. By drawing on insights from transitional justice theory
and practice – the dominant framework for addressing state crimes – I consider how we might pursue institutional, structural, and state-level accountability and responsibility for domestic violence. I sketch out what a phasic
justice approach to the state crime dimensions of domestic violence could
look like, considering stages and mechanisms including a survivor tribunal,
institutional accountability, official apology, and restorative, reparative, and
transformative justice. I explore the capacity of these initiatives to address
domestic violence in a more comprehensive manner, accounting for multiple
levels of responsibility for the harm and dealing with individual, collective,
and society-wide needs for truth, accountability, atonement, expiation, restoration, and substantive transformation.

Notes

1 I constructed this brief account of these crimes by integrating information from
   several media sources including Brook and Foster (2020), Gleeson (2020), and
   McGowan (2020).
2 My focus on male domestic violence against women is not intended to dismiss
   women's violence against men, nor violence within same-sex and non-binary
   relationships. I acknowledge the value in exploring continuities and differences
   between different types of partner violence (see Nowinski & Bowen 2012;
   Frankland & Brown 2014; Kubicek et al. 2016; Register 2018; Stark & Hester
   2019).
3 Throughout this book, I use the term domestic violence to refer to a range of
   violent, abusive, controlling, and coercive behaviours perpetrated by men against
   female intimate partners and ex-partners. This reflects data showing that this
   constitutes the vast majority of serious cases and that domestic violence encompasses a spectrum of harmful behaviours (Johnson 1995; Stark 2007; Meyer &
   Frost 2019). At times, and notably when discussing family law, I use the terms
   'family violence' or 'domestic and family violence' to indicate a broader phenomenon that also includes men's violence against children in the family. This
   expanded definition is important because of the frequent overlap between the

perpetration of intimate partner and child abuse. Where it is useful to explicitly distinguish between these forms of family violence, I sometimes use the terms 'intimate partner violence' or 'child abuse'. I also acknowledge that domestic and family violence can encompass elder abuse and abuse of people with a disability by carers or co-residents; it can also refer to violence involving members of a broader family structure, which, notably for Indigenous Peoples, can include kinship and community networks (Cunneen & Tauri 2016). Unfortunately, I was not able to pursue these nuances in this research.

4 I use the terms 'victim', 'survivor', and 'victim-survivor' variously throughout this book as appropriate, intending to acknowledge both the vulnerability and resilience of those who have experienced domestic violence. The term 'survivor' is often preferred by those who have endured it, in order to emphasise their courage and strength (Meyer & Frost 2019); however, this term can be problematic if it excludes women who did not survive. I also use the term 'victim' without connotations of weakness, but rather to emphasise that offenders perpetrate serious harms which victimise others (Meyersfeld 2010). I note that person-first language such as "people with lived experience of family violence" has value and is preferred by some individuals (see e.g. State Government of Victoria 2019: n.p.), although unfortunately this was not manageable for repeated use here.

5 Royal Commissions are important institutions in Australian political and public life. They represent official acknowledgement of an issue's urgency and import, the need for thorough and contemporary investigation, and a receptivity to innovative insights and ideas for understanding and addressing it.

6 The term 'family violence' is quite unique to the Victorian context in which this Royal Commission was held. It is generally synonymous with 'intimate partner violence by men against women', and thus with the more common international term 'domestic violence' (see Yates 2020).

References

Babcock, Julia & Armenti, Nicholas & Cannon, Clare & Lauve-Moon, Katie & Buttell, Fred & Ferreira, Regardt & Solano, Ingrid. 2016. Domestic violence perpetrator programs: A proposal for evidence-based standards in the United States. *Partner Abuse* 7(4). 355–460.

Balint, Jennifer. 2012. *Genocide, State Crime and the Law.* Abingdon: Routledge.

Barak, Gregg. 1994. Crime, criminology, and human rights: Toward an understanding of state criminality. In Barak, Gregg (ed.), *Varieties of Criminology: Readings from a Dynamic Discipline.* 253–68. Westport: Praeger.

Barak, Gregg. 2008. Towards an integrative study of international crimes and state-corporate criminality: A reciprocal approach to gross human rights violations. In Smeulers, Alette & Haveman, Roelof (eds.), *Supranational Criminology: Towards a Criminology of International Crimes.* 51–74. Antwerp: Intersentia.

Barry, Kathleen. 1979. *Female Sexual Slavery.* New York: New York University Press.

Bernat, Ignasi & Whyte, David. 2017. State-corporate crime and the process of capital accumulation: Mapping a global regime of permission from Galicia to Morecambe Bay. *Critical Criminology* 25(1). 71–86.

Boserup, Brad & McKenney, Mark & Elkbuli, Adel. 2020. Alarming trends in US domestic violence during the COVID-19 pandemic. *The American Journal of Emergency Medicine* 38(12). 2753–5.

Boxall, Hayley & Morgan, Anthony & Brown, Rick. 2020. *The Prevalence of Domestic Violence among Women during the COVID-19 Pandemic*. Canberra: Australian Institute of Criminology.

Bradel, Lauren & Rosenbaum, Alan & Orcutt, Holly. 2019. The prevalence and co-occurrence of the forms of violence against women. *Journal of Aggression, Maltreatment & Trauma* 28(7). 870–87.

Breiding, Matthew & Smith, Sharon & Basile, Kathleen & Walters, Mikel & Chen, Jieru & Merrick, Melissa. 2014. Prevalence and characteristics of sexual violence, stalking, and intimate partner violence victimization: National intimate partner and sexual violence survey, United States, 2011. *Morbidity and Mortality Weekly Report* 63(8). 1–18.

Brook, Benedict & Foster, Ally. 2020. Sacrificed everything: Hannah Clarke's family speaks out after her murder. *News.com.au.* (https://www.news.com.au/entertainment/tv/current-affairs/sacrificed-everything-hannah-clarkes-family-speaks-out-after-her-murder/news-story/e5429bf030fb5c8e07ca557885cc3acc)

Brownmiller, Susan. 1975. *Against Our Will: Men, Women and Rape*. London: Secker and Warburg.

Caulfield, Susan & Wonders, Nancy. 1993. Personal AND political: Violence against women and the role of the state. In Tunnell, Kenneth (ed.), *Political Crime in Contemporary America: A Critical Approach*, 79–100. New York: Garland Publishing.

Chambliss, William. 1989. State organised crime. *Criminology* 27(2). 183–208.

Charlesworth, Hilary & Chinkin, Christine. 2000. *The Boundaries of International Law: A Feminist Analysis*. Manchester: Manchester University Press.

Copelon, Rhonda. 1994. Recognising the egregious in the everyday: Domestic violence as torture. *Columbia Human Rights Law Review* 2. 291–367.

Cunneen, Chris. 2008. State crime, the colonial question and Indigenous Peoples. In Smeulers, Alette & Haveman, Roelof (eds.), *Supranational Criminology: Towards a Criminology of International Crimes*, 159–79. Antwerp: Intersentia.

Cunneen, Chris & Tauri, Juan. 2016. *Indigenous Criminology*. Bristol: Policy Press.

Curthoys, Ann & Tedeschi, Mark & Balint, Jennifer & Joyce, Daniel. 2018. Forum: The Myall Creek Massacre of 1838: Genocide, war crimes, crimes against humanity? *Law and History* 5(1). 146–68.

DeKeseredy, Walter. 2016. Understanding woman abuse in intimate heterosexual relationships: The enduring relevance of feminist ways of knowing. *Journal of Family Violence* 31. 1043–6.

DeKeseredy, Walter & Schwartz, Martin. 2013. *Male Peer Support and Violence against Women: The History and Verification of a Theory*. Boston: Northeastern University Press.

Department of Health and Human Services. 2018. *Free from Violence: Victoria's Strategy to Prevent Family Violence and All Forms of Violence against Women: First Action Plan 2018–2021*. Melbourne: Victorian Government, State of Victoria.

Douglas, Heather. 2019. Policing domestic and family violence. *International Journal for Crime, Justice and Social Democracy* 8(2). 31–49.

Elizabeth, Vivienne & Gavey, Nicola & Tolmie, Julie. 2012. "He's just swapped his fists for the system": The governance of gender through custody law. *Gender and Society* 26(2). 239–60.

Flood, Michael. 2012. *He Hits, She Hits: Assessing Debates Regarding Men's and Women's Experiences of Domestic Violence*. Sydney: Australian Domestic and Family Violence Clearinghouse.

Flood, Michael. 2015. Work with men to end violence against women: A critical stocktake. *Culture, Health & Sexuality* 17. 159.

Frankland, Andrew & Brown, Jac. 2014. Coercive control in same-sex partner violence. *Journal of Family Violence* 29. 15–22.

Fulu, Emma & Warner, Xian & Miedema, Stephanie & Jewkes, Rachel & Roselli, Tim & Lang, James. 2013. *Why Do Some Men Use Violence against Women and How Can We Prevent It? Quantitative Findings from the United Nations Multi-Country Study on Men and Violence in Asia and the Pacific.* Bangkok: United Nation Development Program, United Nations Population Fund, United Nations Women and United Nations Volunteers.

Garcia-Moreno, Claudia & Zimmerman, Cathy & Morris-Gehring, Alison & Heise, Lori & Amin, Avni & Abrahams, Naeemah & Montoya, Oswaldo & Bhate-Deosthali, Padma & Kilonzo, Nduku & Watts, Charlotte. 2015. Addressing violence against women: A call to action. *The Lancet* 385. 1685–95.

Gleeson, Hayley. 2020. Hannah Clarke did everything she could to protect herself and her children. Experts explain why it wasn't enough. *ABC News.* (https://www.abc.net.au/news/2020-03-10/hannah-clarke-domestic-violence-law-cant-keep-women-safe/12041184?nw=0)

Goodmark, Leigh. 2018. *Decriminalizing Domestic Violence: A Balanced Policy Approach to Intimate Partner Violence.* Oakland: University of California Press.

Green, Penny & Ward, Tony. 2000. State crime, human rights and the limits of criminology. *Social Justice* 27(1). 101–15.

Groves, Nicola & Thomas, Terry. 2014. *Domestic Violence and Criminal Justice.* London: Routledge.

Guggisberg, Marika & Fisher, Colleen. 2010. Abused women's double jeopardy interacting with law enforcement on issues of intimate partner violence. *Women against Violence* 22. 18–27.

Haggard, Ulrika & Freij, Ingrid & Danielsson, Maria & Wenander, Diana & Langstrom, Niklas. 2017. Effectiveness of the IDAP treatment program for male perpetrators of intimate partner violence: A controlled study of criminal recidivism. *Journal of Interpersonal Violence* 32(7). 1027–43.

Hegarty, Kelsey & Tarzia, Laura & Murray, Elizabeth & Valpied, Jodie & Humphreys, Cathy & Taft, Angela & Gold, Lisa & Glass, Nancy. 2015. Protocol for a randomised controlled trial of a web-based healthy relationship tool and safety decision aid for women experiencing domestic violence (I-DECIDE). *BMC Public Health* 15. 736–45.

Henry, Nicola. 2011. *War and Rape: Law, Memory and Justice.* Abingdon: Routledge.

Henry, Nicola. 2015. From reconciliation to transitional justice: The contours of redress politics in established democracies. *International Journal of Transitional Justice.* July 9(2). 199–218.

Jepsen, Belinda. 2020. For years, Hannah Clarke didn't have bruises or broken bones. But her abuse was just as brutal. *Mamamia.* (https://www.mamamia.com.au/hannah-clarke-coercive-control/)

Johnson, Michael. 1995. Patriarchal terrorism and common couple violence: Two forms of violence against women. *Journal of Marriage and the Family* 57. 283–94.

Kauzlarich, David & Mullins, Christopher & Matthews, Rick. 2003. A complicity continuum of state crime. *Contemporary Justice Review* 6(3). 241–54.

Kimmel, Michael. 2013. The gender of violence. *The Gendered Society,* 421–52. 5th edn. New York: Oxford University Press.

Kubicek, Katrina & McNeeley, Miles & Collins, Shardae. 2016. Young men who have sex with men's experiences with intimate partner violence. *Journal of Adolescent Research* 31(2). 143–75.

Laing, Lesley. 2017. Secondary victimization: Domestic violence survivors navigating the family law system. *Violence against Women* 23(11). 1314–35.

Liel, Christoph. 2017. Treatment of domestic violence perpetrators: Impact on the risk for recidivism. *Forensic Psychiatry, Psychology, Criminology* 11(1). 59–68.

MacKinnon, Catharine. 1989. *Toward a Feminist Theory of the State.* Cambridge, MA: Harvard University Press.

MacKinnon, Catharine. 1993. On torture: A feminist perspective on human rights. In Mahoney, Kathleen & Mahoney, Paul (eds.), *Human Rights in the Twenty-first Century: A Global Challenge*, 21–31. Boston: M. Nijhoff.

MacKinnon, Catharine. 1994. Rape, genocide and women's human rights. *Harvard Women's Law Journal* 17. 5–16.

McGowan, Michael. 2020. Brisbane car fire: Hannah Clarke's family say they tried to rescue her and children from violent husband. *The Guardian.* (https://www.theguardian.com/australia-news/2020/feb/20/brisbane-car-fire-hannah-baxters-family-say-they-tried-to-rescue-her-and-children-from-violent-husband)

McGowan, Michael & Smee, Ben. 2020. Queensland police spark anger with 'open mind' comment on murder of Hannah Clarke and children. *The Guardian.* (https://www.theguardian.com/australia-news/2020/feb/20/queensland-police-spark-anger-with-open-mind-comment-on-of-hannah-clarke-and-children)

Meyer, Silke. 2016. Still blaming the victim of intimate partner violence? Women's narratives of victim desistance and redemption when seeking support. *Theoretical Criminology* 20(1). 75–90.

Meyer, Silke & Frost, Andrew. 2019. *Domestic and Family Violence: A Critical Introduction to Knowledge and Practice.* Abingdon: Routledge.

Meyersfeld, Bonita. 2010. *Domestic Violence and International Law.* Oxford: Hart Publishing.

Mills, Linda. 1999. Killing her softly: Intimate abuse and the violence of state intervention. *Harvard Law Review* 113(2). 550–613.

Mlambo-Ngcuka, Phumzile. 2020. *Violence against Women and Girls: The Shadow Pandemic.* Statement by Executive Director of UN Women. (https://www.unwomen.org/en/news/stories/2020/4/statement-ed-phumzile-violence-against-women-during-pandemic)

Moreira, Diana Nadine & Pinto da Costa, Mariana. 2020. The impact of the Covid-19 pandemic in the precipitation of intimate partner violence. *International Journal of Law and Psychiatry* 71. (doi:10.1016/j.ijlp.2020.101606)

National Coalition against Domestic Violence. 2017. *Domestic Violence Gun-related Fatalities.* (http://ncadv.org/)

National Coalition against Domestic Violence. 2020. *Domestic Violence National Statistics.* (https://ncadv.org/statistics)

Nowinski, Sabrina & Bowen, Erica. 2012. Partner violence against heterosexual and gay men: Prevalence and correlates. *Aggression and Violent Behavior* 17(1). 36–52.

Office for National Statistics. 2019. *Homicide in England and Wales: Year ending March 2018.* (https://www.ons.gov.uk/peoplepopulationandcommunity/crimeandjustice/articles/homicideinenglandandwales/yearendingmarch2018#how-are-victims-and-suspects-related)

Pain, Rachel. 2012. *Everyday Terrorism: How Fear Works in Domestic Abuse.* Centre for Social Justice and Community Aid, Durham University and Scottish Women's Aid.

Pfitzner, Naomi & Fitz-Gibbon, Kate & True, Jacqui. 2020. *Responding to the 'Shadow Pandemic': Practitioner Views on the Nature of and Responses to Violence against Women in Victoria, Australia during the COVID-19 Restrictions.* Melbourne: Monash Gender and Family Violence Prevention Centre, Monash University.

Price, Jenna. 2018. We can't fix violence against women until we see this as an epidemic. *Sydney Morning Herald.* (https://www.smh.com.au/national/we-can-t-fix-violence-against-women-until-we-see-this-as-an-epidemic-20181213-p50m02.html)

Quinney, Richard. 1980. *Class, State and Crime.* New York: Longman.

Radcliffe, Polly & Gilchrist, Gail. 2016. You can never work with addictions in isolation: Addressing intimate partner violence perpetration by men in substance misuse treatment. *International Journal of Drug Policy* 36. 130–40.

Reeves, Ellen. 2020. Family violence, protection orders and systems abuse: Views of legal practitioners. *Current Issues in Criminal Justice* 32(1). 91–110.

Register, Sophie. 2018. Maybe it's just different with girls: A social-ecological analysis of intimate partner violence in female-on-female relationships. *International Social Science Review* 94(2). 1–28.

Romany, Celia. 1993. Women as aliens: A feminist critique of the public / private distinction in international human rights law. *The Harvard Human Rights Journal* 6. 87–125.

Royal Commission into Family Violence. 2015. *Terms of Reference.* Melbourne: State Government of Victoria. (http://www.rcfv.com.au/MediaLibraries/RCFamily-Violence/UploadedDocs/Terms-of-Reference.pdf)

Royal Commission into Family Violence. 2016. *Report and Recommendations.* Melbourne: State Government of Victoria.

Russell, Diana. 1982. *Rape in Marriage.* New York: Macmillan.

Russell, Diana & Radford, Jill (eds.). 1992. *Femicide: The Politics of Woman Killing.* Buckingham: Open University Press.

Salter, Michael. 2016. Real men don't hit women: Constructing masculinity in the prevention of violence against women. *Australian and New Zealand Journal of Criminology* 49(4). 463–79.

Simm, Gabrielle. 2018. Peoples' tribunals, women's courts and international crimes of sexual violence. In Byrnes, Andrew & Simm, Gabrielle (eds.), *Peoples' Tribunals and International Law*, 61–83. Cambridge: Cambridge University Press.

Stark, Evan. 2007. *Coercive Control: How Men Entrap Women in Personal Life.* New York: Oxford University Press.

Stark, Evan & Hester, Marianne. 2019. Coercive control: Update and review. *Violence against Women* 25(1). 81–104.

State Government of Victoria. 2019. *Three Years on from the Royal Commission into Family Violence.* Melbourne: Family Violence Branch, Department of Premier and Cabinet.

Tatz, Colin. 1985. Racism, responsibility, and reparation: South Africa, Germany, and Australia. *Australian Journal of Politics and History* 31(1). 162–72.

Tatz, Colin. 1999. Genocide in Australia. *Journal of Genocide Research* 1(3). 315–52.

Taylor Mill, Harriet. 1869. Enfranchisement of women. In Rossi, Alice (ed.), *Essays on Sex Equality by John Stuart Mill and Harriet Taylor Mill*, 89–122. Chicago: University of Chicago Press.

United Nations General Assembly. 1993. *Declaration on the Elimination of Violence against Women*. UN Doc A/RES/48/104.

United Nations General Assembly. 2003. *Resolution on the Elimination of Domestic Violence against Women*. UN Doc A/RES/58/147.

United Nations Office on Drugs and Crime. 2019. *Global Study on Homicide 2019: Gender-related Killing of Women and Girls*. Vienna. (https://www.unodc.org/documents/data-and-analysis/gsh/Booklet_5.pdf)

Walklate, Sandra & McCulloch, Jude & Fitz-Gibbon, Kate & Maher, JaneMaree. 2019. Criminology, gender and security in the Australian context: Making women's lives matter. *Theoretical Criminology* 23(1). 60–77.

Women's Aid. 2020. *A Perfect Storm: The Impact of the Covid-19 Pandemic on Domestic Abuse Survivors and the Services Supporting Them*. Bristol: Women's Aid.

World Health Organisation. 2013. *Global and Regional Estimates of Violence against Women: Prevalence and Health Effects of Intimate Partner Violence and Non-partner Sexual Violence*. (https://apps.who.int/iris/bitstream/handle/10665/85239/9789241564625_eng.pdf;jsessionid=3798BB58CC00B986FDD892C816A9E480?sequence=1)

Yates, Sophie. 2020. Gender, context and constraint: Framing family violence in Victoria. *Women's Studies International Forum* 78(102321).

Chapter 2

Reasserting radical feminism

Being, feeling, knowing, thinking, doing

Being, feeling

As a feminist, criminologist, and abuse survivor, much of my past, present, and surely my future, is about domestic violence. I've experienced first-hand the domination, degradation, sexual violation, physical assault, threats, and pervasive terror of a coercive control regime. I have been that utterly subjugated woman, although I did not recognise her at the time. Worse, adored pets were murdered and maimed, and my daughter was severely sexually abused in a cone of threatened secrecy and silence and is now a dangerously traumatised young adult. It is from these experiences that grow the passionate outrage and dogged motivation that now drive my work.

Although I didn't fully recall or understand it until adulthood, abuse in my family of origin set me up as a ripe target for later victimisation. As a vulnerable survivor teenager and in the aftermath of the final breakdown of my parents' dysfunctional and harmful marriage, I was groomed by a paedophile 21 years my senior, who managed to convince me that I was the love of his life and he was the solution to my difficult background. By the time I was 16, I was living with him, although of course with the caveat that I had to hide our relationship and whereabouts from everyone. Based on various lies, deception, manipulation, and threats, I stayed with him, got married, and was literally – as he liked to tease – "barefooted and pregnant in the kitchen" and then with a newborn baby at 19. Bizarrely, my highly educated extended family had by then accepted him and did not intervene to protect me or my daughter in any way. It is certainly true that abusers carefully select their victims.

For approximately ten years total, I existed under this man's abusive totalitarian regime. He utilised the complete toolkit of coercion and violence in order to maintain control over me and my daughter. And perhaps because I so confounded the dominant image of the abused woman, no one noticed the signs, saw the problems, or thought I needed help – not even me. I was intelligent, educated, and high functioning throughout this time: completing high school at a competitive select-entry public institution followed by a

DOI: 10.4324/9781003132370-3

bachelor's degree and post-graduate diploma at Melbourne's most prestigious university, fulfilling the role of devoted wife and mother, and even doing some part-time work. I did not look like the stereotypical abused woman: I was not visibly injured, not a fragile weeping mess, not dysfunctional or disadvantaged in every area of life. To the outside world, I was a capable and contented young woman and mother with a husband who adored, cared for, and provided for me and our child. And I will admit that, like all abusive relationships, there *were* times that seemed positive. But the inside story and the pervasive experience were anything but that.

As long as I submitted to the role of hyper-sexual domestic slave-wife-mother who worshipped and never questioned him, he was content. But absolutely anything, including invisible things, would alter this dynamic. The utter unpredictability of this was central to his control strategy. On an ordinary day we might be at the supermarket when suddenly I was being accused of "checking out" another man when I had absolutely no idea what he was talking about. Or at night, he would assume that my reluctance to have sex with him was not merely exhaustion from managing a household, tertiary studies, and a baby with no outside help, but evidence of infidelity. This would set off literally hours of verbal abuse about my being selfish, de-ceitful, cruel, sick, insane, ugly, hairy, smelly, repulsive, and utterly incapable of anything. These tirades would only end when, weeping, utterly confused, and begging for forgiveness for being so insufferable, I would submit to being raped to prove my fidelity, my validity as a woman and wife, and my status as his perpetually available sex object.

He demanded nothing short of total possession of me, and this led to esca-lating obsessive monitoring, control, and unfounded jealousy. He would call me at all hours of the day, demanding information that would momentarily satisfy his insatiable need for control. His first question was never "*How* are you?" but a barked demand: "*Where* are you?" along with the spoken or un-spoken "*Who* are you with?": a sick need to place me, pin me, like a butterfly on a board, exactly where he wanted me. He would regularly check my phone records and internet history to ensure my compliance, he prohibited me from having any male friends, and he would have me followed by his mates to make sure. Once, when I accepted a lift home from a kind male colleague on a wet winter's day, I was subjected to an entire night of inter-rogation because I did not choose to walk many kilometres home and get drenched and freezing rather than "advertise my availability".

His dominance extended to all areas of everyday life. Although we owned and operated a business together, he insisted on total financial decision-mak-ing and control, and would mete out to me what he framed as a generous allowance to cover household expenses. I now know it wasn't even sufficient for a poverty-level subsistence, but he made me believe it was only my stu-pidity and incompetence that made budgeting difficult. As well as convincing me that I desperately needed him to survive, he skilfully balanced this with stories of his own medical and emotional vulnerability which positioned me as heartless if I was anything other than unconditionally loyal and supportive. And to ensure I was sufficiently intimidated, he would regularly demonstrate his violent capacity with stories of fights, evidence of his punching holes in walls or wrecking property, by smashing things in front of me, and eventually by hitting me.

Like countless women the world over, the incremental psychological abuse was the most damaging because it reduced me to a pathetic gullible shadow of myself. He was an expert gaslighter[1]: continually lying, manipulating, and concocting stories and scenarios that would cause me to fear or admire him, doubt or mistrust others, and question my own sanity. Over years, I was conditioned to believe tales that I now recognise as ridiculous: that he had travelled the world seducing rich and beautiful women; that he had so much money he'd bought an apartment with cash but for some reason no longer owned it; that he was a brilliant businessman who was repeatedly shafted by others; that he had trained in special armed forces and led international counter-terrorist missions; that he had the contacts to get anyone killed and disappeared; that he had powerful friends who could erase criminal charges against him or concoct false charges against others; and of course the endless tales about me, designed to confuse, disorient, humiliate, and diminish me as a person.

I'm not sure how, but underneath everything, I preserved sufficient fragments of self to question it all, to believe I didn't deserve it, and to dare hope for a better future. But I avoided leaving him for so long because I believed I was doing the right thing for my child: I thought she was safe and happy, that I was providing her with a cohesive two-parent family, and with some semblance of living standards. But when I realised she was overhearing his aggressive tirades against me and becoming stressed and anxious, I decided we had to go. Separating from him was devastating, distressing, and extremely dangerous. We lived with a friend until I convinced him to leave our rented home so that my daughter could regain some continuity there with me. He then transferred various debts into my name and convinced me – by performing a heartrending tale about a creditor threatening his life – to empty my bank account of the $10,000 I had earned teaching part-time but had not been allowed to touch in our time together. Over the following year or so, he repeatedly broke into my house, damaged property, and on one occasion hacked my computer, stole my personal journal and threatened to print a thousand copies and disseminate it throughout the community in which I lived and worked. He murdered one of our cats and injured the other so badly that it caused temporary paralysis and permanent disability. He made numerous threats to kill me and my friends, and said that if I sought full custody he would disappear with my daughter overseas and I would never see her again.

I sought protection and support from systems and services, but instead mostly faced a range of institutional barriers which hampered and failed me and my child. There were countless moments when my ex-partner's path of devastation could have been thwarted or challenged, but instead it was passively allowed and even actively enabled. At the bank, there were no government or industry checks or balances in place when I withdrew $10,000 in cash at the same time as I disclosed marital separation and discussed the need for a name change. At the state social service agency, Centrelink, I was refused help because they forensically examined by bank records, accused me of hiding $10,000 in liquid assets, and barred me from income support. Despite multiple forms of documentary evidence and multiple appeals, there was total refusal to acknowledge my victimisation or the fact that I had no cash, no assets, no work, only debts, and a young child to provide for. Instead, I was treated as a fraud and a defrauder of the system. Attempting to obtain assistance through the federal Child Support Agency when my ex refused to make parenting contributions was even worse. I never received a cent nor any support from this Agency: only meaningless letters, condescending and abusive treatment over the phone, interrogation about my situation, and repudiation of my claims. In fact, all that really happened was that I was pressured to investigate the employment and tax affairs of a man who I tried to explain was verifiably dangerous, a pathological liar, and who already knew how to game the system. Throughout these processes, I was never recognised as a victim of partner or ex-partner abuse. Rather, I was framed as the problem: a liar, a failed citizen, and a problematic woman who was undeserving of state resources.

I was grateful for the police assistance I received to obtain my first protective order against my ex after he forced his way into my house, smashed up my bed in front of me, brandished the broken pieces of wood as weapons, and threatened to kill me and any man I brought into the house. But I never had criminal or civil options properly explained to me and did not receive any advice or referrals to appropriate services: legal, financial, community, domestic violence victim support, or otherwise. I had to obtain a second protective order on my own because police did not consider stalking, abusive phone calls and emails, nor threats of violence to be valid grounds for their time. Again, I was treated like a bothersome waste of resources. When I undertook the daunting task of self-representing in my protective order application in the Magistrate's Court, I did not even receive a referral to a domestic violence, victim advocacy, or court support service. And these experiences were just the tip of the iceberg of the lonely road as a victim-survivor.

Like many feminist scholars before me, I disclose these experiences because I want to be honest and real and because I want to bring into the open what are often hidden, misunderstood, and solitary experiences. This is not a cathartic exposé or dramatic backdrop for buying authenticity for this book. Exposing oneself can be risky, especially for academics, and it can have negative professional implications (Reilly 2020). However, I believe it is important and worthwhile. The objectivity claims of traditional academic and positivist social science are *passé*, and critical feminist researchers in particular continue to demonstrate the inevitability and value in being located within rather than outside their research (see e.g. Kelly 1988; Stanley & Wise 1993; 2000; Behar 1996; Hayes & Jeffries 2016; Gutowski & Goodman 2019). Identifying as a woman, mother, abuse survivor, and mother of an abuse survivor, I embrace the epistemic positioning this provides. I hope to show, like many survivor scholars before me, that we are strong people and capable researchers with important experiential insights. My years of researching violence against women has given me an enhanced awareness of how common my victimisation experiences are, and further affirmed the value of producing work that places collective insider perspectives at the forefront of theory-building, challenge, and change. If to know women's personal lives is to know the politics of womanhood and thus to enact feminist theory and method (MacKinnon 1982), this experiential backdrop – and its resonance with other women – is central to the theoretical foundations, knowledge, thinking, ethical choices, and practical processes I engaged in order to produce this book.

Knowing, thinking

My work is premised upon a structural or 'radical' feminist understanding of the world, the state, and domestic violence.[2] Aligning with generations of feminist and pro-feminist scholars and activists (e.g. Millett 1969; Burris 1973; Brownmiller 1975; Barry 1979; Dworkin 1981; MacKinnon 1982; Russell 1982; Bumiller 1987; Kelly 1988; Copelon 1994; Johnson 1995; Connell 2005; Stark 2007; DeKeseredy 2016; Salter 2016), I consider biological sex and the social construct of gender as the primary categorising structures of society. Accordingly, I regard the state, its structures, and institutions as patriarchal, hegemonically masculine, and heteronormative.[3] Within this hierarchy, individual and collective men occupy a superior position to that of women. The subjugation of women relates not just to ideas, symbols, and identities, but also to substantive inequality and disadvantage. Sexual inequality underpins domestic and other violence against women, and violence is both a symptom and a tool of male dominance. This is not merely feminist theory; international data confirm these inextricable links (see UNGA 1979; 1991; 1993; UNODC 2019).

Women are the largest – although certainly not the only – group that is subjugated under patriarchy. Indeed, many other forms of oppression and violence emerge from the foundational subjugation of women. For instance, homosexual men and those not conforming to hegemonically masculine behavioural standards tend to occupy an inferior social position to that of hypermasculine heterosexual men (e.g. Polk 1999; Salter 2016). Discrimination and violence based on sex, gender, and sexuality, such as the criminalisation of homosexual acts, denial of same-sex marriage rights, and homophobic and transphobic assault, can also be understood as patriarchal harms. Violence within diverse intimate relationships and family settings also emerges from patriarchal and associated heteronormative ideologies. For example, violent familial responses to queer revelations often arise from the perceived challenge that alternative sexuality poses to heteropatriarchal values (see e.g. Falleiros Braga et al. 2018). Patriarchal notions of power and ownership can also pollute any relationship and have been identified in same-sex and gender-diverse intimate partner abuse (Meyer 2012; Frankland & Brown 2014; Oliffe et al. 2014; Kubicek et al. 2016). Closely related to the subjugation of women under the individual and collective hegemonic male, these harms reflect the violent legal, social, and cultural enforcement of the heteropatriarchal order.

Maintaining a concerted focus on the foundational (and most prevalent and harmful) form of sexual and gender-based violence is important, however. This is perpetrated by men against women. As generations of feminists before me have shown, violence against women is not exceptional nor aberrant; rather, it is normal and central to the practical functioning and maintenance of patriarchal society and a routine part of everyday and everynight life (Kelly 2010). Violence against women is also best understood as a continuum of harm: a spectrum of intimidation, abuse, and violence which pervades all contexts and settings, with acts labelled criminal often shading imperceptibly into what is deemed normal, innocuous, and unremarkable (Enloe 1983; Kelly & Radford 1996). Women's experiences everywhere are best described as a "state of everyday hostilities" (MacKinnon 1994: 5).

Violence within heterosexual relationships and the domestic setting is particularly central to female experiences of harm. Globally, and irrespective of race, class, culture, or religion, women are at greatest risk of violence in the home and from male partners and other relatives (HSRP 2012; UNODC 2019). This is why interrogating the operation of sexual and gendered power in the private realm is such a critical part of the feminist academic and activist project. Radical feminist scholars have consistently shown that it is "in the private relationship between men and women that fundamental inequality is established" (Barry 1979: 194; also Stanley & Wise 1993; Mertus & Goldberg 1994). They have also shown that the broader political oppression of women is an outgrowth of oppression in the domestic sphere. Domestic violence therefore remains a critical phenomenon for continuous conceptual and theoretical development and practical challenge and change.

Radical feminism offers a diversity of concepts for understanding domestic violence against women, the institutions through which it is perpetrated, and their relationship to the state. Through this lens, the nation-state is a political construct which originates from patriarchal ideology and which deliberately and consistently functions in support of men's interests (e.g. Dworkin 1981; Bumiller 1987; 1992; 2008). More broadly, the state can also be understood as a comprehensive system of mutually supportive structures, institutions, ideologies, policies, and practices, which function in concert to maintain a sexual hierarchy (Brownmiller 1975; Barry 1979; MacKinnon 1989).[4]

State-ordained private-sphere institutions are key units of this wider patriarchal whole. Marriage and the family were originally purposefully designed, sanctified, and officially maintained for a specific purpose: to aid patriarchal power and control at the micro-level (Burris 1973; MacKinnon 1982; Romany 1993). Through law, the state assigned men the responsibility for leading their family and guiding, instructing, controlling, and disciplining their wives and children as they saw fit (Pateman 1988; Copelon 1994; Dobash & Dobash 1998; Stevens 1999). Through the state-ordained authority of individual men, this institutional system enabled the patriarchal nation-state's interests to be upheld in the private sphere without the need for constant external involvement and enforcement. It was also a system which both implicitly and explicitly endorsed men's violence in the family, as I will further explore in subsequent chapters.

Beyond state-ordained private-sphere institutions, a radical feminist lens also exposes direct links between nation-state institutions, the subjugation and violation of women, and domestic violence. For example, at its very foundation, law systematically disenfranchises women by imposing male constructs on their unique experiences and continuing to struggle with the fundamental question "are women human?" (MacKinnon 1989; 2006; Romany 1993; Charlesworth & Chinkin 2000). This leaves women and the harms they suffer frequently invisible through official eyes. Victims of domestic violence experience unique challenges, in part arising from the discriminatory legal frameworks that marginalise their experiences. They are also failed by the state when systematic inaction against men's violence violates their basic human rights (MacKinnon 1993; Copelon 1994; Mertus & Goldberg 1994). Domestic violence victims also receive routinely poor treatment from state institutions when seeking help (Guggisberg & Fisher 2010; Ulbrick & Jago 2018; Reeves 2020). When engaging with state institutions causes such significant additional trauma that it constitutes "secondary victimisation", this clearly shows the state harming women (Laing 2017: 1314; also Bumiller 2008; Meyer 2011; Coy et al. 2015; Meyer 2016; Natalier 2017; 2018; Gutowski & Goodman 2019). At its most extreme, when state responses to domestic violence "replicate … violence" and "inadvertently reproduce its most destructive forms" (Mills 1999: 585; also 1996), this shows the state *itself* directly abusing and violating women.

This structural feminist groundwork clearly implicates the state in oppressing and harming all women, and particularly victims of domestic and other sex-based violence. States are clearly responsible for creating structural and institutional sexual inequality, for the ongoing cultural subjugation of women that this inequality produces, and for the interpersonal violence that emerges from this. They are also responsible for victimisation that results from the systematic state failure to protect women's basic rights. States are even more directly implicated in harming women and domestic violence victims through inadequate, harmful, and even traumatising and violent official responses. Therefore, the next logical step in feminist conceptual and theoretical development in this area must be to consistently *centre* the state in domestic violence and to explicitly and comprehensively identify, conceptualise, and theorise domestic violence *as* a state crime. By working in accordance with feminist principles and pursuing a transdisciplinary problem-driven approach, this is what I did.

Doing

Radical feminist researchers generate innovative and useful products through the determined pursuit of key theoretical, ethical, and action principles.[5] As I already indicated by opening this chapter with a personal account, one of these principles is to give particular weight to the subjective positioning of women. Being located on the margins of society provides subjugated groups with unique opportunities to perceive and comprehend the world and the power dynamics within it (Hartsock 1983; Kelly 2010). As one such subjugated group, women offer arguably "the sharpest perspective" on patriarchal oppression and sex-based harms (Mertus & Goldberg 1994: 217). This "epistemic advantage" (Zalewski 1993: 21) is crucial to understanding the everyday and everynight violence that women experience in daily life, the abuse that characterises many intimate partner and other familial relationships, and also the harms that emerge from encounters with state structures, systems, institutions, and officials.

To value and integrate insider perspectives and local knowledges into my work, I drew on diverse but specific materials. I integrated not just official data and academic works but also grey literature[6], consistently prioritising temporal currency, practical relevance, insider insights, and intellectual rigour (see Owens 2016). In incorporating these different materials, I aimed to help challenge hierarchies of knowledge and reinforce that "experience, theory and practice should exist in a mutual and immediate relationship with each other" (Stanley & Wise 1993: 89; also Howe 2014). I purposefully selected data in accordance with theoretical ideas, epistemic principles, and to inform emerging concepts (see Coyne 1997; Fereday & Muir-Cochrane 2006). I strategically focussed on Western liberal democratic geo-political contexts, drawing data from my local Australian context alongside comparable countries like New Zealand, the United States, Canada, and the United Kingdom; I chose these contexts because they are widely considered progressive domestic violence responders. They have all criminalised a broad spectrum of violence within intimate relationships, the family, and the home, and according to large-scale comparative studies, they have relatively low rates of domestic violence (UNODC 2014; Garcia-Moreno et al. 2015). Focussing on these contexts was the most rigorous approach for identifying state complicity in domestic violence that enabled me to point to the broader international applicability of my ideas.

I also deliberately sampled academic and practitioner data which privileged qualitative feminist methods, featured primary data, and centred victim-survivors. Survivors' experiential knowledge of how state agencies deal with domestic violence was critical, and their accounts of interactions with the state and its officials offered vital insight into the daily functioning of state power in relation to domestic violence. In particular, I utilised sources which detailed experiences of state institutions with direct domestic violence interface: the criminal legal system, the civil legal system through family law and the family court, and government social service agencies. Whilst noting subtle differences between individual accounts, I was repeatedly struck by the continuity and overlap in women's experiences of patriarchal oppression, domestic violence, and state harms. This affirmed the importance of using individual testimony to highlight collective histories and experiences (see Graham & Schiele 2010). Recognising that harms against women should be redefined in a manner that privileges victim-survivor perspectives and that grassroots groups should be involved in the process of defining state crime (Green & Ward 2019; also McCulloch & Blair 2012), I used these insights to inform my development of concepts and theory and a grounded, bottom-up understanding of how domestic violence constitutes a state crime.

I also put feminist principles into practice by linking theory to action. If feminism is "a politics seeking radical redress" (Ahmed et al. 2000: 1) and feminist praxis is premised upon "a belief that something is wrong and that it can and should be changed" (Stanley & Wise 2000: 265), it is not enough to merely narrate women's experiences. Insider insights must be transmuted into explanatory concepts and theory, thereby producing work that is not only interpretive but also generative and transformative (see e.g. Reinharz 1992; Stanley & Wise 1993; 2000). Accordingly, I made sure to link conceptual and theoretical insights to a practical platform for reconsidering responses to domestic violence. In Chapter 9, I offer a toolkit of ideas for addressing the institutional, structural, and state dimensions of domestic violence which can both complement and challenge our present response repertoire.

I also observed feminist praxis by actively acknowledging the place of emotion in research. In proposing a theory and practice of humanistic social science, Behar (1996: 177) discusses the profound value in being emotionally connected to and even "heart-broken" by one's work. This means accepting not only the challenge but also the value in being a human researcher and having human responses to confronting content. With subject matter involving extreme human suffering, like domestic violence, authentic research and writing embraces its affective dimensions and actively cultivates empathy and understanding for its victims. For this reason, I have not artificially sanitised my writing throughout this book. A common problem with official and academic discourse on domestic violence is its tendency to obscure uncomfortable realities with vague and euphemistic language. In academia, omitting, softening, or neutralising disturbing content in order to avoid critique has also been linked to the production of inauthentic and inaccurate accounts of abuse, atrocity, and trauma (Gutowski & Goodman 2019). I therefore deliberately preserve my own and other survivors' descriptions of their experiences where meaningful, and use emotive language where appropriate. This is a small but symbolically significant attempt to acknowledge human suffering and the importance of representing difficult issues authentically.

Importantly, and aligning with other radical feminist research, adopting a transdisciplinary and problem-driven approach was key to producing new conceptual and theoretical insights. Transdisciplinarity has been described as "the science and art of discovering bridges between different areas of knowledge and being" (Nicolescu 1987 in Klein 2004: 516) and it entails drawing on a diversity of relevant traditions, theories, subject areas, and tools in order to develop innovative and productive ideas for challenging and changing the central problem under investigation. It is a particularly effective way to research complex and apparently intractable social problems like domestic violence, which defy resolution through conventional means. It demands creativity, imagination, innovation, and a willingness to push boundaries of knowledge, discipline, and convention. The particular mode of transdisciplinary practice I adopted reflects Mills' "sociological imagination" (1970: 233) and Barton et al.'s (2007: 2) similar "criminological imagination": it moves beyond conceptual orthodoxies and boundaries and combines ideas in unusual and experimental ways. By working in this manner, I managed to generate new insights that bridged disciplinary siloes, developed new concepts and theory, and offered practical ideas for rethinking how we understand and approach domestic violence.

To further elucidate the conceptual and theory-building processes I engaged, I developed the descriptive and instructive analogy of *upcycled appliqué*. This analogy and its processes follow the qualitative social science research tradition of *bricolage* (e.g. Rogers 2012; Carlen 2017) and previous mixed methods research and theory advancement in the state crime field (e.g. Kauzlarich et al. 2003; Lasslett 2014; Green et al. 2018). My original contribution was to integrate concepts and technical terminology from the creative fields of craft, textiles, and sewing to evoke the specific ways I combined material to generate new conceptual and theoretical products. Upcycling is a recent craft practice involving the transformation of old, worn, or outdated items by restoring, revamping, and often combining multiple pieces in order to produce updated items with new value. *Appliqué* is an old sewing technique where multiple fabrics and textiles of various textures, styles, and sizes are layered, joined, decorated, and embroidered to transform an old, tired garment into something new and original. Visualising my work as a process of intellectual upcycling and appliquéing helped facilitate the creative processes of combining data, concepts, and theory to generate new ways of thinking about domestic violence and the role of the state. By treating research materials as metaphorical layers of fabric, this analogy helped me to combine them in strategic ways in accordance with the underlying philosophy and aim of producing something that is revitalised, transformed, and with new function and utility.

Specifically, to expand understandings of domestic violence and the role of the state, I combined material from criminology and the broader social sciences; international law and interdisciplinary legal theory; feminist sociological, legal, and political theory; studies of trauma and atrocity; and transitional, restorative, reparative, and transformative justice theory and practice. These fields all offered useful insights about domestic violence, its site of perpetration, its actors and agents, the state, state criminality, and how we might understand these phenomena differently. However, they had long existed in parallel siloes. By approaching these materials as metaphorical layers of fabric, I combined, layered, refurbished, and extended them in strategic ways to overcome gaps and limitations and to generate new ways of thinking about the state, domestic violence, and how harms might be more innovatively approached. Working in accordance with the underlying philosophy and aim to create an upcycled appliquéd product that is richer than the sum of its parts, I developed new meta-concepts and meta-theories and an expansive "explanatory interpretive end product" (Schreiber et al. 1997: 312) which is characteristic of qualitative meta-analytical research. In this case, it was a fresh radical feminist framework for understanding domestic violence and the role of the state, a cohesive theory of domestic violence as state crime, and a fresh platform from which to consider addressing this problem.

Notes

1 A gaslighter is a perpetrator who uses deliberate psychological strategies of manipulation and deceit that cause victims to doubt their own perception and sanity (Meyer & Frost 2019). Hayes and Jeffries (2016: 47) refer to it as "crazy-making", and note that many women find it "the most insidious and most damaging" aspect of their victimisation experience.
2 I specify my approach as *radical* feminist to distinguish it from other feminisms, and not to suggest in any way that its principles are radical in the sense of being extreme or extremist. My use of the term describes an all-encompassing philosophy and perspective of the world that merely goes to the root of the problem, to its essence: in this case, identifying a patriarchal society and system within which women are individually and collectively subjugated beneath men.
3 I acknowledge the existence and utility of a range of feminisms, and particularly of intersectional approaches to studying violence against women. Intersectional feminists highlight the value in considering sex and gender in conjunction with other categorising structures of oppression, notably race (e.g. Ritchie 1985; hooks 1989; Crenshaw 1991; Sokoloff & Pearce 2011). The intersectional relevance of disability and chronic illness to women's vulnerability to and experiences of violence is also gaining increased recognition (e.g. Buck & Curran 2009; Healey et al. 2013). I acknowledge the value of intersectional approaches and do incorporate intersectional insights in my analysis; however, my research has necessarily proceeded along broadly structural and radical feminist lines.
4 Although this broader definition of the state is useful, I henceforth persist with a more standard definition and understanding of the 'state' as nation-state: the ideological and instrumental governing structure of a geopolitical territory or

common territories, along with the official institutions and officials that oversee and implement this governance in practice.

5 Although there is dispute over the existence or content of a distinctly feminist method *per se*, common principles do unite much feminist research, and particularly that in the radical and structural tradition (Kelly 1988; Stanley & Wise 1993).

6 Grey literature is produced outside of formal academic publishing channels and typically includes reports from non-government organisations, independent research bodies, industry practitioners, and advocacy groups.

References

Ahmed, Sarah & Kilby, Jane & Lury, Celia & McNeil, Maureen & Skeggs, Beverly. 2000. Thinking through feminism. *Transformations: Thinking Through Feminism*, 1–24. London: Routledge.

Barry, Kathleen. 1979. *Female Sexual Slavery*. New York: New York University Press.

Barton, Alana & Corteen, Karen & Scott, David & Whyte, David. 2007. Developing a criminological imagination. In Barton, Alana & Corteen, Karen & Scott, David & Whyte, David (eds.), *Expanding the Criminological Imagination: Critical Readings in Criminology*. 1–14. Cullompton: Willan.

Behar, Ruth. 1996. *The Vulnerable Observer: Anthropology that Breaks your Heart*. Boston: Beacon Press.

Brownmiller, Susan. 1975. *Against Our Will: Men, Women and Rape*. London: Secker and Warburg.

Buck, Alexy & Curran, Liz. 2009. Delivery of advice to marginalised and vulnerable groups: The need for innovative approaches. *Public Space: The Journal of Law and Social Justice* 3. 1–29.

Bumiller, Kristin. 1987. Rape as a legal symbol: An essay on sexual violence and racism. *University of Miami Law Review* 42(1). 75–91.

Bumiller, Kristin. 1992. Law at the margins: The symbolic power of professional discourse. In Merelman, Richard (ed.), *Language, Symbolism and Politics*. Boulder: Westview Press.

Bumiller, Kristin. 2008. *In an Abusive State: How Neoliberalism Appropriated the Feminist Movement against Sexual Violence*. Durham: Duke University Press.

Burris, Barbara. 1973. The fourth world manifesto. In Crow, Barbara (ed.), *Radical Feminism: A Documentary Reader*, 238–64. New York: New York University Press.

Carlen, Pat. 2017. Doing imaginative criminology. In Jacobsen, Michael & Walklate, Sandra (eds.), *Liquid Criminology*. Abingdon: Routledge.

Charlesworth, Hilary & Chinkin, Christine. 2000. *The Boundaries of International Law: A Feminist Analysis*. Manchester: Manchester University Press.

Connell, Raewyn. 2005. The social organisation of masculinity. *Masculinities*, 67–86. 2nd edn. Berkeley: University of California Press.

Copelon, Rhonda. 1994. Recognising the egregious in the everyday: Domestic violence as torture. *Columbia Human Rights Law Review* 2. 291–367.

Coy, Maddy & Scott, Emma & Tweedale, Ruth & Perks, Katherine. 2015. "It's like going through the abuse again": Domestic violence and women and children's (un)safety in private law contact proceedings. *Journal of Social Welfare & Family Law* 37(1). 53–69.

Coyne, Imelda. 1997. Sampling in qualitative research: Purposeful and theoretical sampling. *Journal of Advanced Nursing* 26(3). 623–30.

Crenshaw, Kimberle. 1991. Mapping the margins: Intersectionality, identity politics, and violence against women of color. *Stanford Law Review* 43(6). 1241–99.

DeKeseredy, Walter. 2016. Understanding woman abuse in intimate heterosexual relationships: The enduring relevance of feminist ways of knowing. *Journal of Family Violence* 31. 1043–6.

Dobash, Rebecca & Dobash, Russell. 1998. *Rethinking Violence against Women*. Thousand Oaks: Sage.

Dworkin, Andrea. 1981. *Pornography: Men Possessing Women*. London: Women's Press.

Enloe, Cynthia. 1983. *Does Khaki Become You: The Militarisation of Women's Lives*. London: Pluto.

Falleiros Braga, Iara & De Oliveira, Wanderlei Adadio & Da Silva, Jorge Luia & Malta De Mello, Flávia Carvalho & Iossi Silva, Marta Angélica. 2018. Family violence against gay and lesbian adolescents and young people: A qualitative study. *Revista Brasileira de Enfermagem* 71. 1220–7.

Fereday, Jennifer & Muir-Cochrane, Eimear. 2006. Demonstrating rigor using thematic analysis: A hybrid approach of inductive and deductive coding and theme development. *International Journal of Qualitative Methods*. March 5(1). 1–11.

Frankland, Andrew & Brown, Jac. 2014. Coercive control in same-sex partner violence. *Journal of Family Violence* 29. 15–22.

Garcia-Moreno, Claudia & Zimmerman, Cathy & Morris-Gehring, Alison & Heise, Lori & Amin, Avni & Abrahams, Naeemah & Montoya, Oswaldo & Bhate-Deosthali, Padma & Kilonzo, Nduku & Watts, Charlotte. 2015. Addressing violence against women: A call to action. *The Lancet* 385. 1685–95.

Graham, Mekada & Schiele, Jerome. 2010. Equality-of-oppressions and anti-discriminatory models in social work: Reflections from the USA and UK. *European Journal of Social Work* 13(2). 231–44.

Green, Penny & MacManus, Thomas & de la Cour Venning, Alicia. 2018. *Genocide Achieved, Genocide Continues: Myanmar's Annihilation of the Rohingya*. London: International State Crime Initiative.

Green, Penny & Ward, Tony. 2019. *State Crime and Civil Activism: On the Dialectics of Repression and Resistance*. New York: Routledge.

Guggisberg, Marika & Fisher, Colleen. 2010. Abused women's double jeopardy interacting with law enforcement on issues of intimate partner violence. *Women against Violence* 22. 18–27.

Gutowski, Ellen & Goodman, Lisa. 2019. "Like I'm invisible": IPV survivor-mothers' perceptions of seeking child custody through the Family Court system. *Journal of Family Violence* 35. 441–57.

Hartsock, Nancy. 1983. The feminist standpoint: Toward a specifically feminist historical materialism. In McCann, Carole & Seung-Kyung, Kim (eds.), *Feminist Local and Global Theory Perspectives Reader*. New York: Routledge.

Hayes, Sharon & Jeffries, Samantha. 2016. Romantic terrorism? An auto-ethnographic analysis of gendered psychological and emotional tactics in domestic violence. *Journal of Research in Gender Studies* 6(2). 38–61.

Healey, Lucy & Humphreys, Cathy & Howe, Keran. 2013. Inclusive domestic violence standards: Strategies to improve interventions for women with disabilities? *Violence and Victims* 28(10). 50–68.

hooks, bell. 1989. Violence in intimate relationships: A feminist perspective. *Talking Back: Thinking Feminist, Thinking Black*, 84–91. Boston: South End Press.

Howe, Adrian. 2014. Dramatizing intimate femicide: Petitions, plays, and public engagement (with a Shakespearean gloss). *Canadian Journal of Women and the Law* 26. 276–99.

Human Security Report Project. 2012. Sexual violence in war-affected countries. *Human Security Report: Sexual Violence, Education, and War: Beyond the Mainstream Narrative*, 19–144. Vancouver: Human Security Press.

Johnson, Michael. 1995. Patriarchal terrorism and common couple violence: Two forms of violence against women. *Journal of Marriage and the Family* 57. 283–94.

Kauzlarich, David & Mullins, Christopher & Matthews, Rick. 2003. A complicity continuum of state crime. *Contemporary Justice Review* 6(3). 241–54.

Kelly, Liz. 1988. *Surviving Sexual Violence.* Cambridge: Polity.

Kelly, Liz. 2010. The everyday / everynightness of rape: Is it different in war? In Sjoberg, Laura & Via, Sandra (eds.), *Gender, War, and Militarism: Feminist Perspectives*, 114–23. Santa Barbara: Praeger Security International.

Kelly, Liz & Radford, Jill. 1996. "Nothing really happened": The invalidation of women's experiences of sexual violence. In Hester, Marianne & Kelly, Liz & Radford, Jill (eds.), *Women, Violence and Male Power: Feminist Activism, Research and Practice.* 19–33. Buckingham: Open University Press.

Klein, Julie. 2004. Prospects for transdisciplinarity. *Futures* 36. 515–26.

Kubicek, Katrina & McNeeley, Miles & Collins, Shardae. 2016. Young men who have sex with men's experiences with intimate partner violence. *Journal of Adolescent Research* 31(2). 143–75.

Laing, Lesley. 2017. Secondary victimization: Domestic violence survivors navigating the family law system. *Violence against Women* 23(11). 1314–35.

Lasslett, Kristian. 2014. *State Crime on the Margins of Empire: Rio Tinto, the War on Bougainville and Resistance to Mining.* London: Pluto Press.

MacKinnon, Catharine. 1982. Feminism, Marxism, method, and the state: An agenda for theory. *Signs: Journal of Women in Culture & Society* 7(3). 515–44.

MacKinnon, Catharine. 1989. *Toward a Feminist Theory of the State.* Cambridge, MA: Harvard University Press.

MacKinnon, Catharine. 1993. On torture: A feminist perspective on human rights. In Mahoney, Kathleen & Mahoney, Paul (eds.), *Human Rights in the Twenty-first Century: A Global Challenge*, 21–31. Boston: M. Nijhoff.

MacKinnon, Catharine. 1994. Rape, genocide and women's human rights. *Harvard Women's Law Journal* 17. 5–16.

MacKinnon, Catharine. 2006. *Are Women Human? And Other International Dialogues.* Cambridge: Harvard University Press.

McCulloch, Jude & Blair, Megan. 2012. Law for justice: The history of Community Legal Centres in Australia. In Stanley, Elizabeth & McCulloch, Jude (eds.), *State Crime and Resistance*, 168–82. Hoboken: Taylor and Francis.

Mertus, Julie & Goldberg, Pamela. 1994. A perspective on women and international human rights after the Vienna Declaration: The inside / outside construct. *New York University Journal of International Law and Politics* 26. 201–34.

Meyer, Doug. 2012. An intersectional analysis of lesbian, gay, bisexual, and transgender (LGBT) people's evaluations of anti-queer violence. *Gender and Society* 26(6). 849–73.

Meyer, Silke. 2011. Seeking help for intimate partner violence: Victims' experiences when approaching the criminal justice system for IPV-related support and protection in an Australian jurisdiction. *Feminist Criminology* 6. 268–90.

Meyer, Silke. 2016. Still blaming the victim of intimate partner violence? Women's narratives of victim desistance and redemption when seeking support. *Theoretical Criminology* 20(1). 75–90.

Meyer, Silke & Frost, Andrew. 2019. *Domestic and Family Violence: A Critical Introduction to Knowledge and Practice.* Abingdon: Routledge.

Millett, Kate. 1969. *Sexual Politics.* London: Virago.

Mills, Charles Wright. 1970. *The Sociological Imagination.* Harmondsworth: Penguin.

Mills, Linda. 1996. On the other side of silence: Affective lawyering for intimate abuse. *Cornell Law Review* 81. 1225–63.

Mills, Linda. 1999. Killing her softly: Intimate abuse and the violence of state intervention. *Harvard Law Review* 113(2). 550–613.

Natalier, Kristin. 2017. Micro-aggressions, single mothers and interactions with government workers: The case of Australia's child support bureaucracy. *Journal of Sociology* 53. 622–36.

Natalier, Kristin. 2018. State facilitated economic abuse: A structural analysis of men deliberately withholding child support. *Feminist Legal Studies* 26(2). 121–40.

Oliffe, John & Han, Christina & Maria, Estephanie & Lohan, Maria & Howard, Terry & Stewart, Donna & MacMillan, Harriet. 2014. Gay men and intimate partner violence: A gender analysis. *Sociology of Health & Illness* 36(4). 564–79.

Owens, Larry. 2016. Reflections of a pracademic: A journey from social work practitioner to academic. *Reflections: Narratives of Professional Helping* 22(1). 37–43.

Pateman, Carol. 1988. *The Sexual Contract.* Stanford: Stanford University Press.

Polk, Kenneth. 1999. Males and honour contest violence. *Journal of Homicide Studies* 3(1). 6–29.

Reeves, Ellen. 2020. Family violence, protection orders and systems abuse: Views of legal practitioners. *Current Issues in Criminal Justice* 32(1). 91–110.

Reilly, Rosemary C. 2020. Reclaiming my sister, Medusa: A critical autoethnography about healing from sexual violence through solidarity, doll-making, and mending myth. *Cultural Studies – Critical Methodologies.* (doi:10.1177/1532708620931132)

Reinharz, Shulamit. 1992. *Feminist Methods in Social Research.* New York: Oxford University Press.

Ritchie, Beth. 1985. Battered black women. *Journal of Black Studies and Research* 16(2). 40–4.

Rogers, Matt. 2012. Contextualising theories and practice of bricolage research. *The Qualitative Report* 17(48). 1–17.

Romany, Celia. 1993. Women as aliens: A feminist critique of the public / private distinction in international human rights law. *The Harvard Human Rights Journal* 6. 87–125.

Russell, Diana. 1982. *Rape in Marriage.* New York: Macmillan.

Salter, Michael. 2016. Real men don't hit women: Constructing masculinity in the prevention of violence against women. *Australian and New Zealand Journal of Criminology* 49(4). 463–79.

Schreiber, Rita & Crooks, Dauna & Stern, Phyllis Noreager. 1997. Qualitative meta-analysis. In Morse, Janice (ed.), *Completing a Qualitative Project: Details and Dialogue.* Thousand Oaks: Sage.

Sokoloff, Natalie J. & Pearce, Susan C. 2011. Intersections, immigration, and partner violence: A view from a new Gateway—Baltimore, Maryland. *Women & Criminal Justice* 21(3). 250–66. (doi:10.1080/08974454.2011.584468)

Stanley, Liz & Wise, Sue. 1993. *Breaking Out Again: Feminist Ontology and Epistemology.* 2nd edn. London: Routledge.

Stanley, Liz & Wise, Sue. 2000. But the empress has no clothes! Some awkward questions about the 'missing revolution' in feminist theory. *Feminist Theory* 1(3). 261–88.

Stark, Evan. 2007. *Coercive Control: How Men Entrap Women in Personal Life.* New York: Oxford University Press.

Stevens, Jacqueline. 1999. Compensatory kinship rules: The mother of gender. *Reproducing the State*, 209–35. Princeton: Princeton University Press.

Ulbrick, Madeleine & Jago, Marianne. 2018. *"Officer She's Psychotic and I Need Protection": Police Misidentification of the Primary Aggressor in Family Violence Incidents in Victoria.* Women's Legal Service Victoria.

United Nations General Assembly. 1979. *Convention on the Elimination of All Forms of Discrimination against Women.* UN Doc A/RES/34/180.

United Nations General Assembly. 1991. *Vienna Declaration and Programme of Action.* UN Doc A/CONF.157/23.

United Nations General Assembly. 1993. *Declaration on the Elimination of Violence against Women.* UN Doc A/RES/48/104.

United Nations Office on Drugs and Crime. 2014. *Global Study on Homicide 2013: Trends, Contexts, Data.* (https://www.unodc.org/documents/gsh/pdfs/2014_GLOBAL_HOMICIDE_ BOOK_web.pdf)

United Nations Office on Drugs and Crime. 2019. *Global Study on Homicide 2019: Gender-Related Killing of Women and Girls.* Vienna. (https://www.unodc.org/documents/data-and-analysis/gsh/Booklet_5.pdf)

Zalewski, Marysia. 1993. Feminist standpoint theory meets international relations theory: A feminist version of David and Goliath? *Fletcher Forum of World Affairs,* Summer.

Part II

The state crime dimensions of domestic violence

Chapter 3

Domestic violence as state crime against humanity

This chapter details the first of five standalone frameworks for understanding domestic violence as a state crime. Here, I argue that domestic violence can be understood as an *international crime* and a *state crime against humanity*. By strategically integrating international criminal law, interdisciplinary legal and state crime literature, domestic violence data, and feminist theory into a productive analytical lens, I demonstrate how domestic violence can be understood not just as an individual interpersonal crime but as a systematic collective harm which impacts all women and which functions with distinct organised patterns and dynamics. I also identify how domestic violence operates with the wider ideological, political, and policy support of patriarchal states and how state complicity can be understood at a deeper foundational level through states' generative role in the institutional and ideological frameworks through which domestic violence occurs.

Theorising international crimes and crimes against humanity

International crimes are codified in the Rome Statute of the International Criminal Court. They are classified as "grave crimes ... of concern to the international community as a whole" which "threaten the peace, security and well-being of the world" (ICC 1998: Preamble). Crimes against humanity are a particular category of international crime stipulated in the Statute as "inhumane acts ... intentionally causing great suffering or serious injury to body or to mental or physical health" (ICC 1998: Art 7.1.k). Cited examples include enslavement, imprisonment, torture, sexual violence, murder, collective persecution, and apartheid; however, what makes this category of crime distinctive is not the gravity of offences but rather that they involve the "multiple commission of acts" (ICC 1998: Art 7.2.a) and are "committed as part of a widespread or systematic attack ... directed against a specific civilian population" (ICC 1998: Art 7.1; 2011: Art 7.3). Crimes against humanity are also distinctive because they are associated with "state or organisational policy" to "promote or encourage such an attack" (ICC 2011: Art 7.3).[1]

DOI: 10.4324/9781003132370-5

Crimes against humanity have been considered not just in actionable legal terms, but in philosophical, political, moral, and normative conceptual terms. The notion appeals to a visceral human morality, implying something "particularly heinous" (Schabas 2007: 83) that violates an "inherent humanness" that is common to all people (Meyersfeld 2003: 425). It also alludes to a shared human bond and collective conscience (Robertson 2002; Geras 2011; Jalloh 2013). Regardless of definitional variations, however, the consensus across legal documents, legal literature, and interdisciplinary scholarly and activist commentary is that crimes against humanity are unique in both severity and character. They are not only harms of extreme gravity, scale, impact, and multi-level threat; they also involve repetitive and systematic patterns of perpetration and victimisation, a collective dimension, and an organised or state dimension. In Vernon's (2002; 2013) view, what is distinctive about crimes against humanity is that the state or authorities themselves become involved in violating citizens. In fact, according to many legal, socio-legal and state crime scholars, crimes against humanity are considered "one of the quintessential crimes of state" (Bassiouni 2011: 47).

This final distinguishing feature of crimes against humanity – their association with "a state or organisational policy" (ICC 2011: Art 7.3) – is arguably their most ambiguous component. Across legal documents and interpretive scholarship, the notion of state 'policy' can refer to diverse and even diffuse forms of state connection and involvement (see e.g. ICC 1998; 2011; ICTR 1998; ICTY 2001; Vernon 2002; 2013; Schabas 2008; Bassiouni 2011; Geras 2011; Balint 2012; Shenkman 2012; Jalloh 2013). Whilst policy of course encompasses official written laws, rules, or guidelines, it can also refer to unwritten but widely accepted norms and precedents concerning the everyday functioning of the state, its institutions, and the practical interpretation and implementation of policy. Notably, it can also relate to state inaction as well as action, since the failure to prevent grave harms of a collective nature qualifies as policy (see Copelon 2000). This is particularly salient when it comes to violence against women.

Despite its in-principle equal applicability to women and men, international criminal law has been widely critiqued for its discriminatory focus. MacKinnon (e.g. 1994; 2006) argues that legal and political institutions have always conceived of human as a male concept and have thus fundamentally struggled to expand this to include women. International (and indeed all) law has developed according to the presumption that men are its sole subjects, leading to its broad development along masculine lines and to the exclusion of distinctively female experiences of harm (also Smart 1989; Charlesworth & Chinkin 2000; Meyersfeld 2010; Otto 2012). Where international crimes and crimes against humanity against women have been officially recognised, it has generally been in conflict contexts. For instance, following genocidal atrocities in Rwanda and the former Yugoslavia in the early 1990s, mass rapes of women were pursued through *ad hoc* International Criminal Tribunals, with case outcomes seeing the codification of a range of sexual violence as international crimes and crimes against humanity (e.g. *Prosecutor v. Akayesu* ICTR 1998; *Prosecutor v. Kunarac, Kovac and Vukovic (Foca)* ICTY 2001). War-time rape was explicitly named a war crime, form of torture, and, in certain circumstances, an act of genocide (Copelon 2000; Simpson 2007; Henry 2011; Simm 2018). In these landmark cases, sexual crimes were acknowledged as grave violations resulting from organised and purposeful state action and inaction.

However, these advances have not been accompanied by a corresponding increase in the recognition of harms against women in peacetime and the private sphere. Although far more prevalent than war-time violence, everyday atrocities against women such as men torturing their wives or murdering prostitutes are rarely recognised as grave harms of urgent social or political import (Copelon 1994; MacKinnon 1994; Sideris 2001; Enloe 2012). These "everyday" violations against women (Kelly 2010: 114) tend to be perpetrated in relative obscurity and with impunity. Violence against women in the domestic sphere in particular – despite being perpetrated on a greater scale and causing greater global harm (HSRP 2012; UNODC 2014; Guggisberg 2018) – has not received the same level of attention or recognition as conflict-related violence against women. In fact, unfortunately, the focus on war-time atrocities and their framing as an urgent international concern can, and has, fostered the problematic impression that they are more serious, prevalent, and worthy of action than other forms of violence against women (MacKenzie 2010; Meger 2016). This has tended to elicit condemnation of violence in war, but implicit acceptance of it in peacetime and in everyday lives and homes.

Framing war-time violence against women as exceptional and actionable has also contributed to the problematic differentiation and ranking of violations of women. This practice involves specific forms of victimisation and suffering being compared and categorised according to their perceived level of seriousness, generating an unethical hierarchy which "privileges some [harms against women] while excluding or trivialising others" (Mertus & Goldberg 1994: 218; also Henry 2013; 2014). Although accurately identifying and describing harms is worthwhile, "to rank the egregious demeans it" (Copelon 1995: 208; also Tatz 2011). Ranking violations is also problematic because it differentiates and compares the suffering of the innocent war victim and the supposedly willing victim in everyday life (Heineman 2011; Henry 2011). The lack of attention to women's most common experiences of violence in everyday life, in so-called peacetime, and in the private sphere, directly contributes to their obscurity and their disturbing normalisation. This is what I now confront. By bringing domestic violence data and a radical feminist theoretical lens to bear on an international criminal legal framework, I show that domestic violence can, both empirically and conceptually, be theorised as an international crime and a crime against humanity.

Theorising domestic violence as an international crime

Like other crimes deemed internationally significant, domestic violence is a harm of extreme gravity. Official data from a range of national and international contexts routinely detail severe criminal acts including beating, burning, strangulation, rape, reproductive violence, imprisonment, isolation, systematic psychological and physical torture, threats of extreme violence, and of course murder (Chan & Payne 2013; Breiding et al. 2014; CPS 2017; Bradel et al. 2019). Individually, many of these acts are already codified within the Rome Statute: for example, systematic persecution, severe deprivation of liberty, enslavement, imprisonment, rape, forced pregnancy, and murder are all specifically identified as examples of international crimes (see ICC 1998; 2011). Additionally, when specific incidents of severe violence are perpetrated as part of an abusive regime, they constitute terrorism and torture, which are also codified within these international frameworks. In moral and normative terms, there can be no doubt that these heinous harms are violations of the highest order. Domestic violence therefore fulfils the gravity requirement.

Domestic violence is also perpetrated on a mass scale across national and international contexts. It is the most prominent health risk for women internationally, regardless of geo-political context, race, class, language, culture, or religion (UNGA 1993; Garcia-Moreno et al. 2015; Guggisberg 2018).[2] Indeed, the extreme prevalence of this harm across diverse global contexts has led many commentators to refer to it as an international 'epidemic' or 'pandemic' (e.g. Price 2018; Moreira & Pinto da Costa 2020). The Executive Director of United Nations Women recently described violence against women and girls as the "shadow pandemic" of the Covid era (Mlambo-Ngcuka 2020: n.p.). Notwithstanding the problematic connotations of such terminology (see e.g. Deer 2015; Rose 2017), these are accurate descriptors for the pure magnitude of domestic and family violence. United Nations homicide statistics show that in 2017 alone, over 30,000 women worldwide were intentionally killed by a current or former intimate partner, that a further 20,000 were killed by other family members, and that these figures are on the increase (UNODC 2019).[3]

Domestic violence is a genuinely global problem. Across diverse contexts, World Health Organisation data show that between 15% and 71% of women have experienced intimate partner violence, with a third generally accepted as the global mean (WHO 2013; Garcia-Moreno et al. 2015; Bradel et al. 2019). Although cross-contextual rates do vary, comparable developed liberal democratic Western countries still have alarmingly high rates of domestic violence, with approximately a third of women reporting physical or sexual violation by a partner at some point in their lives (Guggisberg 2018; UNODC 2019; NCADV 2020). In the United States, over ten million women have been raped by an intimate partner, and every fourteen hours a woman is fatally shot by a current or former partner (NCADV 2017). In England and Wales, two women every week become intimate partner homicide victims (ONS 2019), and despite Australia's relatively small population, an average of one woman is similarly killed every week (Walklate et al. 2019). The uncomfortable reality is that no society, no matter how progressive, is free of domestic violence.

The severity and scale of domestic violence across the world indicates its widespread impact and positions it as a security threat on several levels. Firstly, domestic violence affects the short- and long-term health and well-being of victim-survivors. It causes significant immediate damage to physical, sexual, and psychological health and also correlates with complex and chronic physical and mental illness, self-harm, and suicide (NCRVAWAC 2009; Guggisberg 2018; Campbell et al. 2020). Domestic violence is also closely connected to lifetimes of heightened vulnerability to other forms of disadvantage and suffering including poverty, unemployment, and housing insecurity (WLSV 2018; Voth Schrag et al. 2019). Breiding et al.'s (2014) United States-based study, for example, shows that women experiencing food insecurity are four to five times more likely to have experienced domestic violence, indicating the intersection between this harm and other human rights and security issues. Although security discourses tend to be dominated by nation-state-level concerns, "security is also an everyday phenomenon" (Walklate et al. 2019: 62) and domestic harms are central to women's experiences of insecurity.

Domestic violence is also closely connected to other forms of sexual and gender-based violence. War-time violence against women is not aberrant or exceptional, nor is so-called 'post-conflict' or 'peacetime' safe for women (Moser 2001; MacKenzie 2010; Enloe 2012). In fact, "there is unfortunately not so sharp a difference between war and everyday life. Torture and rape in conflict situations have too much in common with rape in the marital bedroom [and] battering in the home" (Copelon 2000: 230). The continuities and causal connections between domestic and other violence further signify the threat it poses to the security of individuals, communities, societies, and the world.

Theorising domestic violence as a crime against humanity

Domestic violence also meets the criteria that distinguish crimes against humanity as a specific type of international crime. The first of these relates to repetitive and systematic patterns of harm. This can be identified with domestic violence firstly because each case of abuse involves repeated violations of the individual victim. The majority of cases reported to authorities in Western jurisdictions involve multiple, systematic, and often escalating violations, as they are part of coercive control regimes (Stark 2007; Flood 2012; Breiding et al. 2014; DeKeseredy 2016). Coercive control is a constellation of strategies designed to undermine, intimidate, manipulate, and threaten the victim, and maintain total control over the relationship and family. It often involves social and cultural isolation, repetitive verbal, psychological, sexual, and economic abuse, and various monitoring and surveillance strategies. Whilst it can involve injurious physical assault, coercive control is often specifically designed not to cause visible marks so as to remain undetected by others. In public, a coercive controlling relationship may appear benign and even caring, yet most perpetrators have a repertoire of verbal references, facial expressions, gestures, and body language that can subtly intimidate, degrade, and threaten the victim. Without exception, each case of coercive control involves multiple forms of abuse which are repetitive, intersecting, and which escalate over time (Johnson 2008; Meyer & Frost 2019; Stark & Hester 2019). The consistent and persistent abuse within each of these domestic violence regimes shows why it can be understood as a harm involving repetitive and systematic patterns.

Domestic violence also involves systematic broader patterns of perpetration and victimisation. Data consistently show that this violence is overwhelmingly perpetrated by men against women and that neither female offending nor male victimisation compare in terms of frequency, severity, power dynamic, overall pattern of domination, or victim impact (Johnson 2010; Enander 2011; Flood 2012; Kimmel 2013; Meyer & Frost 2019). As feminist human rights scholars have demonstrated, this clear group dynamic positions domestic violence as a sex-based harm, since it so disproportionately affects women (Beasley & Thomas 1994; MacKinnon 1994; Romany 1994; Bettinger-Lopez 2008; Meyersfeld 2010). I also argue that this global perpetrator-victim dynamic shows that domestic violence constitutes a systematic collective harm perpetrated against a "specific civilian population" (ICC 1998: Art 7.1; 2011: Art 7.3), which is another stipulation of the crimes against humanity framework. Additionally, I nominate conceptualising any individual woman's domestic victimisation as part of a "widespread or systematic attack" (ICC 1998: Art 7.1; 2011: Art 7.3) because her experience of abuse occurs within the broader context of similar, simultaneous attacks against other women in her community and around the world. This is evidenced by figures showing that, in 2017 alone, over 50,000 women worldwide were intentionally killed by a current or former intimate partner or other family member (see UNODC 2019).

Systematic and collective patterns in domestic violence are also identifiable through the notably consistent perpetration tactics adopted by individual offenders. Despite there being no official perpetrator training courses or manuals – although such written material abounds online in the absence of state censure or regulation – the frequency of cases with identical patterns and minute details is remarkable. Across diverse temporal, geographic, and cultural contexts, perpetrators' use of particular derogatory phrases in precise settings, complex threats using identical language, specifically timed escalating tactics, and sophisticated gaslighting[4] techniques have led scholars, practitioners, and commentators to describe the abstract existence of scripts, toolkits, handbooks, textbooks, and even schools of men's domestic abuse (e.g. Barry 1979; Kelly 1988; 2010; Graham 1994; Radford & Stanko 1996; Evans 2006; Cameron 2014; Kelly et al. 2014; Hill 2019). In the United States, Stark (2007: 259) notes how, regardless of race, class, or culture, variations on insults such as bitch, pig, slut, and whore are virtually universal in abusive relationships. These labels denote women as dirty and sexually corrupt: confirming their subordinate status as tainted, sexualised sinners who deserve male derogation and violation. This pattern of verbal and psychological abuse is also identified in McKenzie et al.'s (2016: 58) Australian study of domestic homicides, where compulsive unfounded suspicions of infidelity and the use of "derogatory gendered terms" including slut, bitch, and whore were documented in a significant number of cases and across different cultural and linguistic backgrounds. Eleven out of the fifty-one men who were tried for killing their (ex-)partner used almost identical language and phrasing to either directly or indirectly abuse their victims. This evidence demonstrates how domestic abuse of women by men in diverse contexts is unified by continuities and patterns.

Sexed and sexualised patterns in domestic violence are further revealed when considering continuities in assault and injury. Stark (2007) notes that humiliating and degrading sexual treatment is routine in abusive relationships around the world and that partner assaults of women by men invariably have a sexual component. This is evidenced by the prevalence of injuries to body parts associated with female sexuality: the face, breasts, and genitals. In the United States, Reckdenwald et al. (2019) identify the face as a common area for injurious intimate partner assaults, which they suggest is targeted by abusers in order to visibly mark and dehumanise their victim. Further indicating the sexualised nature of much domestic violence, Boxall et al.'s (2020) Australian study shows that, amongst women who reported recent domestic abuse, almost half were victims of specifically *sexual* partner abuse. In United States-based interview research with women who reported losing consciousness due to their partner striking them in the head, St. Ivany et al. (2018) found that medical attention was often denied because women were raped immediately after being physically assaulted, whilst they were either conscious or semi-conscious. Researchers found that this was a common way that perpetrators further asserted their physical and sexual dominance and ensured that their victim was isolated from potential sources of help whilst critically injured. This disturbing range of evidence illustrates the deeply sexualised nature of domestic violence and how it is used as a tool to reinforce women's status as sexual objects to be owned, used, and abused by men.

The collective harm caused by domestic violence can also be understood through its pervasive group impact. This is because all forms of violence against women affect all women. Generations of data reveal the all-encompassing nature of violation and violence that girls and women experience throughout their lives. Spanning childhood sexual objectification and incest; harassment in schools, universities, and workplaces; confrontation with sexualised obscenities and degrading advertising in public; surveillance, stalking, sexual assault, and of course a spectrum of intimate partner and family violence; this diversity of harms is described by Radford and Stanko (1996: 67) as the "permanent backdrop" for women's existence and relationships. Feminist scholars have documented how this "legacy of terror" creates "a way of life for women" (Barry 1979: 43). The knowledge, awareness, and for many the experience of violence has a cumulative and pervasive effect because this ever-present threat is a perpetual source of concern. Researchers have documented the extensive, complex, and constant ways that women order their daily lives around minimising risks of victimisation in both the private and public spheres; on the other hand, men demonstrate no comparable adaptive behaviours to real or perceived risks (see e.g. Kelly 1988; 2010; Graham 1994; Connell 2005; Katz 2006). As the most common form of violence against women, domestic violence has a negative impact that extends beyond individuals to families, neighbourhoods, communities, and societies (Pain 2012; Walklate et al. 2019). It profoundly affects the personal safety, well-being, and ability to enjoy a peaceful existence for half the world's population.

Domestic violence can also in broader terms be understood as a systematic, collective harm with political, policy, and state elements. This relates to the final distinguishing feature of crimes against humanity: they are strategic, organised, and associated with the state. Conventionally, crimes against humanity are most often understood in terms of racial or ethnic ideologies, violations, and state interests; however, these are not the only dimensions through which they occur. A distinguishing feature of crimes against humanity and other state crimes is that their perpetration furthers the interests of either the state or of elite groups controlling the state (Kauzlarich et al. 2003). In other words, these crimes have the underlying aim of creating or maintaining the state in a particular political image or according to particular political ideologies (Balint 2012). Arguably the most well-known example of a crime against humanity, the World War II Holocaust involved the systematic subjugation, persecution, mass murder, genocide, and attempted annihilation of Jewish people as an ethnic and cultural group (Tatz 1985; Kolin 2008). South African apartheid is another widely cited example involving the systematic segregation, oppression, enslavement, and violation of Peoples of Colour (SATRC 1998; Boraine 2000; Stanley 2005; Rose 2015). In both these contexts, crimes against humanity were based on ideologies of white supremacy and were perpetrated with the aim of creating a particular racial and ethnic state.

A radical feminist lens illuminates crimes against humanity not only along the lines of race and ethnicity, but along the lines of sex. Caputi and Russell (1990 in Caulfield & Wonders 1993: 88) allude to the crime against humanity of racial and ethnic genocide when theorising violence against women thus:

> *Most people understand that lynchings and pogroms are motivated by political objectives: preserving white and gentile supremacy. Similarly, the aim of violence against women – conscious or not – is to preserve male supremacy.*

In fact, systematic patriarchal harms like domestic violence have already been referred to as femicide and gynocide (see e.g. Barry 1979; Caputi 1989; Russell & Radford 1992; Howe 2014). The term 'femicide' is even used by United Nations bodies (e.g. UNGA 2006; UNODC 2019), which acknowledge that violent hate crimes are systematically committed against women and girls because of their sex and with misogynistic motives.[5] When many tens of thousands of females worldwide are killed by partners and family every year in the process of policing sex-based subordination (see UNODC 2019), oppressive patriarchal ideology is clearly at play. These women and girls are victims of the systematic private policing of their inferior political and social status and these atrocities are directly related to maintaining male supremacy. Thinking about this violence as aligned with *patriarchal* interests underscores that it is not just individual or interpersonal, but distinctly *collective* and *political*.

By highlighting the patriarchal character and interests of the nation-state, domestic victimisation can also be illuminated as a critical cog within an organised, systematic, group-based subjugation project. Through a radical feminist lens, female subjugation is pervasive, simultaneously occurring at different sites, by different individual and collective men, yet with common features and aims. As Connell (2005: 83) explains:

> *… the privileged group use violence to sustain their dominance. Intimidation of women ranges across the spectrum from wolf-whistling in the street, to office harassment, to rape and domestic assault, to murder by a woman's patriarchal 'owner', such as a separated husband… [all] commonly accompanied by verbal abuse of women.*

All these harms target women "precisely because they are women" (True 2012: 9; also Jeffreys 1997) and function in tandem to systematically subjugate this group and sustain male supremacy. Domestic violence in particular is a unique form of female subjugation with specific features which enhance its impact. It is perpetrated within a private and relatively hidden context; it is also perpetrated by those who are closest to the victim and upon whom the victim is often reliant – for example, for protection from poverty, social stigma, or outside threats of violence. In this sense, the abuse of power and trust inherent in any act of domestic violence makes it all-encompassing in its impact, arguably rivalling that of any other source (McQuigg 2011). This positions it a crucial element within the wider subjugation project.

Additionally implicating the state, the private institutions in which domestic violence occurs can be understood as state-created structures of harm. Across common law systems, marriage and the family were historically established as part of the overarching patriarchal political structure. As important building blocks of the patriarchal state, these institutions were, by design, inherently unequal and harmful. Men's ownership of women was officially documented in law to ensure control over their wives, with married women assuming the status of their husband's property (Cobbe 1878; Deer 2015). Ideologically, because men were considered spiritually, morally, and intellectually superior, they were nominated the rulers of the family unit and required by law to lead, guide, instruct, and control their wife and children (Pateman 1988; Stevens 1999; McQuigg 2011). Men were directed not only to use instructive corporal punishment on their children but to physically discipline their wives to aid the maintenance of patriarchal private-sphere order (Dobash & Dobash 1998; Hattery & Smith 2012). In fact, through specifying what were perceived to be reasonable bounds of men's violence in the family (Dworkin 1981), state law explicitly endorsed the harm. The state therefore created the institutional foundations for domestic violence.

Domestic violence has also been afforded particular state protection. By officially designating the domestic sphere an exceptional zone which should be free from outside interference or intervention, the state legitimised inaction against men's domestic and family violence (Pateman 1988; Mertus & Goldberg 1994; Sullivan 1995; Stevens 1999; Hildebrandt 2006). This ensured that it could be systematically obscured and overlooked. Feminist human rights scholars have already comprehensively identified that the "legalised disregard" for domestic violence and the "official impunity" afforded perpetrators represents state support for the violation (MacKinnon 1993: 29; also Romany 1993; Copelon 1994; Meyersfeld 2003; Libal & Parekh 2009; Hakimi 2010).[6] Since crimes against humanity require a "state or organisational policy" element that "promote[s] or encourage[s the] attack" (ICC 2011: Art 7.3) and since this can include policy failures (Copelon 2000), purposeful and demonstrable state inaction against domestic violence is further evidence of this harm constituting a crime against humanity. As I further explore in the following chapter, despite the official criminalisation of domestic violence in common law contexts, private-sphere exceptionalism endures in the present, limiting legal intervention in the harm and enabling men to offend with impunity.[7]

Because state inaction against domestic violence reinforces patriarchal power, it can also be understood as ideological and political in the sense that it further entrenches women's subordinate position in society. Caulfield and Wonders (1993: 92) nominate the term "political crime" to describe domestic and other violence against women because it is an outcome of states' refusal to appropriately criminalise harms, sanction men's violence, or provide full legal protections to women. State failures in this area have also been identified as the deprivation of citizenship rights on the basis of sex (Beasley & Thomas 1994; MacKinnon 1994; Naranch 1997). In the United States, Stark (2007) extends this to conceptualise domestic violence as a liberty crime, due to the way that men's violence – coupled with state inaction – prevents women from exercising their constitutional rights to equality, liberty, safety, and integrity. This further underscores the ideological and political nature of domestic abuse and its connections to the state.

These state roles in domestic violence align with a broad understanding of state liability – or 'policy', in the language of international criminal law – as creating the harmful frameworks from which violations emanate. A holistic understanding of state criminality also encompasses the nation-state's creation of the structural and institutional frameworks within which atrocities can be perpetrated with widespread impunity. The 'Mau Mau' litigation is illustrative here (see Bowcott 2016; also Balint 2016; 2019). This lawsuit was brought by Kenyans against the British state for extreme violations perpetrated in various detention centres under the 1950s colonial administration. The British High Court not only adjudicated the state's liability for specific acts of torture and brutality perpetrated against detainees; it also considered the idea that state complicity encompasses states' creation of the structural and institutional frameworks, and thus the possibilities, for systematic violence to occur. In case judgements, the High Court conceptualised the system of abuse and detention established by the British colonial administration as the foundation of the violence since it set up the official framework within which atrocities could be perpetrated in obscurity and with impunity. This was narrated as creating vicarious liability for the state. I argue that this is a comparable framework of state liability for domestic violence because states created, sanctified, and protected the legal and political institutions in which domestic atrocities are perpetrated, thus further positioning domestic violence as a state crime against humanity.

In more explicit terms also, marriage and the family systematically produce domestic violence harms that are already stipulated as crimes against humanity: enslavement, torture, and terrorism. Over a century and a half ago, revolutionary feminists were already documenting incisive critiques of marriage and the family, their foundation upon men's violent dominion, and the systematic harms perpetrated within these institutions. Harriet Taylor Mill (1869: 160–2), for example, theorised marriage as a state-supported institution of "domestic slavery". She likened the status of wives to that of ancient Greek or Roman slaves, but noted that slaves had the right to refuse sexual advances from their owners whereas wives did not, meaning that a woman's husband could "claim from her and enforce the lowest degradation of a human being, that of being made the instrument of an animal function contrary to her inclinations". Later, Pateman (1988: 154) similarly identified the family as an institution which enabled men to "exercise the power of a slave-owner over [their] wife". The grossly inferior status of women in the family has been widely documented as men's literal "chattel property", since their value was established in the same way as with other moveable property such as slaves (Dworkin 1981: 101; also Deer 2015).

Torture within the state-ordained framework of marriage has also been documented by generations of feminist scholars and activists. An early critique by Francis Power Cobbe (1878: 48–9) challenged the familiar legal terminology of her times, 'wife-beating', labelling it a euphemism and arguing that it disguised "the extremity of the cruelty involved" with men's violence in the home. She identified that the typically escalating nature of marital violence meant that "wife-beating,… in numberless cases, advances to wife-torture, and the wife-torture usually ends in wife-maiming, wife-blinding, or wife-murder". Feminists of the modern era elaborated on this insight by systematically identifying how certain domestic abuse actually constitutes torture in accordance with the Universal Declaration of Human Rights (UNGA 1948) and the Convention against Torture (UNGA 1984) (see Russell 1982; MacKinnon 1993; Copelon 1994; Meyersfeld 2003; Sifris 2014).

The domestic sphere has also been exposed as a site of officially disregarded terrorism. Kelly's (1988) early critique of the incongruity of political attention to international terrorism highlighted that the domestic terrorism of intimate partner abuse threatened far greater numbers of people on an everyday basis. Other feminist scholars joined Kelly in challenging the disproportionate media focus on random international terrorist acts, when compared to the stark silence and normalisation of the "everyday taken-for-granted campaign of terror" waged against women in the home (Finn 1989: 376). Drawing on the psycho-social theory of Stockholm Syndrome[8], Graham's (1994) work shows that abusive intimate relationships have parallel power dynamics to those between international terrorists and their hostages. Many authors have further conceptualised "everyday terrorism" in the home by identifying how specific and intersecting oppressive tactics create an overall regime of isolation, intimidation, and ever-present fear for the victim (Pain 2012: 8; also Johnson 1995; 2008; 2011; Stark 2007; Hayes & Jeffries 2016). Since enslavement, torture, and terrorism are all stipulated as crimes against humanity, domestic violence is clearly appropriate for conceptualisation within this framework.

Considering the machinations of crimes against humanity further illuminates how domestic violence can be understood through this lens. Green et al. (2018) argue that genocide and other crimes against humanity are best understood not as "a legal construction, which reifies individual intent" but "as a complex social process" (22) "with no clearly defined end" (14). To understand and accurately identify these crimes, they posit that it is essential to scrutinise not just specific violations and individual perpetrators, but historical, political, structural, and institutional dimensions of state and elite power that underpin violent acts (also Laplante 2009; Henry 2013; Balint 2014; Stanley 2014). For example, Kolin's (2008) analysis of genocide illuminates the diverse facets of state power that undergird, precede, disguise, and facilitate the commission of atrocities. This work highlights how states can perpetrate gross, heinous, and systematic harms in a normalised and even invisible manner over time by ensuring that "ordinary violence is woven into the social fabric" (68). At diverse sites and through often subtle processes that differentiate and stigmatise certain social groups, the wider population can become desensitised to the concept and practice of mass coercion and violence against certain groups. This work emphasises the importance of considering wider processes and practices which provide the groundwork for state crimes against humanity to become possible; it also sheds light on how particular conditions and practices can normalise and justify harms against certain groups in society.

This type of nuanced analysis is especially important for identifying crimes against humanity and state crimes in so-called developed liberal democracies, which often unfold over long historical periods. Whilst these societies may appear peaceful and non-violent, this façade masks state criminality in the form of systematic repression, violation, and subtle attempts to undermine or destroy certain social groups. For example, the treatment of Indigenous populations in colonial contexts like Australia has been identified as a complex process of genocide (Tatz 1985; 2003; Manne 2004; Henry 2015; Curthoys et al. 2018).[9] This state harm encompasses states' establishment of the ideological foundations of group inferiority and indispensability, symbolically violent politics, systematically unequal structural conditions, and the conscious administration of generations of racist policies. But because this symbolic and state violence unfolds over an extended historical period, the subordinate status of the target group comes to be widely regarded as normal, natural, and unremarkable, and thus undeserving of critique or remedy (see Shelby 2014; Haslanger 2017). Careful attention must therefore be paid to identifying and deconstructing complex state crimes like these.

Similarly, recognising and understanding state crimes against women must involve nuanced attention to how they variously manifest in subtle ways and over long historical periods. When certain types of violence, perpetrated either directly or indirectly by the state, have been systematically tolerated by the state over an extended timeframe, this has long-term impacts. Even when these harms are eventually criminalised, little may change. This is because although the contemporary state might in one sense communicate official intolerance of the harm, the powerful structural, institutional, and cultural forces which first endorsed it endure (MacKinnon 2019). This is certainly the case with domestic violence, which continues to be reproduced at epidemic levels despite its criminal codification and official condemnation. The underlying structural violence that originally produced systematic inequality endures, as do the institutional frameworks that reified and enabled group supremacy in the first place. Thus, the systematic collective violence continues as part of a long-term patriarchal state crime event.

A similar feminist analysis of the state foundations for domestic violence and other systematic harms against women highlights the historical and contemporary processes that produce and reproduce male dominance and the system-wide conditions "that support, condone, or ignore gross power imbalances including the subjugation of women" (Mertus & Goldberg 1994: 228). It looks at the harmful but invisible and normalised ideologies, narratives, and practices that obscure, minimise, and legitimise male control, entitlement, and aggression; it considers the complementary frameworks that stigmatise women and position them as responsible for, or deserving of, domestic abuse. It also examines state structures, institutions, agencies, individual officials, and public and private actors, considering how these function together towards patriarchal aims and contribute to the production and reproduction of domestic and other violence against women. It is these multiple state dimensions of domestic violence that the following chapters of Part II will further explore.

Conclusion

Conceptualising domestic violence as an international crime and a state crime against humanity highlights the international significance of this harm as well as broader dimensions of perpetration, victimisation, and responsibility. Thinking about domestic violence against women as a crime against humanity in particular offers a constructive new way of understanding it. Firstly, it situates specific violations of individual women by individual men within the context of similar, simultaneous attacks against other women. Secondly, it effectively captures how domestic violence is not just a series of heinous criminal acts but also a form of systematic and collective group persecution, since women are members of the same subjugated group and are so disproportionately victimised. Thirdly, it provides a framework through which to begin considering the state's implication in domestic violence, since crimes against humanity are widely understood as a type of state crime.

I argue that thinking about domestic violence in this way can also help prompt useful shifts in how we respond to it. Firstly, this conceptual frame elevates domestic violence from merely a type of interpersonal violence criminalised by local jurisdictions to a harm of wider significance for which there are multiple layers of culpability and responsibility. The framework also highlights the impact of domestic violence on women not just individually, but collectively. It therefore offers a valuable counterpoint to the individualised, interpersonal narratives of domestic violence that dominate contemporary discourse and practice. Conceiving of domestic violence in this way underscores the need for more holistic approaches to prevention and redress and points towards a multi-faceted approach to addressing complicity, impact, and responsibility – including at the state level.

Notes

1 This necessarily distilled account highlights key definitional principles using the language of the Rome Statute but is the product of diverse consultations of

statutory law, case law, and a variety of legal and interdisciplinary scholarship on what constitutes international crimes and crimes against humanity. The citations throughout this section are indicative of the sources I consulted.

2 Beyond being female, other markers of subordination and disadvantage can increase the risk of experiencing domestic violence. In both the United States and Australia, for example, sex intersects with race, ethnicity, socio-economic status, and other factors in impacting risk and harm (Graham-Bermann & Halabu 2004; Murray & Powell 2009; Kimmel 2013). Important recent progress is also being made in recognising the heightened vulnerability of disabled and chronically ill women to domestic violence (e.g. Buck & Curran 2009; Engnes & Lundgren 2013; Healey et al. 2013).

3 The broader data set includes an additional significant number of women who were killed by perpetrators with an unknown or unspecified relationship to the victim, indicating that the domestic homicide figure represents an underestimation of the actual number of such cases.

4 Gaslighting is a deliberate psychological abuse strategy where perpetrators manipulate and deceive victims into doubting their own perception and sanity (Meyer & Frost 2019). Hayes and Jeffries (2016: 47) aptly term it "crazy-making" and note that many women experience it as "the most insidious and most damaging" aspect of domestic victimisation.

5 Certain Latin American countries have also codified femicide as a specific criminal offence, recognising that women and girls are sometimes killed (often by family) specifically because of their subordinate status or role as female (see UN-ODC 2019).

6 These arguments have more recently been upheld in transnational courts, where rulings confirm that systematic state failures to respond to women's pleas for domestic violence protection constitute gender-based discrimination (e.g. ECHR 2009; IACHR 2011). For analyses of these cases, their principles, and their relevance to evolving human rights law, see Bettinger-Lopez (2008; Bettinger-Lopez 2013), Goldfarb (2008), Meyersfeld (2010), Andrews and Khavinson (2013), and Cabrera (2015).

7 This will be further explored in subsequent chapters, where I identify the uniquely lenient treatment afforded to men's domestic crimes and demonstrate the endurance of this exceptionalist ideology through persistently inadequate state responses to these harms.

8 This term was coined following the curiously sympathetic and supportive attitudes that hostages developed towards their captors during a siege in Stockholm, Sweden, in 1973. It is now widely accepted to explain the tendency of certain victims to adopt the worldview of their abuser and to hide, minimise, and even excuse the violations they have suffered.

9 In a landmark legal case in 1998, Supreme Court Justice Crispin determined that there was ample evidence to indicate that acts of genocide were committed during Australian colonisation (see Balint 2014 for further discussion).

References

Andrews, Averil & Khavinson, Jenny. 2013. From international to domestic approaches: Battling domestic violence in the United States. *Family and Intimate Partner Violence Quarterly* Summer. 17–34.

Balint, Jennifer. 2012. *Genocide, State Crime and the Law*. Abingdon: Routledge.

Balint, Jennifer. 2014. Transitional justice and state crime. *Macquarie Law Journal* 13. 147–63.

Balint, Jennifer. 2016. The 'Mau Mau' legal hearings and recognising the crimes of the British colonial state: A limited constitutive moment. *Critical Analysis of Law* 3(2). 261–85.

Balint, Jennifer. 2019. Prosecuting and partnering for social change: Law, social movements, and Australia's mandatory detention for refugees and asylum seekers. In Sarat, Austin (ed.), *Studies in Law, Politics and Society*, 169–89. Emerald Group Publishing Limited.

Barry, Kathleen. 1979. *Female Sexual Slavery*. New York: New York University Press.

Bassiouni, Mahmoud Cherif. 2011. Crimes of state and other forms of collective group violence by non-state actors. In Rothe, Dawn & Mullins, Christopher (eds.), *State Crime: Current Perspectives*, 1–22. New Brunswick: Rutgers University Press, Introduction.

Beasley, Michele & Thomas, Dorothy. 1994. Domestic violence as a human rights issue. In Fineman, Martha & Mykituik, Roxanne (eds.), *The Public Nature of Private Violence: The Discovery of Domestic Violence*, 323–48. New York: Routledge.

Bettinger-Lopez, Caroline. 2008. Human rights at home: Domestic violence as a human rights violation. *Columbia Human Rights Law Review* 40. 19–77.

Bettinger-Lopez, Caroline. 2013. Jessica Lenahan (Gonzales) v United States: Implementation, litigation, and mobilisation strategies. *Journal of Gender, Social Policy and the Law* 21. 207–29.

Boraine, Alex. 2000. *A Country Unmasked: Inside South Africa's Truth and Reconciliation Commission*. Oxford: Oxford University Press.

Bowcott, Owen. 2016. Mau Mau lawsuit due to begin at high court. *The Guardian*. (https://www.theguardian.com/law/2016/may/22/mau-mau-kenya-compensation-lawsuit-high-court)

Boxall, Hayley & Morgan, Anthony & Brown, Rick. 2020. *The Prevalence of Domestic Violence among Women during the COVID-19 Pandemic*. Canberra: Australian Institute of Criminology.

Bradel, Lauren & Rosenbaum, Alan & Orcutt, Holly. 2019. The prevalence and co-occurrence of the forms of violence against women. *Journal of Aggression, Maltreatment & Trauma* 28(7). 870–87.

Breiding, Matthew & Chen, Jieru & Black, Michele. 2014. *Intimate Partner Violence in the United States – 2010*. Atlanta: National Center for Injury Prevention and Control, Centers for Disease Control and Prevention.

Breiding, Matthew & Smith, Sharon & Basile, Kathleen & Walters, Mikel & Chen, Jieru & Merrick, Melissa. 2014. Prevalence and characteristics of sexual violence, stalking, and intimate partner violence victimization: National intimate partner and sexual violence survey, United States, 2011. *Morbidity and Mortality Weekly Report* 63(8). 1–18.

Buck, Alexy & Curran, Liz. 2009. Delivery of advice to marginalised and vulnerable groups: The need for innovative approaches. *Public Space: The Journal of Law and Social Justice* 3. 1–29.

Cabrera, Deborah Mas. 2015. Domestic violence and equal protection of the laws: A look at Town of Castle Rock v Gonzales and Lenahan v United States. *Revista Juridica Universidad De Puerto Rico* 84(2). 321–36.

Cameron, Prue. 2014. *Relationship Problems and Money: Women Talk about Financial Abuse*. Melbourne: Women's Information and Referral Exchange.

Campbell, Andrew M. & Hicks, Ralph A. & Thompson, Shannon L. & Wiehe, Sarah E. 2020. Characteristics of intimate partner violence incidents and the environments in which they occur: Victim reports to responding law enforcement officers. *Journal of Interpersonal Violence* 35(13/14). 2583–606.

Caputi, Jane. 1989. The sexual politics of murder. *Gender and Society* 3(4). 437–56.

Caulfield, Susan & Wonders, Nancy. 1993. Personal AND political: Violence against women and the role of the state. In Tunnell, Kenneth (ed.), *Political Crime in Contemporary America: A Critical Approach*, 79–100. New York: Garland Publishing.

Chan, Andy & Payne, Jason. 2013. *Homicide in Australia: 2008–9 to 2009–10 National Homicide Monitoring Program Annual Report*. Canberra: Australian Institute of Criminology.

Charlesworth, Hilary & Chinkin, Christine. 2000. *The Boundaries of International Law: A Feminist Analysis*. Manchester: Manchester University Press.

Cobbe, Frances Power. 1878. Wife torture in England. In Radford, Jill & Russell, Diana (eds.), *Femicide: The Politics of Woman Killing*, 46–52. Buckingham: Open University Press.

Connell, Raewyn. 2005. The social organisation of masculinity. *Masculinities*, 67–86. 2nd edn. Berkeley: University of California Press.

Copelon, Rhonda. 1994. Recognising the egregious in the everyday: Domestic violence as torture. *Columbia Human Rights Law Review* 2. 291–367.

Copelon, Rhonda. 1995. Women and war crimes. *St Johns' Law Review* 69. 61–8.

Copelon, Rhonda. 2000. Gender crimes as war crimes: Integrating crimes against women into International Criminal Law. *McGill Law Journal*. November 46(1). 217–40.

Curthoys, Ann & Tedeschi, Mark & Balint, Jennifer & Joyce, Daniel. 2018. Forum: The Myall Creek Massacre of 1838: Genocide, war crimes, crimes against humanity? *Law and History* 5(1). 146–68.

Deer, Sarah. 2015. *The Beginning and End of Rape: Confronting Sexual Violence in Native America*. Minnesota: University of Minnesota Press.

DeKeseredy, Walter. 2016. Understanding woman abuse in intimate heterosexual relationships: The enduring relevance of feminist ways of knowing. *Journal of Family Violence* 31. 1043–6.

Dobash, Rebecca & Dobash, Russell. 1998. *Rethinking Violence against Women*. Thousand Oaks: Sage.

Dworkin, Andrea. 1981. *Pornography: Men Possessing Women*. London: Women's Press.

Enander, Viveka. 2011. Violent women? The challenge of women's violence in intimate heterosexual relationships to feminist analyses of partner violence. *Nordic Journal of Feminist and Gender Research, June* 19(2). 105–23.

Engnes, Eva Lidén Kristin & Lundgren, Ingela. 2013. Women's experiences of important others in a pregnancy dominated by intimate partner violence. *Scandinavian Journal of Caring Sciences* 27(3). 643–50.

Enloe, Cynthia. 2012. How long does 'post-war' last? Feminist warnings, Fred Halliday distinguished lecture. *London School of Economics and Political Science*. (http://www2.lse.ac.uk/newsAndMedia/videoAndAudio/channels/publicLecturesAndEvents/player.aspx?id=1633)

European Court of Human Rights. 2009. *Opuz v Turkey*. (http://www.refworld.org/docid/4a2f84392.html)

Evans, Patricia. 2006. *The Verbally Abusive Man: Can he change? A Woman's Guide to Deciding Whether to Stay or Go*. New York: Adams Media.

Finn, Geraldine. 1989. Taking gender into account in the theatre of terror: Violence, media, and the maintenance of male dominance. *Canadian Journal of Women & the Law*. December 3(2). 375–94.

Flood, Michael. 2012. *He Hits, She Hits: Assessing Debates Regarding Men's and Women's Experiences of Domestic Violence*. Sydney: Australian Domestic and Family Violence Clearinghouse.

Garcia-Moreno, Claudia & Zimmerman, Cathy & Morris-Gehring, Alison & Heise, Lori & Amin, Avni & Abrahams, Naeemah & Montoya, Oswaldo & Bhate-Deosthali, Padma & Kilonzo, Nduku & Watts, Charlotte. 2015. Addressing violence against women: A call to action. *The Lancet* 385. 1685–95.

Geras, Norman. 2011. *Crimes against Humanity: Birth of a Concept*. Manchester: Manchester University Press.

Goldfarb, Sally. 2008. *The Legal Response to Violence against Women in the United States of America: Recent Reforms and Continuing Challenges, Expert Paper Prepared for the United Nations Division for the Advancement of Women*. UN Doc EGM/GPLVAW/2008/EP.06.

Graham, Dee. 1994. *Loving to Survive: Sexual Terror, Men's Violence, and Women's Lives*. New York: New York University Press.

Graham-Bermann, Sandra & Halabu, Hilda. 2004. Fostering resilient coping in children exposed to violence: Cultural considerations. In Jaffe, Peter & Baker, Linda & Cunningham, Alison (eds.), *Protecting Children from Domestic Violence: Strategies for Community Intervention*, 71–88. New York: Guildford Press.

Green, Penny & MacManus, Thomas & de la Cour Venning, Alicia. 2018. *Genocide Achieved, Genocide Continues: Myanmar's Annihilation of the Rohingya*. London: International State Crime Initiative.

Guggisberg, Marika. 2018. The impact of violence against women and girls: A life span analysis. In Guggisberg, Marika & Hendricksen, Jessamy (eds.), *Violence against Women in the 21st Century: Challenges and Future Directions*, ch 1. New York: Nova Science Publishers.

Hakimi, Monica. 2010. State bystander responsibility. *The European Journal of International Law* 21(2). 341–85.

Haslanger, Sally. 2017. Racism, ideology and social movements. *Res Philosophica* 94(1). 1–22.

Hattery, Angela & Smith, Earl. 2012. *The Social Dynamics of Family Violence*. Boulder: Westview Press.

Hayes, Sharon & Jeffries, Samantha. 2016. Romantic terrorism? An auto-ethnographic analysis of gendered psychological and emotional tactics in domestic violence. *Journal of Research in Gender Studies* 6(2). 38–61.

Healey, Lucy & Humphreys, Cathy & Howe, Keran. 2013. Inclusive domestic violence standards: Strategies to improve interventions for women with disabilities? *Violence and Victims* 28(10). 50–68.

Heineman, Elizabeth. 2011. The history of sexual violence in conflict zones. In Heineman, Elizabeth (ed.), *Sexual Violence in Conflict Zones: From the Ancient World to the Era of Human Rights*. 1–24. Philadelphia: University of Pennsylvania Press.

Henry, Nicola. 2011. *War and Rape: Law, Memory and Justice*. Abingdon: Routledge.

Henry, Nicola. 2013. Memory of an injustice: The 'Comfort Women' and the legacy of the Tokyo Trial. *Asian Studies Review* 37(3). 362–80.

Henry, Nicola. 2014. The fixation on wartime rape: Feminist critique and International Criminal Law. *Social & Legal Studies* 23(1). 93–111.

Henry, Nicola. 2015. From reconciliation to transitional justice: The contours of redress politics in established democracies. *International Journal of Transitional Justice.* July 9(2). 199–218.

Hildebrandt, Mireille. 2006. Privacy and identity. In Claes, Eric & Duff, Antony & Gutwirth, Serge (eds.), *Privacy and Criminal Law*, 43–57. Antwerp: Intersentia.

Hill, Jess. 2019. *See What You Made Me Do: Power, Control and Domestic Violence.* Melbourne: Black Inc.

Howe, Adrian. 2014. Dramatizing intimate femicide: Petitions, plays, and public engagement (with a Shakespearean gloss). *Canadian Journal of Women and the Law* 26. 276–99.

Human Security Report Project. 2012. Sexual violence in war-affected countries. *Human Security Report: Sexual Violence, Education, and War: Beyond the Mainstream Narrative*, 19–144. Vancouver: Human Security Press.

Inter-American Court of Human Rights. 2011. *Lenahan (Gonzales) v. United States.* (https://www.oas.org/en/iachr/decisions/2011/USPU 12626EN.DOC)

International Criminal Court. 1998. *Rome Statute.* ISBN No. 92-9227-227-6. (https://www.refworld.org/docid/3ae6b3a84.html)

International Criminal Court. 2011. *Elements of Crimes.* (http://www.icc-cpi.int/NR/rdonlyres/336923D8-A6AD-40EC-AD7B-45BF9DE73D56/0/ElementsOfCrimesEng.pdf)

International Criminal Tribunal for Rwanda. 1998. (http://ictrcaselaw.org/docs/15154.pdf)

International Criminal Tribunal for the former Yugoslavia. 2001. (https://www.refworld.org/docid/3dda28414.html)

Jalloh, Charles. 2013. What makes a crime against humanity a crime against humanity? *American University Law Review* 28(2). 381–442.

Jeffreys, Sheila. 1997. *The Idea of Prostitution.* North Melbourne: Spinifex Press.

Johnson, Michael. 1995. Patriarchal terrorism and common couple violence: Two forms of violence against women. *Journal of Marriage and the Family* 57. 283–94.

Johnson, Michael. 2008. *A Typology of Domestic Violence: Intimate Terrorism, Violent Resistance, and Situational Couple Violence.* Boston: Northeastern University Press.

Johnson, Michael. 2010. Lanhinrichsen-Rolling's confirmation of the feminist analysis of intimate partner violence. *Sex Roles* 62. 212–9.

Johnson, Michael. 2011. Gender and types of intimate partner violence: A response to an anti-feminist literature review. *Aggression and Violent Behaviour* 16. 289–96.

Katz, Jackson. 2006. *The Macho Paradox.* Naperville: Sourcebooks.

Kauzlarich, David & Mullins, Christopher & Matthews, Rick. 2003. A complicity continuum of state crime. *Contemporary Justice Review* 6(3). 241–54.

Kelly, Liz. 1988. *Surviving Sexual Violence.* Cambridge: Polity.

Kelly, Liz. 2010. The everyday / everynightness of rape: Is it different in war? In Sjoberg, Laura & Via, Sandra (eds.), *Gender, War, and Militarism: Feminist Perspectives*, 114–23. Santa Barbara: Praeger Security International.

Kelly, Liz & Sharp, Nicola & Klein, Renate. 2014. *Finding the Costs of Freedom: How Women and Children Rebuild their Lives after Domestic Violence.* London: Solace Women's Legal Aid and Child and Woman Abuse Studies Unit.

Kimmel, Michael. 2013. The gender of violence. *The Gendered Society*, 421–52. 5th edn. New York: Oxford University Press.

Kolin, Andrew. 2008. *State Structure and Genocide*. Lanham: University Press of America.

Laplante, Lisa. 2009. Transitional justice and peace-building: Diagnosing and addressing the socio-economic roots of violence through a human rights framework. *International Journal of Transitional Justice* 2. 331–55.

Libal, Kathryn & Parekh, Serena. 2009. Reframing violence against women as a human rights violation. *Violence against Women* 15(12). 1477–89.

MacKenzie, Megan. 2010. Securitising sex? Towards a theory of the utility of war-time sexual violence. *International Feminist Journal of Politics*. June 12(2). 202–21.

MacKinnon, Catharine. 1993. On torture: A feminist perspective on human rights. In Mahoney, Kathleen & Mahoney, Paul (eds.), *Human Rights in the Twenty-first Century: A Global Challenge*, 21–31. Boston: M. Nijhoff.

MacKinnon, Catharine. 1994. Rape, genocide and women's human rights. *Harvard Women's Law Journal* 17. 5–16.

MacKinnon, Catharine. 2006. *Are Women Human? And Other International Dialogues*. Cambridge: Harvard University Press.

MacKinnon, Catharine. 2019. *Where #MeToo Came From, and Where It's Going*. (https://www.theatlantic.com/ideas/archive/2019/03/catharine-mackinnon-what-metoo-has-changed/585313/)

Manne, Robert. 2004. Aboriginal child removal and the question of genocide, 1900–1940. In Moses, Dirk (ed.), *Genocide and Settler Society: Frontier Violence and Stolen Indigenous Children in Australian History*, 217–38. New York: Berghahn.

McKenzie, Mandy & Kirkwood, Deborah & Tyson, Danielle & Naylor, Bronwyn. 2016. *Out of Character? Legal Responses to Intimate Partner Homicides by Men in Victoria 2005–2014*. Melbourne: Domestic Violence Resource Centre Victoria.

McQuigg, Ronagh. 2011. *International Human Rights Law and Domestic Violence: The Effectiveness of International Human Rights Law*. London: Routledge.

Meger, Sara. 2016. *Rape Loot Pillage: The Political Economy of Sexual Violence in Armed Conflict*. Oxford: Oxford University Press.

Mertus, Julie & Goldberg, Pamela. 1994. A perspective on women and international human rights after the Vienna Declaration: The inside / outside construct. *New York University Journal of International Law and Politics* 26. 201–34.

Meyer, Silke & Frost, Andrew. 2019. *Domestic and Family Violence: A Critical Introduction to Knowledge and Practice*. Abingdon: Routledge.

Meyersfeld, Bonita. 2003. Reconceptualising domestic violence in international law. *Albany Law Review* 67. 371–426.

Meyersfeld, Bonita. 2010. *Domestic Violence and International Law*. Oxford: Hart Publishing.

Mlambo-Ngcuka, Phumzile. 2020. *Violence against Women and Girls: The Shadow Pandemic*. Statement by Executive Director of UN Women. (https://www.unwomen.org/en/news/stories/2020/4/statement-ed-phumzile-violence-against-women-during-pandemic)

Moreira, Diana Nadine & Pinto da Costa, Mariana. 2020. The impact of the Covid-19 pandemic in the precipitation of intimate partner violence. *International Journal of Law and Psychiatry* 71. (doi:10.1016/j.ijlp.2020.101606.)

Moser, Caroline. 2001. The gendered continuum of violence and conflict. In Moser, Caroline & Clark, Fiona (eds.), *Victims, Perpetrators or Actors? Gender, Armed Conflict and Political Violence*. 30–52. London: Zed Books.

Murray, Suellen & Powell, Anastasia. 2009. What's the problem? Australian public policy constructions of domestic and family violence. *Violence against Women* 15(5). 532–52.

Naranch, Laurie. 1997. Naming and framing the issues: Demanding full citizenship for women. In Daniels, Cynthia (ed.), *Feminists Negotiate the State: The Politics of Domestic Violence.*21–34. Lanham: University Press of America.

National Coalition against Domestic Violence. 2017. *Domestic Violence Gun-related Fatalities.* (http://ncadv.org/)

National Coalition against Domestic Violence. 2020. *Domestic Violence National Statistics.* (https://ncadv.org/statistics)

National Council to Reduce Violence against Women and their Children. 2009. *Time for Action: The National Council's Plan for Australia to Reduce Violence against Women and their Children 2009–21.* Department of Families, Housing, Community Services and Indigenous Affairs, Commonwealth of Australia.

Office for National Statistics. 2019. *Homicide in England and Wales: Year ending March 2018.* (https://www.ons.gov.uk/peoplepopulationandcommunity/crime-andjustice/articles/homicideinenglandandwales/yearendingmarch2018#how-are-victims-and-suspects-related)

Otto, Dianne. 2012. *Feminist Approaches to International Law.* New York: Oxford University Press.

Pain, Rachel. 2012. *Everyday Terrorism: How Fear Works in Domestic Abuse.* Centre for Social Justice and Community Aid, Durham University and Scottish Women's Aid.

Pateman, Carol. 1988. *The Sexual Contract.* Stanford: Stanford University Press.

Price, Jenna. 2018. We can't fix violence against women until we see this as an epidemic. *Sydney Morning Herald.* (https://www.smh.com.au/national/we-can-t-fix-violence-against-women-until-we-see-this-as-an-epidemic-20181213-p50m02.html)

Radford, Jill & Stanko, Elizabeth. 1996. Violence against women and children: The contradictions of crime control under patriarchy. In Hester, Marianne & Kelly, Liz & Radford, Jill (eds.), *Women, Violence and Male Power: Feminist Activism, Research and Practice.* Buckingham: Open University Press.

Reckdenwald, Amy & Szalewski, Alec & Yohros, Alexis. 2019. Place, injury patterns, and female-victim intimate partner homicide. *Violence against Women* 25(6). 654–76.

Robertson, Geoffrey. 2002. *Crimes against Humanity: The Struggle for Global Justice.* London: Penguin.

Romany, Celia. 1993. Women as aliens: A feminist critique of the public / private distinction in international human rights law. *The Harvard Human Rights Journal* 6. 87–125.

Romany, Celia. 1994. State responsibility goes private: A feminist critique of the public / private distinction in international human rights law. In Cook, Rebecca (ed.), *Human Rights of Women: National and International Perspectives*, 85–115. Philadelphia: University of Pennsylvania Press.

Rose, Evelyn. 2015. Twenty years since democracy in South Africa: Reconsidering the contributions of the Truth and Reconciliation Commission. *Melbourne Journal of Politics* 37. 61–77.

Rose, Evelyn. 2017. Book review of 'The Beginning and End of Rape: Confronting Sexual Violence in Native America' by Sarah Deer. *Law and Society Review* 15(1). 232–5.

Russell, Diana. 1982. *Rape in Marriage*. New York: Macmillan.

Russell, Diana & Radford, Jill (eds.). 1992. *Femicide: The Politics of Woman Killing*. Buckingham: Open University Press.

Schabas, William. 2007. *An Introduction to the International Criminal Court*. 3rd edn. Cambridge: Cambridge University Press.

Schabas, William. 2008. State policy as an element of international crimes. *Journal of Criminal Law and Criminology* 98(3). 953–82.

Shelby, Tommie. 2014. Racism, moralism and social criticism. *Du Bois Review: Social Science Research on Race* 11(1). 57–74.

Shenkman, Carey. 2012. Catalyzing national judicial capacity: The ICC's first crimes against humanity outside armed conflict. *New York University Law Review* 87. 1210–48.

Sideris, Tina. 2001. Rape in war and peace: Social context, gender, power and identity. In Meintjes, Sheila & Pillay, Anu & Turshen, Meredith (eds.), *The Aftermath: Women in Post-Conflict Transformation*, 142–58. London: Zed Books.

Sifris, Ronli. 2014. *Reproductive Freedom, Torture, and International Human Rights: Challenging the Masculinisation of Torture*. Abingdon: Routledge.

Simm, Gabrielle. 2018. Peoples' tribunals, women's courts and international crimes of sexual violence. In Byrnes, Andrew & Simm, Gabrielle (eds.), *Peoples' Tribunals and International Law*, 61–83. Cambridge: Cambridge University Press.

Simpson, Gerry. 2007. *Law, War and Crime*. Cambridge: Polity.

Smart, Carol. 1989. *Feminism and the Power of Law*. London: Routledge.

South African Truth and Reconciliation Commission. 1998. *Truth and Reconciliation Commission Report*. (http://www.justice.gov.za/trc/report/)

St. Ivany, Amanda & Kools, Susan & Sharps, Phyllis & Bullock, Linda. 2018. Extreme control and instability: Insight into head injury from intimate partner violence. *Journal of Forensic Nursing* 14(4). 198–205.

Stanley, Elizabeth. 2005. Truth commissions and the recognition of state crime. *British Journal of Criminology*. July 45(4). 582–97.

Stanley, Elizabeth. 2014. The victimisation of children in state-run homes in New Zealand. In Rothe, Dawn & Kauzlarich, David (eds.), *Towards a Victimology of State Crime*, 46–65. London: Routledge.

Stark, Evan. 2007. *Coercive Control: How Men Entrap Women in Personal Life*. New York: Oxford University Press.

Stark, Evan & Hester, Marianne. 2019. Coercive control: Update and review. *Violence against Women* 25(1). 81–104.

Stevens, Jacqueline. 1999. Compensatory kinship rules: The mother of gender. *Reproducing the State*, 209–35. Princeton: Princeton University Press.

Sullivan, Donna. 1995. The public / private distinction in international human rights law. In Peters, Julie & Wolper, Andrea (eds.), *Women's Rights, Human Rights: International Feminist Perspectives*, 126–34. New York: Routledge.

Tatz, Colin. 1985. Racism, responsibility, and reparation: South Africa, Germany, and Australia. *Australian Journal of Politics and History* 31(1). 162–72.

Tatz, Colin. 2003. *With Intent to Destroy: Reflecting on Genocide*. New York: Verso.

Tatz, Colin. 2011. Genocide studies: An Australian perspective. *Genocide Studies and Prevention: An International Journal* 6(3). 231–44.

Taylor Mill, Harriet. 1869. Enfranchisement of women. In Rossi, Alice (ed.), *Essays on Sex Equality by John Stuart Mill and Harriet Taylor Mill*, 89–122. Chicago: University of Chicago Press.

True, Jacqui. 2012. *The Political Economy of Violence against Women*. New York: Oxford University Press.

United Kingdom Crown Prosecution Service. 2017. *Controlling or Coercive Behaviour in an Intimate or Family Relationship in the Serious Crime Act 2015*. United Kingdom. (https://www.cps.gov.uk/legal-guidance/controlling-or-coercive-behaviour-intimate-or-family-relationship)

United Nations General Assembly. 1948. *Universal Declaration of Human Rights*. Resolution 217 A(III).

United Nations General Assembly. 1984. *Convention against Torture and Other Cruel, Inhuman or Degrading Treatment or Punishment*. UN Doc A/RES/39/46.

United Nations General Assembly. 1993. *Vienna Declaration and Programme of Action*. Tabled at the World Conference on Human Rights, Vienna, 14–25 June 1993, UN Doc A/CONF.157/23.

United Nations General Assembly. 2006. *In-Depth Study on All Forms of Violence against Women*. UN Doc A/61/122/Add.1.

United Nations Office on Drugs and Crime. 2014. *Global Study on Homicide 2013: Trends, Contexts, Data*. (https://www.unodc.org/documents/gsh/pdfs/2014_GLOBAL_HOMICIDE_ BOOK_web.pdf)

United Nations Office on Drugs and Crime. 2019. *Global Study on Homicide 2019: Gender-related Killing of Women and Girls*. Vienna. (https://www.unodc.org/documents/data-and-analysis/gsh/Booklet_5.pdf)

Vernon, Richard. 2002. What is a crime against humanity? *The Journal of Political Philosophy* 10(3). 231–49.

Vernon, Richard. 2013. Crime against humanity: A defence of the subsidiarity view. *Canadian Journal of Law and Jurisprudence*. 26(1). 229–41.

Voth Schrag, Rachel J. & Robinson, Sarah R. & Ravi, Kristen. 2019. Understanding pathways within intimate partner violence: Economic abuse, economic hardship, and mental health. *Journal of Aggression, Maltreatment & Trauma* 28(2). 222–42.

Walklate, Sandra & McCulloch, Jude & Fitz-Gibbon, Kate & Maher, JaneMaree. 2019. Criminology, gender and security in the Australian context: Making women's lives matter. *Theoretical Criminology* 23(1). 60–77.

Women's Legal Service Victoria. 2018. *Small Claims, Large Battles: Achieving Economic Equality in the Family Law System*. Report by Women's Legal Service Victoria.

World Health Organisation. 2013. *Global and Regional Estimates of Violence against Women: Prevalence and Health Effects of Intimate Partner Violence and Non-partner Sexual Violence*. (https://apps.who.int/iris/bitstream/handle/10665/85239/9789241564625_eng.pdf;jsessionid=3798BB58CC00B986FDD892C816A9E480?sequence=1)

Chapter 4

Domestic violence as micro-state crime

In this chapter, I put forward the argument that domestic violence constitutes a *micro-state crime*. Based on radical feminist thinking on the family, the state, and domestic violence, this conceptual framework challenges and expands common understandings of these key phenomena in order to advance state crime theory into the private sphere. By identifying the family as a microcosm of the nation-state, the individual patriarch as sovereign of this micro-state, and his family as his subjects, I show how domestic and family violence can be understood as a crime perpetrated within a state territory by a sovereign entity. As part of this theoretical argument, I explore how domestic violence constitutes a system, method, and tool of state governance in the private sphere and at the micro-level and how it is comparable to repressive nation-state governance.

Micro-state crime is underpinned by what I term *micro-state ideology*: the framework that establishes and upholds patriarchal micro-sovereignty as morally, culturally, and legally defensible. This ideology provides the foundation for domestic violence because it normalises patriarchal authority and justifies its abusive and violent enforcement. Because micro-state ideology is originated and supported by the nation-state through its reification of marriage and the family and the private sphere, domestic violence is both a micro-state crime in itself as well as a state crime which is simultaneously supported by the nation-state. In this way, it is also indicative of nation-state criminality. To examine the contemporary relevance of understanding domestic violence in this way, I draw together evidence of enduring support for micro-state ideology through official policy, practice, and discourse of nation-state institutions across the legal and social service systems. I explore how, symbolically and substantively, these institutions function in support of patriarchal micro-sovereignty and, in turn, how they perpetuate domestic and family violence.

Conceptualising patriarchal sovereignty and the micro-state

Notions of the state and sovereignty traditionally centre geographic and legal boundaries and political and cultural interests and are generally

DOI: 10.4324/9781003132370-6

interchangeable with the modern idea of the nation-state and its structures of official governance. These ideas are generally reflected in the state crime literature. For example, Rothe and Mullins (2006: 3) discuss the state as a reified entity governing a territory and a people, and the sovereign as the figurehead of this state entity; state crimes are therefore "committed by a sovereign polity to advance its interests". However, this framework can be expanded to enable the notion of 'state' to be extended into the private domain. Through the lens of early English legal and political theory, the family is also a state-like institution. Thomas Hobbes (1651 in Chapman 1975), for example, saw the state as the structural and political model for the family, and thus the family as a diminutive state. Like the English monarch, the head of the family had absolute authority over his domain. This is reflected in Blackstone's (1765: 1053) common law commentaries, where the family patriarch is named the "sovereign", "baron", or "lord" of the family, and women and children as his subjects. Within his jurisdiction, the family sovereign, just like the nation-state's monarch, was required to "make laws" and "judge ... disputes". Also just as nation-state sovereigns could demand executions of their subjects, the male head of the family could even legitimately order his own children's death (Hobbes 1651 in Chapman 1975: 78). In terms of hierarchical structure and political legitimacy, the family closely resembled the nation-state in miniature: what I shall call a *micro-state*.

A radical feminist lens enables further critique of the patriarchal harms that emerge from this micro-state arrangement. It also uncovers and interrogates the purpose of marriage and the family and the role of men's violence within these institutions. Feminist critique first enables us to challenge the construction of both macro- and micro-patriarchal power structures as normal, natural, and rational (see Hobbes 1651 in Chapman 1975) and to expose this as an ideological process of hegemonic maintenance (see Shelby 2014; Haslanger 2017). The nation-state is then illuminated as a political construct which originates from patriarchal ideology and which deliberately and consistently functions in support of male interests (Bumiller 2008). Marriage and the family are also illuminated as institutions purposefully sanctified and supported by the nation-state to help sustain patriarchal power in all areas of society (MacKinnon 1989). As a mirror and model of the nation-state, the key role of the micro-state and its sovereign was to oversee the maintenance of patriarchal power, values, and interests in the private sphere. Within what I term this *micro-jurisdiction*, the male figurehead's power to rule over his family constituted *micro-sovereignty*.

To support the individual patriarch's regime, the nation-state designated the family an official zone of non-interference: effectively, a "parallel state" (Romany 1993: 100). Within their micro-jurisdictions, individual men were expected to uphold patriarchal values and order, thereby ensuring that patriarchal nation-state interests were also upheld. Bestowing this power on family patriarchs meant that nation-state power could then be exercised at a distance through its localised representatives – individual male heads of families – and the nation-state could adopt a less direct role in patriarchal maintenance (Stevens 1999; Hildebrandt 2006). As an inviolable space which was relatively free from official intervention, micro-sovereigns were able to administer this power as they chose (Malley-Morrison & Hines 2004; Bumiller 2008). The interaction between the nation-state and the micro-state was therefore one of mutual support.

The foundations for masculine abuse within the family were therefore historically established in early common law. Based on a belief in their spiritual, moral, and intellectual superiority, men, as owners and rulers of the family unit, were allocated responsibility for leading, guiding, instructing, and controlling their wife and children (Pateman 1988; Stevens 1999; McQuigg 2011). To aid the maintenance of domestic order, men were directed not only to use instructive corporal punishment on their children but to physically discipline their wives as they deemed appropriate (Dobash & Dobash 1998; Hattery & Smith 2012).[1] The family was considered a sanctified and inviolable space in which the nation-state should not intervene, and individual men alone determined how they treated their subjects. Because they would not be held to account for violations perpetrated in the domestic sphere, men were effectively positioned "as a *de facto* absolutist state in women's lives" (Copelon 1994: 297; also Subedi 1997; Hildebrandt 2006; Meyersfeld 2010).

The institutionalisation of masculine private-sphere violence was also established through the denial of women and children's legal independence and their designation as male property. Historically, men's ownership of women was officially documented in law. Like other moveable property such as cattle or slaves, women and children were considered part of a man's estate and were commodified in terms of their value to their patriarch (Cobbe 1878; Burris 1973; Dworkin 1981; Deer 2015). Specifically, a female's rights and interests were subsumed beneath the relevant male figure, depending on her age and circumstances. Initially, she was under the rule of her father or other male blood relative, but upon marriage her interests were considered "merged" into her husband's (Peach 2000: 58). This is confirmed in Blackstone's (1765: 1052) common law commentary:

> By marriage, the husband and wife are one person in law: that is, the very being or legal existence of the woman is suspended during the marriage, or at least is incorporated and consolidated into that of the husband.

This patriarchal framework effectively dissolved any legal status – along with the identity and humanity – of a woman, rendering her an item of property under her husband's control. Since a man could treat his property as he chose, this equated to an endorsement of any violence against her.

Under such conditions, a patriarch's power was absolute. He could legitimately order his wife to do anything he pleased, beat her, imprison her, and recapture and punish her if she attempted to leave (see Blackstone 1765; for critique, see Mill 1869; Pateman 1988; Harne & Radford 2008; Lesses 2014). Women had no moral or legal capacity to question or challenge the authority of their micro-sovereign and the law provided grave consequences for any such attempt. Any circumstances in which a woman contravened her husband's authority or interests was considered "a sort of *petty treason*" (Cobbe 1878: 47) and provided a legitimate explanation for his use of extreme and even lethal violence against her. For this reason, Taylor Mill argued that marriage was enacted via a totalitarian dynamic and "a law of despotism" (1869: 156). Furthermore, if a victim of domestic abuse killed her husband in self-defence, it was also considered an act of treason punishable by death. It is from these official historical foundations that micro-state ideology emerged: the discursive frameworks of thought and action that construct patriarchal micro-sovereignty, ownership, and control as legitimate and necessary; that deny female autonomy, rights, and agency; and that consider any challenge to patriarchal sovereignty problematic and punishable.

Domestic violence as micro-state governance

If the domestic sphere can be conceptualised as a patriarchal micro-state, domestic violence can accordingly be understood as a mode of micro-state governance, since it is a crucial tool of power and control within the micro-state regime. Understanding the family patriarch as a sovereign state in himself – indeed, as an "absolutist state" (Copelon 1994: 297) – also illuminates the power dynamics which underpin domestic violence. An absolutist figure like a sovereign or monarch is one who simultaneously inspires both terror and adoration in their subjects. With supposedly divine authority, they are revered but feared, since they have unmitigated power to determine the fate of their subjects. Understanding individual domestic violence victims as the subjects of an absolutist and totalitarian state regime also illuminates the state crime features of domestic violence. Both macro- and micro-state regimes construct a similar power dynamic between sovereign and subject: one where absolute loyalty and deference are required. The familiar political notions of despotism and treason mentioned above also indicate the comparability of nation-state power and individual patriarchs' exercise of micro-state power.

The nation-state and micro-state are also comparable in terms of specific repressive governance techniques. Both utilise "well-developed tactics of intimidation and coercion" to impose "discipline and a strategy of ... governance" over their subject-victims (Marcus 1994: 31–2). The systematic and calculated forms of oppression, threat, and violence used by totalitarian nation-states to ensure the conformity and compliance of their subject-citizens are thoroughly documented (e.g. Cohen 1995; Robertson 2002; May 2005; Balint 2012). Two particularly common tools used towards this aim are terror and torture. State terrorism involves various forms of measured violence which function as messages of intimidation to the populace, creating mass fear and submission (Green & Ward 2004; Kolin 2008). Torture can also be understood as a particular "mode of governance" (Chomsky & Herman 1979: 361) when it involves calculated and deliberately administered forms of violence that are designed to subjugate and control citizens through a process of terror. In such societies, terror is also

> *diffuse, violence is always latent, pressure is exerted from all sides on its members … terror cannot be located, for it comes from everywhere and from every specific thing. … The citizen in this kind of society is always the object of the gaze of the state, whether physically … or symbolically … or both.*
>
> (Khatib 2013: 7–8)

Such regimes sustain and extend their power through fear, intimidation, and the ever-present threat of violence.

A radical feminist lens challenges us to think about political repression and terror-based governance not just along nation-state lines, but also at the sites and in the ways that are most often experienced by women: in the home, from their patriarch, and in the form of coercive control. As mentioned in previous chapters, these regimes involve a constellation of abusive tactics which together aim to maintain the perpetrators' absolute control over his partner and family, and there are grave consequences for dissent or disloyalty (Stark 2007; Johnson 2008). Such a regime is aptly illustrated in the Canadian context through the experiences of Teresa Craig (see Sheehy 2018), who eventually killed her husband after spending years under his totalitarian control. As detailed in extensive evidence presented at the murder trial, Teresa's husband had terrorised her and their son for years, isolating them geographically and socially, forcing them to live in abject poverty, monitoring and surveilling them, repeatedly degrading and physically abusing the child, threatening to kill them if they tried to leave, and regularly displaying his power and capacity to carry out his threats by brandishing weapons, damaging property, and assaulting other people. Extensive evidence presented at the trial detailed conditions of absolute imprisonment and overwhelming terror which led Teresa to genuinely fear for her and her son's lives and to see no possibility for escape other than by killing her husband.

Because parallel oppressive and violent techniques are used by micro-sovereigns to maintain control over the family, this positions domestic violence as a form of totalitarian governance and as a micro-state crime. Coercive controlling domestic violence has already been shown to constitute terrorism and torture (e.g. MacKinnon 1993; Copelon 1994; Johnson 1995). Clear parallels have been identified between international terrorism and the domestic terrorism in everyday lives and homes, with "fear, terror and control" operating consistently across these contexts (Pain 2012: 8; also Kelly 1988; Finn 1989; Stark 2007; Hayes & Jeffries 2016). Although analysing different sites, perpetrators, and examples of torture, Chomsky and Herman's (1979)

and Marcus' (1994) analyses perfectly align. Both examine torture as a strategic mode of governance, and although with different perpetrator actors –
totalitarian nation-states and coercive control perpetrators – they reveal that
the use of torture in nation-state and family contexts has parallel aims, strategies, and modes of operation. This highlights the continuities between totalitarian patriarchy at the macro- and micro-institutional levels, positioning
systematic domestic violence regimes as totalitarian regimes.

Parallels can also be drawn between destructive micro-state and nation-
state regimes' organised methods of subjugating and degrading their subjects.
In his insightful analysis of "techniques of genocide", Lemkin (1944: 82–90)
documents the intricate, interconnected techniques that Nazi Germany employed against the Jewish people to systematically subjugate, alienate, disen-
franchise, degrade, destroy, and disable their capacity for asserting individual
or collective identity, integrity, beliefs, or rights. These genocidal techniques
comprehensively addressed all areas of life: political, social, cultural, economic, biological, physical, religious, and moral. Employed in concert, they
were a method for the degradation and ultimate destruction of a group in
order to extend state rule and to advance the state in a particular direction
and image (see e.g. Kolin 2008; Balint 2012).

This framework is also useful for illuminating coercive control as a systematic and comprehensive method of maintaining and extending micro-state
rule. With marriage and the family as the micro-state, the patriarch as head
of state, and his wife as the singular subject (although replicated all over the
world by other women in the same position), coercive controlling domestic violence can be understood as a method for the systematic subjugation
of state subject/object beneath the sovereign and within the framework of
micro-state governance. Indeed, it is well established that this type of abuse
must be understood not in terms of single or even multiple incidents of harm
but as a comprehensive regime of power (e.g. Marcus 1994; Stark 2007; Elizabeth 2015).

As I discussed in Chapter 3, coercive control perpetrators employ specific, mutually reinforcing techniques to gain and maintain complete control
over their victim. They deliberately degrade the victim's physical, sexual,
psychological, and emotional health and isolate them from social, moral, or
spiritual sources of connection and support. They deny their victim's dignity
and humanity and comprehensively disable their capacity to assert selfhood
in any form. In cases where victims do attempt to assert independence or
agency, this is perceived as illegitimate and directly provocative to the perpetrator's reign of control and can even be the precipitating factor in severe
intimate partner assault and murder. In other words, if the perpetrator cannot completely control and subjugate his victim, she is best annihilated. A
coercive controlling regime of domestic abuse can therefore be understood
as a technology of state-administered power and to resemble dehumanising
and destructive genocidal techniques in form, method, and aim. Like the

systematically unequal structures upon which racial and ethnic genocide is premised, coercive control is also premised upon symbolic and substantive (sexual) inequality (Stark 2007), with wider patriarchal power structures and networks at the macro-level enabling this degradation and destruction at the micro-level.

The contemporary endurance of micro-state ideology

Conceptualising domestic violence as a micro-state crime is not only relevant for illuminating its historical origins, purpose, function, and governance techniques. It is also relevant for analysing persistent justificatory narratives for domestic violence and for critiquing contemporary responses to the problem. Despite significant progress in institutional recognition of and responses to domestic violence, what I term *micro-state ideology* demonstrably endures in the policy, practice, and discourse of nation-state institutions. Symbolically and substantively, these institutions provide ongoing support for patriarchal micro-sovereignty and, in turn, contribute to the perpetuation of domestic violence.

Through criminal law

The enduring principle of state non-interference in the domestic sphere – and in violence perpetrated within it – is a particularly tenacious aspect of original micro-state ideology that endures in contemporary law. Through official policy, practice, and discourse, law continues to reproduce the notion that the family is an inviolable space which should be subject to minimal oversight, intervention, or adjudication. This is firstly reflected in the fact that domestic violence was not widely criminalised across the Western liberal-democratic world until the early 1990s. Marital rape, for example, was protected by law in England and Wales until 1990 and 1991 (Lees 1996; Harne & Radford 2008). In the United States, the last state to lift the marital rape exemption was North Carolina, in 1993 (Hong 2018). Across all Australian criminal jurisdictions, marital sexual violence was officially recognised by 1994 (ALRC 2010a). Even following its codification as a crime, however, domestic violence has consistently been treated as a non-criminal, private, and a relatively insignificant matter in law, highlighting the enduring impact of micro-state ideology through private-sphere exceptionalism. Well after its official censure in the United States, law has not only continued to allow men to "get away with" criminal violence in the home but has "positively excus[ed]" it (Stevens 1999: 218–9).

A particular facet of micro-state ideology with direct ongoing relevance to domestic violence and law is male proprietariness. This stems from the original legal notion of a husband's ownership of his wife and the associated denial of female subjectivity or autonomy in intimate relationships (see Pateman

1988; Deer 2015). In general legal terms, being a proprietor – as indeed a husband was over his wife in common law until recently – means to have exclusive possession of and rights to an object. In an intimate relationship, proprietariness denotes a general attitude of ownership over a partner which can manifest as the perceived entitlement of a man to exclusively access his partner's body at any time and in any manner of his choosing (DeKeseredy & Schwartz 2013). Across contexts and cultures, proprietariness underpins the justification of intimate partner sexual violence, since the greater a man's sense of sexual entitlement, the more readily he will justify his use of sexual coercion and violence (Kelly 1988). In the United States, Hattery (2009: 135) concludes that this specifically sexual ownership of women by men continues to constitute the "crux of gender relations". In her research with domestic violence victims and perpetrators, Hattery found that both groups regarded men's unrestricted access to women's bodies as normal and legitimate, with men frequently rationalising violence against partners after they refused sex.

Male proprietariness continues to be sanctioned in contemporary law around the world through the marital rape exemption.[2] Vestiges of this exemption endure today, meaning that in practice, rape within legal or de facto marriage is still widely permitted. In Australia, Lesses (2014) notes that marital rape remains very difficult to prosecute because a range of legal technicalities preclude its formal adjudication. In the United States, whether through explicit justification or tacit support, the spirit of the marital exemption endures in law in practice (Copelon 2000; DeKeseredy & Schwartz 2013). Randall and Venkatesh (2017: 190) argue that the persistent contemporary inadequacy of state law around marital rape around the world "effectively facilitates and condones a private legal space ... where sexual assault and coercion are permissible". By tacitly approving of sexually entitled and abusive male behaviour within marriage, these weak legal frameworks reflect nation-states' ongoing support for patriarchal micro-sovereignty and violent methods of maintaining it.

Men's use of violence to defend ownership of their female partner also continues to be legally and culturally endorsed. Again, this stems from the notion that a woman is the exclusive sexual property of her husband and that it is legitimate for a man to violently enforce his perceived rights and needs in this domain. This underpins the enduring sexual double standard whereby men's infidelity is widely accepted, yet women are expected to be devoted and faithful to their male partner. Since a woman can only be owned by one man at a time, a woman's infidelity is constructed as an act of this theft in which she aids and abets the thief (Hattery 2009). It is for these reasons that sexual jealousy and often baseless suspicions of female infidelity are central to controlling and abusive relationships. Indeed, "infidelity is the most frequent 'violation' used to justify domestic violence" (Stark 2007: 248).

Sexual jealousy and accusations of female infidelity are consistently identified in domestic violence cases across time and context. In an early study in the United Kingdom which investigated the dynamics of violent incidents with domestic perpetrators and victims, Davidson (cited in Barry 1979: 173) found that 66% of assaults directly related to male sexual jealousy, even though in 83% of these cases the women had confidentially informed researchers that there was no reason for their partner to be jealous. These findings bear striking similarities to Hattery's (2009: 95) later United States-based research, where male suspicion and jealousy, although again most often unfounded, was a "primary cause" of violence in the relationships under study (also Stark 2007). Chan and Payne's (2013) recent Australian research also provides strong evidence of the direct connection between proprietariness and intimate partner homicide, since some of the most common motives offered by perpetrators were revenge, jealousy, and desertion, with the latter referring to when the victim had attempted to separate from them. Considering that these themes remain central to first-hand accounts of domestic abuse over time (see e.g. Pfitzner et al. 2020), they indicate the strong endurance of proprietary ideology and the persistent justification of male ownership and control within contemporary intimate relationships.

In law, proprietary ideology manifests specifically through the provocation defence and its various modern iterations. This legal doctrine upholds male ownership of women and provides a justificatory framework for men's domestic violence against female partners. Cobbe (1878: 47) identifies the earliest documented form of provocation: a formal legal defence which justified a man's murder of his wife in "attenuating circumstances". The defence was based on male sovereignty and the associated belief that an "offence of the wife against her husband [constituted] ... treason". It established that for a woman to contravene her husband's demands or interests was a legitimate explanation for him using extreme and even lethal violence against her. Of course, the defence was not available for a woman who killed her husband in response to systematic victimisation. This effectively meant that women were "liable to capital punishment without judge or jury for transgressions which, in the case of a man, would never be punished at all". Early provocation law is a demonstrable outgrowth of micro-state ideology and proprietariness and represents official justification for the lethal enforcement of patriarchal sovereignty.

Although provocation law has evolved and in some contexts has been officially abolished, its principles persist. In Victoria, Australia, the provocation defence itself was available until 2005, and subsequently defensive homicide continued to operate in a similar manner until 2014 (Naylor & Tyson 2017). As Tyson's (2011) research shows, provocation could include a woman nagging, taunting, insulting, or goading her partner. It was considered particularly provocative if a woman flirted with another man, flaunted infidelity, or expressed a desire to leave the relationship. For any such behaviours, a man could easily make provocation claims because it reinforced accepted cultural notions of his partner as his sexual property. These doctrines have provided either a complete or partial defence to murder, thereby offering either complete exoneration for an offender or a reduction in culpability (Freiberg et al. 2015). The provocation defence, for example, could reduce the liability and penalty from murder to manslaughter in cases where the accused killed his partner after "losing control" because of an accepted category of provocation (Naylor & Tyson 2017: 73). Given that these accepted categories for invoking the provocation defence clearly reflect notions of male sexual ownership, they represent enduring legislative expressions, and thus official endorsements, of male proprietary ideology.

Through law enforcement

State law enforcement responses to domestic violence also continue to be directly influenced by micro-state ideology, and notably the notion of private-sphere exceptionalism. Prior to the official criminalisation of domestic violence across the Western world, police recognition of and response to this harm was minimal. Even severe and repeated victimisation of women – provided it was by a male partner – was dismissed as a private matter unworthy of nation-state concern or intervention (Dobash & Dobash 1998; Hildebrandt 2006; Harne & Radford 2008). Since widespread criminalisation in the 1990s, there have been notable improvements as the official recognition of domestic violence filters down to police policy and practice. But, even post 2000, well after significant reform to law enforcement frameworks, domestic violence has continued to be treated as less serious than comparable non-domestic offences (Fernandez 2010; Meyersfeld 2010; Birdsey & Snowball 2013). The notion that domestic violence is a 'family matter' best obscured from public view and resolved behind closed doors continues to play out in police attitudes and practices (Meyer 2011; 2016; Segrave et al. 2018). These ideas are a direct outcome of the historical reification of marriage and the family and demonstrate the enduring influence of the exceptional status of the private sphere.

Across diverse Western contexts, official police apathy is often caused by the enduring perception that domestic violence is not serious and that it should be resolved privately rather than through formal intervention. In the United States, Johnson (2008: 75) notes that, over a decade after criminalisation, "we continue to encounter cases in which such violence is treated more as a minor personal problem than as the crime that it is". In Australia, police attitudes also reveal the enduring notion that violence in the home is a trivial interpersonal matter rather than a crime. In research with police officers in Victoria, Segrave et al. (2018) repeatedly encountered the view that intimate partner violence did not warrant law enforcers' attention, with officers expressing their annoyance at being asked to assist with what they perceived as petty private problems. Overwhelmingly, police considered attending domestic violence incidents an illegitimate use of their time and resources, and in fact regarded such cases as "the archetypal form of [what is considered] *not* real police work" (107; emphasis original).

Some comments by Victorian police officers in the study even pointed towards enduring reluctance to limit a man's authority and presence in the home. "If you think he's going to hit you then leave. Don't stay around and expect us to come and kick him out of your house", asserted one anonymous Senior Constable (in Segrave et al. 2018: 105). These comments are particularly illuminating, given that in most Australian jurisdictions, the law does allow for the removal of perpetrators from the family home in order to protect victims (see ALRC 2010b). As Diemer et al. (2017) explain, since 2005 there have been significant shifts in Victoria, across Australia, and internationally, towards supporting women with the option of remaining in the family home while the perpetrator is excluded. Yet these police responses point to the enduring impact of states' reification of the domestic sphere as an exceptional zone of individual patriarchal authority and non-intervention. Micro-state ideology clearly continues to influence police perceptions of their role and the priority they afford various offences based on the identity and relationship of victim and perpetrator and the site of harm.

Enduring official law enforcement support for micro-state ideology can also be identified in police narratives of lethal domestic violence. In the Swiss context, Gloor and Meier's (2013) analysis of police reports of intimate partner homicides reveals the official reproduction of male proprietary narratives. These official accounts frequently normalised possessive, jealous, and aggressive masculine behaviour and focussed on debates about whether the woman's behaviour had been questionable or had provoked relationship conflict. For example, in Report 37 (Gloor & Meier 2013: 71–2), police specifically mentioned a history of sexual jealousy in the marriage, that the perpetrator "assumed [his wife] was having a fling", and that these suspicions led to him to "hit his wife on at least one occasion for certain". Yet police did not identify this as problematic male violence, nor as relevant to the eventual homicide. Rather, they depicted this violent history as benign and unimportant. This account echoes the traditional notion of domestic violence as a relationship conflict issue to be resolved in private, as well as the idea that male sexual jealousy – even when unfounded – is natural, normal male behaviour and an anticipated, accepted part of marriage.

Gloor and Meier's (2013) study also reveals law enforcers' discursive reinforcement of the legitimacy of violent patriarchal micro-sovereignty. For example, Report 22 (p. 72) documented an extensive history of the man's psychological, emotional, and physical violence against his wife and children, with police detailing that

> *within his family, he is said to have been the 'absolute boss', never allowing any 'ifs and buts' … It wasn't rare that he beat her in front of the children … the children had also been subjected mercilessly and had to suffer all kinds of beatings.*

Yet, the official police summary of this case was merely the mild assertion that the woman "has been noticed every now and again with a black eye or other kinds of sores" and that the children "*had* to suffer all kinds of beatings" (my emphasis). This account clearly normalises, and even depicts an inevitability about, masculine violence in the home and towards women and children. Indeed, across many cases in this study, police consistently depicted male control, abuse, and physical violence as normal, unremarkable, and even necessary behaviour for a husband and father figure. This clearly reflects and reinforces the original common law expectation that men act as the "sovereign" or "lord" of the family and assume responsibility for leading, instructing, and even violently disciplining their wife and children in the maintenance of patriarchal domestic order (see Blackstone 1765: 1053).

Through criminal courts

Micro-state ideology is also identifiable in the recent and contemporary operation of criminal courts. Through the adjudication of domestic violence crimes, the sexist historical frameworks which endorsed patriarchal control in the domestic sphere continue to create problematic lenses through which male and female behaviours are interpreted. Looking further at two particular domestic violence offences mentioned previously – marital rape and intimate partner homicide – I identify their continued judicial interpretation in accordance with micro-state ideology. In turn, this discursive framework becomes the basis from which men's domestic violence is obscured, normalised, tolerated, and effectively decriminalised.

The notorious case of *R v Johns*, heard in South Australia in 1992, clearly illustrates official judicial support for patriarchal sovereignty, micro-state ideology, and sexual domestic violence. This marital rape case was heard *after* the relevant offences were officially criminalised in the jurisdiction. Yet, Supreme Court Justice Bollen apparently set this fact aside when he informed the jury that "there is, of course, nothing wrong with a husband, faced with his wife's … refusal to engage in intercourse, [to use] rougher than usual handling" (Bollen 1992 in Kaspiew 1995: 350). These comments clearly articulate the notion of the man as sovereign entity and his wife's body as sovereign territory, thereby communicating overall support for patriarchal micro-sovereignty. They also reveal a series of normative assumptions that reflect micro-state ideology and can indeed be understood as ideology in the true critical sense: an expression of normative beliefs which are considered inherently valid and self-evident but which specifically function to rationalise unjust relations (see Shelby 2014; Haslanger 2017). In this case, the specific ideology these comments supported was patriarchal sovereignty and male sexual proprietariness, both of which legitimate and perpetuate the injustice of sexual inequality and the routineness of female violation.

Firstly, Justice Bollen takes as given the notion men have sexual needs and that it is rightful and reasonable for them to make sexual demands of women. Additionally, he implies that women are and should be sexually subservient to men and should make themselves permanently sexually available. This reflects the early common law notion that "by marriage, the husband and wife are one person in law" (Blackstone 1765: 1052) and that women had no independent status, rights, or the capacity to assert their physical integrity. Indeed, the concept of marital rape did not even exist, since a woman's body was considered her husband's property (Pateman 1988; Lesses 2014; Deer 2015). The absence of the concept or requirement of sexual consent in Justice Bollen's narrative reflects the endurance of this notion. Further, by asserting that there is "nothing wrong" (Bollen 1992 in Kaspiew 1995: 350) with a man using force against his wife should she not be appropriately sexually compliant, the commentary expresses support for the ideological and literal subordination of women beneath their husbands and justifies men's violent enforcement of this subordination.

Justice Bollen's commentary also supports domestic violence as micro-state crime because it positions the woman's body as sovereign territory. By negating the post-criminalisation concept of the need for ongoing sexual consent within marriage, the judge's comments again hark back to Blackstone's (1765: 1052) common law commentaries, which stipulate that "by marriage, ... the *very being* ... of the woman is incorporated and consolidated into that of the husband". In this sense, marriage is a vehicle for female colonisation (see Burris 1973; Barry 1979), where women's bodies are territory to be occupied, governed, or plundered as the imperial man chooses. This indicates parallels between the conceptualisation of female bodies as empty vessels without status and the designation of land as *terra nullius*, just as Australia supposedly was prior to European invasion – both are supposedly free and available for patriarchal occupation and colonisation. Justice Bollen's commentary is thus exposed as official discursive support for a patriarch's sovereignty and use of violence through positioning his wife's body as *his* colonised territory. As an expression of micro-state ideology, it negates the possibility of the man's violence constituting a criminal act, and in turn, officially enables marital sexual coercion and rape.

The Justice's commentary in this case can be understood as official judicial support for patriarchal micro-sovereignty, micro-state ideology, and domestic sexual violence. It also illustrates why domestic violence should be understood as a micro-state crime which is reinforced by the macro-state and its institutions. It communicates that a sovereign has, and should have, unfettered authority and autonomy to manage his subjects. It also communicates the idea that a man's choices and conduct in the family should be free from scrutiny or interference, thereby also reinforcing micro-state ideology. In this case, judicial power functioned to uphold micro-state ideology by authorising and excusing the defendant's violence, even though the relevant offence was criminalised at the time. It illustrates how normative sexist ideologies of male sovereignty, dominance, sexual entitlement, and the denial of women's autonomy and bodily sovereignty endure after legislative reform and are disseminated at the highest official levels.

The adjudication of intimate partner homicide also provides demonstrable evidence of contemporary support for micro-state ideology. This is particularly obvious in various modern forms of the provocation defence, which I introduced in the earlier section on criminal law. In adjudicative practice, these legal doctrines have readily framed women as responsible for their own victimisation and have functioned to excuse, minimise, or justify men's violence. Hall et al.'s (2016) analysis of sentencing remarks in intimate partner homicide cases in two Australian jurisdictions identifies prevalent provocation and victim-blaming narratives. In *R v Roesner* (2002 in Hall et al. 2016: 401), Justice Teague suggested that the victim was "the source of the conflict" and thus responsible for her own death because she had attempted to separate from the defendant and gain custody of their children. Consistent with other cases in the study, a woman's decision to leave her partner was considered a legitimate rationale for lethal male violence. Even as provocation is phased out, judicial narratives of men's violence continue to draw on provocation themes to blame women for men's violence and reduce male culpability (Hunter 2006; Tyson 2011; Douglas 2012). McKenzie et al.'s (2016) study of intimate partner homicide cases in Victoria identifies prevalent narratives of women as the cause of the stress that led to their husband killing them; it also identifies these narratives being used at sentencing to mitigate the defendant's culpability. This study also reveals courts routinely accepting defence narratives of male violence as a legitimate response to women's sexual disinterest, interest in other men, ambivalence about the relationship, or desire to separate. As former Supreme Court Justice Cummins stated in a speech at the release of McKenzie et al.'s (2016) report, "these tales are nothing short of character assassination where the living man … is trying to colonise the status of the victim, when he is in fact perpetrator" (Cummins 2016: n.p.).

In contrast, studies show that women rarely succeed with provocation defences in court and are disproportionately punished for using violence against men, even as a response to long-term abuse. In the United States, Peach's (2000) research reveals disproportionate treatment of male and female domestic violence offenders in the adjudication of law. Even when a woman's violence against a male partner followed a protracted history of victimisation, she was still treated far more harshly than a comparable male offender. In McKenzie et al.'s (2016) study, the cohort of *female-perpetrated* intimate partner homicides also reflects these findings, with judges not consistently recognising domestic victimisation histories as relevant background to women's use of lethal defensive violence. The Canadian cases of *R v Craig* (2008 and 2011 in Sheehy 2018) which I outlined earlier in the chapter also show contemporary judicial resistance to recognising male domestic abuse as relevant to women's lethal violence. In both these cases, despite an extensive, documented history of the deceased man's coercive controlling violence and the reign of terror he had maintained over his wife and child, the court was reluctant to consider this history when adjudicating his eventual killing by his wife.

Despite their official abolition, the influence of provocation and similar defences endures in the adjudication of law and reinforces the notion of patriarchal sovereignty and ownership of women. Tyson (2011; 2013) concludes that, regardless of whether they officially exist in law at the time of adjudication, these defence frameworks continue to function as a specifically sexed excuse for men's violence towards women but not for women's violence towards men. They are consistent with the original spirit of the provocation defence which blames women for their victimisation and which suggests that for a woman to challenge a man and assert her independence is to be responsible for her own death. Recent research in Victoria, Australia, shows that these doctrines continue to inform case narratives and sentencing decisions in cases of men's lethal domestic violence (Hunter & Tyson 2016; Naylor & Tyson 2017). Contemporarily, women are still blamed for their victimisation, and men's lethal violence is still minimised and justified. The judiciary and the criminal court system therefore continue to reinforce the original idea of male ownership of women and to condone the violent enforcement of patriarchal sovereignty, further revealing domestic violence as a micro-state crime which functions with nation-state support.

Through family law

Micro-state ideology is also contemporarily perpetuated in civil law through family law. This notably occurs through pro-contact ideology. Identifiable across Western systems, this ideology consists of principles and practices which privilege the presence of men and fathering, based on the belief that fathers are inherently necessary to families and to children's development and upbringing (Harne & Radford 2008; Flood 2012; Coy et al. 2015; Morrison 2015). It clearly echoes the construction of patriarchal authority in the private sphere as normal, natural, and necessary (see Hobbes 1651 in Chapman 1975) and has evolved from ideas concerning the unconditional importance of patriarchal leadership and guidance within the family (see Blackstone 1765). Pro-contact culture is detrimental to women and children because it systematically privileges and reinforces patriarchal values, favours men's and fathers' interests over those of women and children, normalises male control and abuse within the family, and prioritises fathers' ongoing involvement in children's lives without adequate regard for the risk of violence or for the safety or quality of parenting.

Pro-contact ideology and culture are ingrained in family law and remain central to legal practice and decision-making across the United States, the United Kingdom, and Australia. In these contexts, pro-contact ideology and culture reproduce the ideology of patriarchal sovereignty and are directly implicated in tolerating, excusing, and perpetuating domestic and family violence (Hunter 2006; Kelly et al. 2014; Coy et al. 2015). In Australia, through Laing's (2010) research with women accessing the family law system, participants described how state officials – spanning solicitors, court-appointed assessors, mediators, and magistrates – frequently stressed the importance of fathering without accounting for whether it might be consistent, positive, or even safe. Some of the most common beliefs encountered by participants were that children need a relationship with their father even if it has been abusive and that contact is inevitable, irrespective of prior violence. Cross-contextually, the misconception that children "want to see their fathers and must have affection for them" even if they have been violent and abusive remains widespread (Harne & Radford 2008: 67). Since pro-contact ideology generates narratives that ignore, minimise, and dismiss masculine violence within the family, it represents law's support for patriarchal sovereignty and micro-state ideology and its normalisation of patriarchal violence.

Across contexts, the critical importance of fathers to children's lives is consistently emphasised in family court cases, with little regard for the safety or quality of this fathering. Hunter's (2006) study of both United States and Australian child custody cases found that judgements consistently minimised histories of male violence in favour of narratives which emphasised the value of the patriarch and the nuclear family. In cases where parental separation was unavoidable, the maintenance of regular contact with fathers was afforded paramount importance. Even where fathers' prior violence had caused serious injury to their partner, and in some cases killed them, the maintenance of regular child-father contact was prioritised in judicial decision-making. Research in the United Kingdom and Australia also confirms that even in the presence of a documented history of violent offending, family law decision-makers commonly deem fathers valuable and suitable parents (Patrick et al. 2008; Laing 2010; 2013; Flood 2012; Coy et al. 2015; Conte 2018).

Research into victim-survivors' experiences with family courts in England also shows men's violence being consistently dismissed in favour of their perceived 'rights' as men and fathers. As one anonymous participant in Kelly et al.'s (2014: 98) study recalled, it was impossible to influence the powerful pro-contact ideological undercurrent in the system:

> I was battling to prove that actually it's not his right to see the children … it's their right for them to be safe from whoever's being abusive. [But] if you've been within the family court system you know what your own solicitor will say to you: 'Well it's a father's 'right' to see his children'.

Women who attempted to raise histories of male violence were also consistently told it was irrelevant to parenting and paternal 'rights'. For example,

Erika (in Coy et al. 2015: 58) was told that her ex-partner's extensive history of violence against her had

> *nothing to do with [father-child] contact at all. I've never been able to raise that, I've never been allowed to speak about it. The court don't want to know about his conduct, his behaviour, when I've been there it's all about his rights to see the children, have contact, and when I said I [had] concerns about him emotionally abusing them, they wouldn't hear of it … All they wanted to know is when he could see them.*

Even in the face of extensive evidence of intimate partner violence which was admitted by the father, judges dismissed this in favour of supporting and enabling men's perceived 'rights' and their ongoing influence over children. This indicates the enduring operation of a hierarchy of interests in these systems, where men and fathers are at the top, including when they have not only violated women and children but have offended against the law and the state itself.

In Australia, family law's pro-contact ideology and the associated belief in the importance of fathers continues even to override evidence of direct physical and sexual abuse of children. Prior to 2012, shared parental responsibility in child custody cases was determined around 75% of the time where direct violence allegations and child safety concerns were raised (Fehlberg et al. 2015). But despite a significant round of legislative amendments in 2012 which explicitly prioritised child safety, little has changed to diminish the dominance of pro-contact principles. Kaspiew et al.'s (2015a; 2015b) large-scale research for the Federal Government's Australian Institute of Family Studies identifies negligible differences in the determination of fathers' access to children since the 2012 reforms, even in the presence of child abuse allegations. This shows the enduring prominence of pro-contact principles in family court practice. It also shows how this institutional arm of the state functions in support of patriarchal sovereignty and micro-state ideology and to normalise domestic and family violence.

Through state social services

In state social service systems, policy discourse and practice also reflect micro-state ideology similar to that operating in the family law. Within social services, micro-state ideology is particularly evident in child support policy. Across comparable Western contexts, child support policy narratives are dominated by men's 'rights' and interests, functioning to the detriment of women and children and particularly domestic violence victim-survivors. In Australia, child support policy analyses reveal highly gendered notions of parental identities, roles, and responsibilities, with a particularly strong trope being the perceived entitlement of men to independence from state interference in their personal affairs (Branigan 2007; Laing 2010; Cook & Natalier 2013; Cameron 2014; Natalier et al. 2015). This male entitlement is based on a starkly unequal conceptualisation of parental responsibility where separated fathers are perceived as financially responsible for themselves alone, whereas mothers are expected to not only be primary caregivers but to unconditionally shoulder all financial responsibility for themselves and their children. Women's right to autonomy is essentially "written out of the picture" in these policy discourses at the expense of upholding men's independence, autonomy, and financial security (Cook & Natalier 2013: 44). This reinforces the ideology of male sovereignty and perpetuates sexed and gendered inequality in the family.

Another micro-state discourse which is actively reproduced in child support policy and practice in Australia and the United States is the grossly disproportionate reification of fathers' contributions. In these discourses, child support payments made by men are framed as generous 'gifts' offered by honourable fathers. This is again underpinned by patriarchal ideology which assigns great value to fathers and fathering, regardless of the quality of their presence, contributions, or behaviours. It means that any financial or other input made by fathers towards their children's lives is greatly extolled (Laing 2010; Beller 2015), whereas single mothers' constant caring, financial, and other contributions to their children are invisible and assumed. This ideology is evident in Australian research of single mothers' experiences with the government social welfare and child support systems (e.g. Cameron 2014; Cook 2015; Natalier et al. 2015; Cook & Natalier 2016). Researchers found that women who attempted to obtain Child Support Agency assistance with late, partial, or unpaid child support from their ex-partner were not only consistently dismissed but were encouraged to be grateful for any payments they received, no matter how tokenistic or paltry. Wendy (in Natalier et al. 2015: 25), for example, was told by staff to "count yourself lucky" because she received a few irregular and partial payments. This resonates with Harris' (2015) research in the United States, which also identifies the idea of fathers' financial contributions as a gift. In fact, underscoring the cultural reification of male rather than female contributions to society, both mothers and fathers considered fathers' parenting payments as generous offerings rather than obligations or necessary contributions to their child's subsistence and well-being.

Over the past fifteen years in Australia, child support policy reform has further entrenched male privilege and non-custodial fathers' control over ex-partners and children (see Fehlberg & Maclean 2009). Mothers' rights to receive reasonable financial input from their children's father, or child rights to a decent standard of living, have remained peripheral. Intense lobbying from men's rights' groups has ensured that the reforms uphold men's symbolic position as autonomous subjects who should be free to control their lives and finances; reforms have also given fathers greater choice over the form and manner of their contributions and enhanced their ability to dictate how contributions are to be used by the custodial parent (Flood 2012; Cook & Natalier 2013). This has further normalised and entrenched male control over the former family, enhancing a power relationship whereby men have the socially constructed entitlement to exert ongoing economic power over women and children (Cook & Natalier 2016). Additionally, this particular policy provision has helped to perpetuate the sexist idea that masculine rationality is vital for tempering the unreasonable and irrational tendencies of mothers and that fathers' decision-making is inherently necessary to children's upbringing. In the Californian context, Harris' (2015) study indicates similar patterns in the re-inscribing of patriarchal ideology and interests through child support policy. In both the Australian and United States contexts, sexed and gendered narratives and norms prevail, ensuring that fathers have the perceived right to personal independence, financial autonomy, and control, whereas mothers do not. By reifying and privileging men and their interests, the nation-state actively reproduces inequality and perpetuates micro-state ideology and male dominance, thereby reinforcing the symbolic and substantive frameworks that facilitate and justify male control in the domestic domain.

Conclusion

In this chapter, I have shown how domestic violence can be understood as a *micro-state crime*. By bringing together legal, political, and feminist theory on the state and the family, I explained how the family constitutes a diminutive patriarchal state which is both a reflection and reinforcement of the patriarchal nation-state, and which positions the male head of the family as sovereign and his wife and children as his subjects. I showed the enduring relevance of understanding domestic violence as a micro-state crime through recent and contemporary evidence of micro-state support via official institutional channels. I showed how nation-state institutions' treatment of and responses to men, women, and domestic and family violence uncovers powerful and enduring micro-state ideology manifesting through policy, practice, and discourse. Overall, I identified that, in real terms and with substantive impact, these nation-state institutions continue to normalise, legitimise, and reinforce patriarchal micro-sovereignty and the idea of the family as micro-state, thereby actively contributing to the perpetuation and legitimation of men's domestic violence.

Understanding the family as a micro-state and domestic violence as a micro-state crime is a revolutionary way of expanding state crime theory into the private sphere. It helps illuminate the purpose, methods, and techniques of domestic violence as well as the parallels between the exercise of power in repressive and violent regimes of the nation-state and the family. It also highlights the continuities and connections between patriarchal power at the micro- and macro-levels, across private and public institutions, and in the past and present. This lens compels us to confront the origins of domestic violence, its official historical authorisation, and its enduring legitimation.

Notes

1 This is reflected in the following distasteful Old English proverb:

> *A spaniel, a woman, a hickory tree,*
> *The more ye beat them, the better they be.*

2 Lesses (2014) discusses the origins of the marital rape exemption, and in particular the question of whether a man's immunity from prosecution for raping his wife derived directly from English common law itself, from the influential early development of common law through Blackstone's (1765) work, from biblical assertions around marriage, from the development of the concept through legal adjudication and precedent, or from various combinations of these factors. In any case and as Lesses acknowledges, there is no question that the marital rape exemption has been applied across common law contexts and over time. For the purposes of my argument, it is not crucial which factors most influenced the development of this legal principle, since they all relate to organised, state-level patriarchal structures which were based on ideologies that privileged men and their interests.

References

Australian Law Reform Commission. 2010a. *Family Violence: A National Legal Response.* (Report 114.)

Australian Law Reform Commission. 2010b. *Police Powers in Dealing with Family Violence.* (https://www.alrc.gov.au/publication/family-violence-a-national-legal-response-alrc-report-114/9-police-and-family-violence-2/police-powers-in-dealing-with-family-violence/)

Balint, Jennifer. 2012. *Genocide, State Crime and the Law.* Abingdon: Routledge.

Barry, Kathleen. 1979. *Female Sexual Slavery.* New York: New York University Press.

Beller, Lynn. 2015. When in doubt, take them out: Removal of children from victims of domestic violence ten years after Nicholson v Williams. *Duke Journal of Gender, Law and Policy* 22. 205–39.

Birdsey, Emma & Snowball, Lucy. 2013. *Reporting Violence to Police: A Survey of Victims Attending Domestic Violence Services.* Sydney: New South Wales Bureau of Crime Statistics and Research.

Blackstone, William. 1765. *Commentaries on the Laws of England.* Project Gutenberg Online Resources. (https://www.gutenberg.org/files/30802/30802-h/30802-h.htm)

Branigan, Elizabeth. 2007. Who pays in the end? The personal and political implications of financial abuse of women in intimate partner relationships. *Just Policy* 44. 31–6.

Bumiller, Kristin. 2008. *In an Abusive State: How Neoliberalism Appropriated the Feminist Movement against Sexual Violence.* Durham: Duke University Press.

Burris, Barbara. 1973. The fourth world manifesto. In Crow, Barbara (ed.), *Radical Feminism: A Documentary Reader*, 238–64. New York: New York University Press.

Cameron, Prue. 2014. *Relationship Problems and Money: Women Talk about Financial Abuse*. Melbourne: Women's Information and Referral Exchange.

Chan, Andy & Payne, Jason. 2013. *Homicide in Australia: 2008–9 to 2009–10 National Homicide Monitoring Program Annual Report*. Canberra: Australian Institute of Criminology.

Chapman, Richard. 1975. Leviathan writ small: Thomas Hobbes on the family. *American Political Science Review*. March 69(1). 76–90.

Chomsky, Noam & Herman, Edward. 1979. *The Political Economy of Human Rights*. Boston, MA: South End Press.

Cobbe, Frances Power. 1878. Wife torture in England. In Radford, Jill & Russell, Diana (eds.), *Femicide: The Politics of Woman Killing*, 46–52. Buckingham: Open University Press.

Cohen, Stanley. 1995. State crimes of previous regimes: Knowledge, accountability, and the policing of the past. *Law and Social Inquiry* 20. 7–50.

Conte, Isabella. 2018. *The (In)visible Victim: Characterisations of Child Victims of Intrafamilial Child Sexual Abuse in the Family Court of Australia*. School of Social and Political Sciences, University of Melbourne. (Graduate Thesis.)

Cook, Kay. 2015. *Financial Responsibility for Children Following Parental Separation: Welfare-to-work and Child Support Policy Winners and Losers*. Melbourne: Royal Melbourne Institute of Technology Centre for Applied Social Research Symposium.

Cook, Kay & Natalier, Kristin. 2013. The gendered framing of Australia's child support reforms. *International Journal of Law, Policy and the Family*. April 27(1). 28–50.

Cook, Kay & Natalier, Kristin. 2016. Gender and evidence in family law reform: A case study of quantification and anecdote in framing and legitimising the 'problems' with child support in Australia. *Feminist Legal Studies* 24. 147–67.

Copelon, Rhonda. 1994. Recognising the egregious in the everyday: Domestic violence as torture. *Columbia Human Rights Law Review* 2. 291–367.

Copelon, Rhonda. 2000. Gender crimes as war crimes: Integrating crimes against women into International Criminal Law. *McGill Law Journal*. November 46(1). 217–40.

Coy, Maddy & Scott, Emma & Tweedale, Ruth & Perks, Katherine. 2015. "It's like going through the abuse again": Domestic violence and women and children's (un)safety in private law contact proceedings. *Journal of Social Welfare & Family Law* 37(1). 53–69.

Cummins, Phillip. 2016. *How is Family Violence Recognised in Legal Responses to Intimate Partner Homicides?* Melbourne: Domestic Violence Resource Centre Victoria Public Forum.

Deer, Sarah. 2015. *The Beginning and End of Rape: Confronting Sexual Violence in Native America*. Minnesota: University of Minnesota Press.

DeKeseredy, Walter & Schwartz, Martin. 2013. *Male Peer Support and Violence against Women: The History and Verification of a Theory*. Boston, MA: Northeastern University Press.

Diemer, Kristin & Humphreys, Cathy & Crinall, Karen. 2017. Safe at home? Housing decisions for women leaving family violence. *Australian Journal of Social Issues* 52(1). 32–47.

Dobash, Rebecca & Dobash, Russell. 1998. *Rethinking Violence against Women*. Thousand Oaks: Sage.

Douglas, Heather. 2012. A consideration of the merits of specialised homicide offences and defences for battered women. *Australian and New Zealand Journal of Criminology.* 45(3). 367–82.

Dworkin, Andrea. 1981. *Pornography: Men Possessing Women.* London: Women's Press.

Elizabeth, Vivienne. 2015. From domestic violence to coercive control: Towards the recognition of oppressive intimacy in the Family Court. *New Zealand Sociology* 30(2). 26–43.

Fehlberg, Belinda & Kaspiew, Rae & Millbank, Jenni & Kelly, Fiona & Behrens, Juliet. 2015. *Australian Family Law: The Contemporary Context.* 2nd edn. Melbourne: Oxford University Press.

Fehlberg, Belinda & Maclean, Mavis. 2009. Child support policy in Australia and the United Kingdom: Changing priorities but a similar tough deal for children. *International Journal of Law, Policy and the Family* 23(1). 1–24.

Fernandez, Marilyn. 2010. *Restorative Justice for Domestic Violence Victims: An Integrated Approach to their Hunger for Healing.* Lanham: Lexington Books.

Finn, Geraldine. 1989. Taking gender into account in the theatre of terror: Violence, media, and the maintenance of male dominance. *Canadian Journal of Women & the Law.* December 3(2). 375–94.

Flood, Michael. 2012. Separated fathers and the fathers' rights movement. *Journal of Family Studies* 18(2/3). 235–45.

Freiberg, Arie & Gelb, Karen & Stewart, Felicity. 2015. Homicide law reform, provocation and sentencing. In Freiberg, Arie & Fitz-Gibbon, Kate (eds.), *Homicide Law Reform in Victoria: Retrospect and Prospects,* 42–56. Leichhardt, NSW: Federation Press.

Gloor, Daniela & Meier, Hanna. 2013. "Clouds darkening the blue marital sky": How language in police reports (re)constructs intimate partner homicides. In Klein, Renate (ed.), *Framing Sexual and Domestic Violence through Language,* 57–86. New York: Palgrave Macmillan.

Green, Penny & Ward, Tony. 2004. *State Crime: Governments, Violence and Corruption.* London: Pluto Press.

Hall, Guy & Whittle, Marion & Field, Courtney. 2016. Themes in judges' sentencing remarks for male and female domestic murders. *Psychiatry, Psychology and Law* 23(3). 395–412.

Harne, Lynne & Radford, Jill. 2008. *Tackling Domestic Violence: Theories, Policies and Practice.* Maidenhead: Open University Press.

Harris, Deborah. 2015. "You just have to look at it as a gift": Low-income single mothers' experiences of the child support system. *Journal of Poverty* 19(1). 88–108.

Haslanger, Sally. 2017. Racism, ideology and social movements. *Res Philosophica* 94(1). 1–22.

Hattery, Angela. 2009. *Intimate Partner Violence.* Lanham: Rowman and Littlefield.

Hattery, Angela & Smith, Earl. 2012. *The Social Dynamics of Family Violence.* Boulder: Westview Press.

Hayes, Sharon & Jeffries, Samantha. 2016. Romantic terrorism? An auto-ethnographic analysis of gendered psychological and emotional tactics in domestic violence. *Journal of Research in Gender Studies* 6(2). 38–61.

Hildebrandt, Mireille. 2006. Privacy and identity. In Claes, Eric & Duff, Antony & Gutwirth, Serge (eds.), *Privacy and Criminal Law,* 43–57. Antwerp: Intersentia.

Hong, Kari. 2018. A new mens rea for rape: More convictions and less punishment. *American Criminal Law Review.* Spring 55(2). 259–332.

Hunter, Rosemary. 2006. Law's (masculine) violence: Reshaping jurisprudence. *Law and Critique* 17. 26–46.

Hunter, Rosemary & Tyson, Danielle. 2016. The implementation of feminist reforms: The case of post-provocation sentencing. *Social & Legal Studies* 26(2). 129–65.

Johnson, Michael. 1995. Patriarchal terrorism and common couple violence: Two forms of violence against women. *Journal of Marriage and the Family* 57. 283–94.

Johnson, Michael. 2008. *A Typology of Domestic Violence: Intimate Terrorism, Violent Resistance, and Situational Couple Violence.* Boston, MA: Northeastern University Press.

Kaspiew, Rae. 1995. Rape lore: Legal narrative and sexual violence. *Melbourne University Law Review* 20(2). 350–82.

Kaspiew, Rae & Carson, Rachel & Dunstan, Jessie & Qu, Lizia & Horsfall, Briony & De Maio, John & Moore, Sharnee & Moloney, Lawrie & Coulson, Melissa & Tayton, Sarah. 2015a. *Evaluation of the 2012 Family Violence Amendments.* Melbourne: Australian Institute of Family Studies.

Kaspiew, Rae & Carson, Rachel & Dunstan, Jessie & Qu, Lizia & Horsfall, Briony & De Maio, John & Moore, Sharnee & Moloney, Lawrie & Coulson, Melissa & Tayton, Sarah. 2015b. *Experiences of Separated Parents Study.* Melbourne: Australian Institute of Family Studies.

Kelly, Liz. 1988. *Surviving Sexual Violence.* Cambridge: Polity.

Kelly, Liz & Sharp, Nicola & Klein, Renate. 2014. *Finding the Costs of Freedom: How Women and Children Rebuild their Lives after Domestic Violence.* London: Solace Women's Legal Aid and Child and Woman Abuse Studies Unit.

Khatib, Lina. 2013. *Image Politics in the Middle East: The Role of the Visual in Political Struggle.* I.B.Tauris & Co.

Kolin, Andrew. 2008. *State Structure and Genocide.* Lanham: University Press of America.

Laing, Lesley. 2010. *No Way to Live: Women's Experiences of Negotiating the Family Law System in the Context of Domestic Violence.* Sydney: University of Sydney.

Laing, Lesley. 2013. *"It's Like This Maze that You Have to Make Your Way Through":* Women's Experiences of Seeking a Domestic Violence Protection Order in NSW. Sydney: University of Sydney.

Lees, Sue. 1996. Unreasonable doubt: The outcomes of rape trials. In Hester, Marianne & Kelly, Liz & Radford, Jill (eds.), *Women, Violence and Male Power: Feminist Activism, Research and Practice,* 99–116. Buckingham: Open University Press.

Lemkin, Raphael. 1944. Genocide. *Axis Rule in Occupied Europe: Laws of Occupation, Analysis of Government, Proposals for Redress,* 79–95. Washington: Carnegie Endowment for International Peace.

Lesses, Kos. 2014. PGA v The Queen: Marital rape in Australia: The role of repetition, reputation and fiction in the common law. *Melbourne University Law Review* 37(3). 786–833.

MacKinnon, Catharine. 1989. *Toward a Feminist Theory of the State.* Cambridge, MA: Harvard University Press.

MacKinnon, Catharine. 1993. On torture: A feminist perspective on human rights. In Mahoney, Kathleen & Mahoney, Paul (eds.), *Human Rights in the Twenty-first Century: A Global Challenge,* 21–31. Boston, MA: M. Nijhoff.

Malley-Morrison, Kathleen & Hines, Denise. 2004. *Family Violence in Cultural Perspective: Defining, Understanding, and Combating Abuse.* Thousand Oaks: SAGE.

Marcus, Isabel. 1994. Reframing 'domestic violence': Terrorism in the home. In Fineman, Martha & Mykituik, Roxanne (eds.), *The Public Nature of Private Violence: The Discovery of Domestic Violence*, 11–35. New York: Routledge.

May, Larry. 2005. *Crimes against Humanity: A Normative Account.* Cambridge: Cambridge University Press.

McKenzie, Mandy & Kirkwood, Deborah & Tyson, Danielle & Naylor, Bronwyn. 2016. *Out of Character? Legal Responses to Intimate Partner Homicides by Men in Victoria 2005–2014.* Melbourne: Domestic Violence Resource Centre Victoria.

McQuigg, Ronagh. 2011. *International Human Rights Law and Domestic Violence: The Effectiveness of International Human Rights Law.* London: Routledge.

Meyer, Silke. 2011. Seeking help for intimate partner violence: Victims' experiences when approaching the criminal justice system for IPV-related support and protection in an Australian jurisdiction. *Feminist Criminology* 6. 268–90.

Meyer, Silke. 2016. Still blaming the victim of intimate partner violence? Women's narratives of victim desistance and redemption when seeking support. *Theoretical Criminology* 20(1). 75–90.

Meyersfeld, Bonita. 2010. *Domestic Violence and International Law.* Oxford: Hart Publishing.

Mill, John Stuart. 1869. The subjection of women. In Rossi, Alice (ed.), *Essays on Sex Equality by John Stuart Mill and Harriet Taylor Mill*, 123–242. Chicago: University of Chicago Press.

Morrison, Fiona. 2015. All over now? The ongoing relational consequences of domestic abuse through children's contact arrangements. *Child Abuse Review* 24. 274–84.

Natalier, Kristin & Cook, Kay & Pitman, Torna. 2015. *Single Mother's Experiences with the DHS-CS.* Research report funded by University of Tasmania and Flinders University.

Naylor, Bronwyn & Tyson, Danielle. 2017. Reforming defences to homicide in Victoria: Another attempt to address the gender question. *International Journal for Crime, Justice and Social Democracy* 6(3). 72–87.

Pain, Rachel. 2012. *Everyday Terrorism: How Fear Works in Domestic Abuse.* Centre for Social Justice and Community Aid, Durham University and Scottish Women's Aid.

Pateman, Carol. 1988. *The Sexual Contract.* Stanford: Stanford University Press.

Patrick, Rebecca & Cook, Kay & McKenzie, Hayley. 2008. Domestic violence and the exemption from seeking child support: Providing safety or legitimising ongoing poverty and fear. *Social Policy and Administration* 42(7). 749–67.

Peach, Lucinda. 2000. Is violence male? The law, gender and violence. In Waller, Marguerite & Rycenga, Jennifer (eds.), *Frontline Feminisms: Women, War and Resistance*, 57–72. New York: Routledge.

Pfitzner, Naomi & Fitz-Gibbon, Kate & True, Jacqui. 2020. *Responding to the 'Shadow Pandemic': Practitioner Views on the Nature of and Responses to Violence against Women in Victoria, Australia During the COVID-19 Restrictions.* Melbourne: Monash Gender and Family Violence Prevention Centre, Monash University.

Randall, Melanie & Venkatesh, Vasanthi. 2017. Criminalizing sexual violence against women in intimate relationships: State obligations under human rights law. *American Journal of International Law Unbound* 190. 189–96.

Robertson, Geoffrey. 2002. *Crimes against Humanity: The Struggle for Global Justice*. London: Penguin.

Romany, Celia. 1993. Women as aliens: A feminist critique of the public / private distinction in international human rights law. *The Harvard Human Rights Journal* 6. 87–125.

Rothe, Dawn & Mullins, Christopher. 2006. *Symbolic Gestures and the Generation of Global Social Control: The International Criminal Court*. Lexington: Lanham.

Segrave, Marie & Wilson, Dean & Fitz-Gibbon, Kate. 2018. Policing intimate partner violence in Victoria (Australia): Examining police attitudes and the potential of specialisation. *Australian & New Zealand Journal of Criminology* 51(1). 99–116.

Sheehy, Elizabeth. 2018. Expert evidence on coercive control in support of self-defence: The trial of Teresa Craig. *Criminology & Criminal Justice* 18(1). 100–14.

Shelby, Tommie. 2014. Racism, moralism and social criticism. *Du Bois Review: Social Science Research on Race* 11(1). 57–74.

Stark, Evan. 2007. *Coercive Control: How Men Entrap Women in Personal Life*. New York: Oxford University Press.

Stevens, Jacqueline. 1999. Compensatory kinship rules: The mother of gender. *Reproducing the State*, 209–35. Princeton, NJ: Princeton University Press.

Subedi, Surya. 1997. Protection of women against domestic violence: The response of international law. *European Human Rights Law Review* 6. 587–606.

Taylor Mill, Harriet. 1869. Enfranchisement of women. In Rossi, Alice (ed.), *Essays on Sex Equality by John Stuart Mill and Harriet Taylor Mill*, 89–122. Chicago: University of Chicago Press.

Tyson, Danielle. 2011. Victoria's new homicide laws: Provocative reforms or more stories of women 'asking for it'? *Current Issues in Criminal Justice* 23(2). 203–33.

Tyson, Danielle. 2013. *Sex, Culpability and the Defence of Provocation*. London: Routledge.

Chapter 5

Domestic violence as structural state crime

In this chapter, I argue that domestic violence can be understood as a *structural state crime*. This is because states play a direct and demonstrable role in generating and sustaining the structures, structural arrangements, and structural conditions that underlie both sexual inequality and domestic violence. As official state accounts themselves acknowledge, sexual inequality is the "root" of domestic violence (e.g. RCFV 2016: 2). Therefore, by looking beneath domestic violence itself and at how state policies produce and reproduce sexual inequality, the foundational role of states in domestic violence becomes clear. After first developing a feminist state crime framework for conceptualising patriarchal structural violence, I look at how states actively contribute to sustaining sexual inequality. I also identify a more immediate state structural role in domestic violence where states create, support, and maintain specific structures that normalise and justify male violence and exacerbate women's vulnerability to it. By looking at socio-economic, industrial, cultural, ideological, and epistemic structures, I identify how the state actively and contemporarily contributes to sustaining the structural dimensions of domestic violence.

A feminist theory of structural violence state crime

When states create economic, social, cultural, and institutional conditions that systematically privilege certain groups and disadvantage others, this has been identified as structural violence (e.g. Galtung 1969; Uvin 1998; Zizek 2008). Socio-economic structural violence has been comprehensively examined by scholars in this area, with authors unpacking how state policies produce and reproduce poverty, unemployment, underemployment, poor educational attainment, and limited opportunities for economic advancement for specific social groups which often extend across generations. Structural violence is frequently obscured by its more apparent violent symptoms: interpersonal crimes like assault, robbery, and drug and weapons offences. But it is structural forces that underlie these specific violent phenomena and align with a

DOI: 10.4324/9781003132370-7

range of vulnerabilities to both offending and victimisation. Authors specifically identify these conditions as state produced. State policy action and inaction which causes systematic inequality is recognised as a serious form of state harm, although not as explicitly criminal. In structural violence literature, the focus is also primarily on socio-economic, racial, and ethnic structural violence rather than its sex or gender dimensions.

In the state crime field, structural violence is widely considered a form of state criminality. This is because structural violence causes systematic disadvantage and suffering for certain oppressed groups and because it originates in and is maintained by state policies (e.g. Barak 1994; Green & Ward 2000). Structural violence generally sits at one end of a spectrum of state criminality: Kauzlarich et al. (2003: 247), for example, identify structural violence as "omission-implicit state crime", which I nominate as *structural violence state crime*. Due to its Marxist origins, much state crime research focusses on the economic dimensions of structural violence state crime, comprehensively critiquing capitalist structures and the harms endemic to their functioning (e.g. Kramer & Michalowski 1990; Barak 1991; 1994; Friedrichs 2010; Rothe & Mullins 2011; Bernat & Whyte 2017).[1] Postcolonial and decolonial state crime literature also identifies race-based structural violence state crime against Indigenous Peoples in a range of supposedly peaceful liberal-democratic societies. In these contexts, systemic and institutional racism – and even hidden structures of genocide – continues to unfold via complex and protracted state crime processes (e.g. Behrendt 2001; Manne 2004; Wolfe 2006; Balint & Evans 2010; Short 2010; Henry 2015; Balint et al. 2016; Curthoys et al. 2018). But the state crime field has not adequately attended to the sex or gender dimensions of structural violence state crime in these contexts, nor to structural factors that contribute to epidemic levels of male violence against women. Ironically, despite detailed analysis of the paternalistic – and thus patriarchy-derived – ideologies and practices of racist imperial and colonial projects, the literature overlooks the value of examining systematic violence against women through the same structural violence lenses.

A feminist reimagining of structural violence state crime in liberal democracies illuminates its operation along sex and gender lines. This is because if the structural harms of capitalism or colonialism can be considered state crimes, then the structural harms of patriarchy can also be considered state crimes, as can specific harms against women that emerge from this sex-based structural hierarchy. Feminist and pro-feminist scholars have already comprehensively shown that state policies, practices, and ideologies sustain a sexual hierarchy and the structural subjugation of women; they have also shown how these unequal conditions are conducive to, and supportive of, male violence against women (e.g. Caulfield & Wonders 1993; Enloe 2000; Jeffreys 2009; MacKinnon 2011). Without necessarily naming it as such, many scholars have analysed the relationship of sex-based structural violence to domestic violence. For example, in analysing coercive control as both a symptom and tool of broader sexual inequality, Stark (2007) argues that states have a direct line of responsibility through maintaining economic, social, and cultural conditions that perpetuate the subordination of women. Stark explains how domestic violence is possible specifically because it functions within, and aligns with, the structural subjugation of women. Without explicitly or comprehensively naming the state's role as criminal, many feminist contributions clearly identify state complicity through the production of persistent inequality and conducive conditions for male violence, particularly in the home. By adding terminology and concepts from the structural violence and state crime fields, I argue that we can illuminate sex-based structural violence state crime and uncover the state's criminal implication in domestic violence.

Conceptualising and identifying structures themselves is not a simple task. Some, like economic structures, are traceable to specific policies around employment, income, or taxation, for example. Others are less visible and more abstract, like ideological structures, which can be an obscure but powerful vehicle for reproducing sexual inequality, upholding male interests, and legitimising the expression of masculine power through control and abuse. In everyday terms, ideology manifests as implicit ideas and patterns of reason and judgement which are treated as inherently valid and self-evident: the taken-for-granted ways of seeing, hearing, thinking, knowing, and speaking about the world that generally escape scrutiny (Patrick et al. 2008). Yet ideology functions to distort reality and reproduce injustice. Through a critical structural lens, ideology can refer to specific structures of knowledge and thought that function to legitimate hegemonic power (e.g. Eagleton 1991; Shelby 2014; Haslanger 2017). From a critical state crime perspective, ideology is a reflection and reinforcement of the interests of dominant groups in society and a tool elites use to sustain their interests (e.g. Kauzlarich et al. 2003). I suggest that ideological structural violence can therefore be understood as an obscure mode of structural power and state criminality as well as key to better understanding the institutional and cultural legitimation of the supremacy and subjugation of certain social groups.

Identifying and illuminating the everyday operation of ideological structural violence means attending to its discursive transmission. This means uncovering how oppressive epistemic structures function through discourse: the written and spoken language, symbols, and verbal patterns that articulate the world and its subjects (see Foucault 1978; 1984; Thompson 2001; Graham & Schiele 2010; Browne et al. 2018). Since discourses do not merely reflect reality but "systematically form the objects of which they speak" (Foucault 1973: 49), they are a powerful vehicle through which social constructs are (re)produced. Through oppressive discursive processes, narratives of powerful groups tend to be accepted as truth and fact whereas those of subjugated groups are relegated or disqualified as inferior or illegitimate. This (re)produces knowledge hierarchies, normalises substantive inequality, and further justifies the oppressive and harmful treatment of certain groups. As a form of state crime, ideological structural violence plays out in substantive terms through official policy, practice, and discourse of state institutions. Given that state entities are composed of individual state agents, each representative – when acting in an official capacity – is also a potential medium of ideological state criminality (see Rothe & Mullins 2011). Through discursive means, state officials express, reproduce and reinforce inequality in ideological form, which can also constitute structural violence when it systematically privileges certain groups, compounds others' vulnerability, and rationalises violence against already-oppressed individuals.

A feminist perspective on ideological structural violence illuminates specifically *patriarchal* ideology and discourse and how it functions to privilege male interests. Under patriarchy, this discursive hierarchy tends to exclude or marginalise uniquely female knowledges and experiences, impede the recognition of uniquely female victimisation, and generate oppressive and discriminatory discourses about women. Specifically, by drawing on sexist ideological tropes concerning male superiority, male power, and the necessity of controlling women, it facilitates the legitimation of masculine violence, particularly in the domestic sphere. Interrogating these patriarchal ideologies *as* structural violence – and therefore state crimes, particularly when they emanate directly from state institutions and agents – means uncovering and challenging the ideas, assumptions, and judgements about men, women, and violence which masquerade as natural and normal, truth and fact, but which actually reproduce symbolic and substantive sexual inequality and violence (see Millett 1969; MacKinnon 1982; 1989).

In the remainder of this chapter, I unpack how structural domestic violence state crime plays out through state policy, practice, and ideology. By looking at how states produce and reproduce sex-based structural violence and how they generate the structural frameworks within which domestic violence can be perpetrated on an epidemic scale and with widespread impunity, I show how domestic violence constitutes a structural state crime.

Socio-economic structures and domestic violence

States can be understood as directly responsible for domestic violence because they produce and sustain the socio-economic structures of sexual inequality which underpin women's vulnerability to domestic control and abuse. Historically, women were structurally subjugated by state laws and policies which deprived them of political and socio-economic rights and opportunities. Effectively excluded from being full and independent citizens in Western democracies (Lake 1996; Park 2015), women were severely constrained in their ability to complete schooling, obtain a higher education or trade, secure paid work, pursue a career, or earn an adequate independent income. Although this situation has notably improved, this historical backdrop continues to have lasting effects on women's capacity for socio-economic autonomy and security and their capacity to resist male control and violence, particularly in the domestic sphere.

In contemporary liberal democracies, women are generally afforded symbolic equality with men; however, this does not translate into substantive economic equality in everyday life. In the developed capitalist West, data from the last twenty years show persistent disparities in income between men and women. In 2005, men's average incomes in the United States were approximately double women's (Connell 2005). In 2012, wage discrimination was still causing American women to earn around 25% less than their male counterparts (Hattery & Smith 2012). Goodmark (2018) notes that whilst the gender pay gap has narrowed over time, it persists for all women and notably for African American and Latina women. In 2014 in Australia, wage disparity in full-time employment was over 20% in favour of men and this gap had widened during the decade prior, suggesting that recent policies exacerbated rather than alleviated the problem (Chang et al. 2014). Amado et al. (2018: 357) confirm that recent studies across European Union countries show women still being paid "considerably less than men". Sex-based inequality on this scale reflects structural factors as it involves "a massive dispossession of social resources" along patriarchal lines (Connell 2005: 83). It is directly linked to state policies which converge to produce women's structural socio-economic disadvantage.

Even as policies have become more progressive, historical frameworks which limited women's participation as full citizens tend to reproduce socio-economic sexual inequality. In labour and employment, for example, traditional state-reified ideology concerning appropriate sex roles for men and women continues to explicitly and implicitly influence policy and practice. As Goodmark (2018) discusses, in different professions requiring comparable education, training, and skills, those traditionally occupied by men continue to be remunerated at significantly higher rates than those traditionally occupied by women. The consistently lower level of importance afforded to women's careers also means that female-dominated professions are still culturally and monetarily devalued. The increasing casualisation of the workforce is a gendered problem too, because insecure employment is and always has been dominated by women, and mothers in particular. In unpaid work, women continue to bear disproportionate burdens due to the persistent gendered division of child care and domestic labour (also Zuckerman 2014). The Covid-19 pandemic has highlighted and exacerbated all these disparities, reflecting the persistence of patriarchal values and ideologies around the gendered division of labour and the greater priority afforded to men's paid work. Despite repeatedly asserting equality- and equity-based principles and rhetoric, states across the liberal-democratic developed world are still failing to adequately address these disparate realities. This ensures the ongoing devaluation of women's contributions to society and, in substantive socio-economic terms, the entrenchment of female disadvantage.

Structural constraints on women's collective socio-economic independence have direct implications for domestic violence. Economic policies which reproduce the feminisation of poverty and economic disadvantage (see True 2012; Zuckerman 2014) lead to the widespread reliance of women on other – overwhelmingly male – figures to survive. Since this dependence is most often on a partner, it enhances possibilities for male control, reinforces female subordination, and fuels inequality within the family. From a socio-economically vulnerable position, it is difficult for women to escape relationships that become abusive. Contrary to the popular notion that victims can miraculously leave abusive relationships and thrive on their own, abused women often lack the socio-economic capital to leave and establish a sustainable independent existence (Qu et al. 2014; Goodmark 2018; Fitz-Gibbon 2020). A common pattern, particularly for the most disadvantaged women, is that once they do manage to leave a violent partner, they are soon relying on a new partner who is also violent. Constrained by the structural conditions which have produced their subordination, women can be literally imprisoned in domestic life and trapped in a revolving door of abusive relationships (Johnson 2008). For women who are also mothers, staying with an abusive partner can be a legitimate and rational decision when leaving is not only extremely dangerous but may also condemn their children to a life of poverty (Brush 2011; McArthur et al. 2013; Cameron 2014).

Cross-contextual studies also show direct connections between state-reified familial roles, economic policies and conditions, and men's domestic violence. Specifically, there are direct links between socio-economic policies and conditions, men's gendered experiences, and their perpetration of violence within the family. It is widely documented that men who strongly identify with the identity of masculine provider can experience difficulties with fulfilling this role as a "dramatic assault" upon their masculine dignity (DeKeseredy & Schwartz 2013: 77). Fearing a breakdown in their patriarchal authority and control, some men use violence to reassert their personal power and reconstitute a sense of masculine identity (Flood 2003; Howson 2006; Kimmel 2010). Specifically, research from different corners of the globe shows perpetrators using violence to reassert household dominance when their traditional role as provider is in jeopardy, for instance when experiencing chronic unemployment (Boonzaier 2005; Hattery 2009; Hattery & Smith 2012; True 2012; Goodmark 2018). Domestic violence also tends to increase in alignment with women's increasing participation in the economic and public spheres and in roles traditionally assigned to men. When high unemployment is structurally entrenched and jobs are a finite resource, women's participation in the workforce can be perceived as a direct threat to men's ability to fulfil their masculine role. The fact that attitudes supportive of restoring masculinity through violence have particular support amongst socio-economically marginalised men (DeKeseredy 1990; DeKeseredy & Schwartz 2013; DeKeseredy et al. 2019) further confirms connections between socio-economic structures and domestic violence. Together, these elements show direct links between the state, socio-economic structures, and domestic violence.

Through social service policy and administration in comparable Western liberal democracies, states also demonstrably contribute to reproducing structural socio-economic disadvantages for women, with unique impacts for domestic violence survivors. Regardless of context, clients of state social services are amongst the most vulnerable of citizens. In Australia and across the Western world, this cohort experiences intersectional disadvantage and vulnerability: not only suffering from domestic violence but also poverty, unemployment, chronic physical and mental ill-health, complex trauma, and substance abuse issues (Fehlberg & Maclean 2009; Brush 2011; ACOSS 2014; Fahmy et al. 2017). Single parents escaping domestic abuse are a prominent sub-group of social service clientele. Large-scale studies in Australia, for example, show a history of violence in over 60% of cases of separating parents with children and that the vast majority of victims are women who become sole parents (De Maio et al. 2013; Qu et al. 2014). Single-mother abuse survivors face unique socio-economic challenges that are exacerbated by state policies and practices. Overwhelmingly, these mothers attempt to support themselves and their children through a combination of social security payments and insecure, low-paid, casual, or part-time employment (Cook 2012; 2015; Cameron 2014; Cook et al. 2015; Natalier 2017; 2018). For single mothers with children under school age, state, institutional, and organisational policies that create high childcare costs and lack of workplace flexibility often exclude them from employment entirely (Fahmy et al. 2017). These factors make income stability and financial security "virtually impossible" (Cameron 2014: 48).

Adequate child support, also known in some contexts as child maintenance, is thus critical for the subsistence of single-parent families. Yet, for single-mother domestic violence survivors, child support and its state administration are central to experiences of systematic disadvantage, poverty, and abuse. Australian and United Kingdom-based studies show that state-facilitated economic abuse through child support withholding directly contributes to chronic economic hardship and poverty for women and children (Branigan 2007; Patrick et al. 2007; Kelly et al. 2014; Coy et al. 2015; Natalier 2018; WLSV 2018). In Australia, the federal-level Department of Human Services and its sub-agencies Centrelink and the Child Support Agency are responsible for ensuring that separated parents share the financial costs of raising children. But data show this state Department directly contributing to the ongoing victimisation and vulnerability of single mothers and their children. Underlying many of the problems facing clients is a system which structurally disadvantages women. The child support system is characterised by inaccurate assessments, low levels of compliance, and inadequate enforcement of child support obligations (Cook 2015). Even when custodial parents do receive assessed rates of child support, these are demonstrably inadequate. Patrick et al. (2007) found that 80% of mothers who were receiving child support received $5 or less per week; Cameron (2014) identified that extremely low assessed rates were often based on fraudulent information provided by payers, which the Agency did not seek to verify. Research continues to show a stark gap between the child support minimum rate and even a small portion of basic parenting costs such as rent, utilities, food, clothing, and school equipment (Natalier et al. 2015; Natalier 2017). In reality, assessed rates of child support do not reflect costs incurred by custodial parents. This government agency therefore contributes to entrenching hardships for single parents and exacerbating women's economic vulnerability.

Australian research further shows that non-custodial parents routinely fail to comply with their child support obligations, with fathers with a history of intimate partner abuse the least likely group to fulfil their obligations (Cameron 2014; Cook et al. 2015; Natalier 2017; 2018). Of mothers who had experienced violence either before, during, or after separation, De Maio et al.'s (2013) study showed that 36% received less than the assessed amount of child support from their ex-partner. The fact that non-paying fathers routinely circumvent obligations without consequence further points towards a state role in these harms. Since the unequal socio-economic power relationship between child support payers and payees is maintained through contemporary policy, it can be understood as officially supported and enabled. Indeed, several researchers have suggested that the oppressive power that child support payers wield over payees can be understood as a state-facilitated harm, since payers are given state-sanctioned power to dictate the quality of life of their former family and can exert this control with impunity (Patrick et al. 2008; Cook 2013; Natalier 2018).

I further nominate child support withholding as a form of *state-facilitated domestic abuse*, since it is systematically institutionally enabled. Inadequate law and policy around child support compliance and demonstrable institutional disinterest in enforcing fathers' economic obligations indicates the low priority afforded to this issue and the system's legitimation of economic abuse. It also highlights the links between child support non-compliance, state policy and practice, and the reproduction of women's disadvantage and vulnerability to domestic violence. More broadly, it shows the social service system's direct role in extending economic abuse beyond relationship separation and its contribution to the feminisation of poverty: a recognised form of structural violence (see True 2012; Zuckerman 2014). Because financial difficulties for single mothers are structurally entrenched and systemically exacerbated by state policies, they should be understood as structural violence state crime. And, because this structural violence uniquely impacts domestic violence victims by enabling financial abuse and exacerbating their economic vulnerability, it also constitutes domestic violence state crime.

Industrial and cultural structures and domestic violence

Another way that states directly contribute to domestic violence is by providing support for industrial and cultural structures which reinforce sexual inequality, normalise female sexual objectification, and both directly and indirectly contribute to domestic violence. By inadequately regulating and thus tacitly endorsing industries which normalise violence against women and produce specific violence themselves, the state plays a demonstrable role in these harms. In Caulfield and Wonders' (1993: 91) words, "the state's support for a culture of violence toward women [includes] failing to regulate industries that market violence against women as a commodity". Regulatory failures on the part of the state then directly contribute to the perpetuation of the harmful cultural structures embedded within these industries which systematically normalise and endorse violence against women. Two lucrative industries which have played an identifiable role in commodifying women and fuelling sex-based violence are the film and television industry and the sex industry. These industries receive neither adequate, appropriate, nor consistent regulation by the state. This positions the state as a complicit actor in the violence against women that both directly and indirectly arises from these industries.

In the film industry, lack of adequate state regulation of representations of male violence against women demonstrates the state's support for cultural structures that normalise and reproduce this harm. One example is the classification frameworks which regulate film distribution in the United States, which indicate systematic lenience towards violent content and steadily increasing levels of violence in films since the late 1980s (Leon & Barowski 2011). Dick's (2006) investigation into these classification and regulation processes reveals a problematic absence of state involvement or oversight, particularly given the serious implications of this regulatory vacuum. The body responsible for film classification, the Motion Picture Association of America, is privately funded by Hollywood studios and is not subject to any government or public scrutiny; its processes are entirely arbitrary and opaque. This, in effect, gives the Motion Picture Association quasi-legal regulatory powers, given that its ratings dictate the frameworks for films' cinema release, audience admission, and retail sales across the country. Under the Association's classification system, the two most restrictive ratings for mainstream film distribution in the United States are R and NC-17. The former allows viewing by mature audiences with parent or guardian accompaniment, whereas NC-17 prohibits any person under 18 from cinema entry or product purchase, regardless of parental presence or supervision. I suggest that comparing the content of films with these respective ratings provides insight into the free dissemination of violent material that this regulatory vacuum allows.

Comparative content analysis of two films with the two most restrictive United States-based ratings illustrates the pervasive normalisation and toleration of male violence against women, yet extreme restrictions around depictions of taboo subject matter. *Blue is the Warmest Colour* (Kechiche 2013) was given the most restrictive NC-17 rating for depicting full-frontal nudity and highly explicit lesbian sex. Problematic undercurrents in the film aside, this rating did not relate to depictions of violence, considering that the film's most extreme depictions of violence involve a minor physical altercation in a schoolyard, and one woman being slapped across the face during an argument. On the other hand, *The Girl with the Dragon Tattoo* (Oplev 2009), also known by the original Swedish title *Men Who Hate Women*, received the lower American R rating, but features extended, repeated, and graphic scenes of brutal oral and vaginal rape, sexual torture, and various sadistic violations of both a sexual and non-sexual nature. Comparing the ratings and content of these films provides illustrative evidence of the pervasive normalisation of extreme male-on-female sexual violence but the stigmatisation of naked bodies and sex within a same-sex relationship. This clearly indicates the existence of a problematic censorship hierarchy. If taboo subject matter such as queer sexuality is subject to strict regulation, whereas brutal and traumatising violence against women is freely disseminated, this suggests that the Motion Picture Association's classification system prioritises the policing of conservative sexual mores over real harms associated with violent content. In the absence of state oversight or intervention, the state is therefore complicit in the ramifications of having this accessible, consumable violence circulate within society.

Extensive research shows direct correlations between the visual consumption of violence and violent behaviour, particularly in relation to male perpetration and female victimisation. As radical feminist research over time has shown (e.g. Dworkin 1985; Dines 2010; MacKinnon 2011; Tyler 2011; DeKeseredy et al. 2019), men's exposure to media depictions of degradation and violence towards women, particularly early in life, demonstrably increases their likelihood of becoming perpetrators of sexual violence. This is because consuming this material tends to normalise sexual inequality and the objectification of women, model men's sexual entitlement, and promote attitudes supportive of masculine violence. Since this research demonstrates strong links between men's media consumption and perpetration of violence, the state's inadequate media regulation and the free availability of sexually violent material implicates the state in violence against women.

Another industry which receives state support and is implicated in violence against women is the sex industry. Through legislating to allow various forms of prostitution, stripping, pornography, and pornographic advertising (and indeed encouraging these as lucrative capitalist enterprises), states provide substantive support and cultural endorsement for these industries and the harms against women that emerge from them. Official policy support for this industry has been identified by generations of feminist scholars as constituting the official legitimation of violence against women (e.g. Dworkin 1981; Jeffreys 1997; 2009; 2010; Coy 2008; Dines 2010; MacKinnon 2011). Violence is both endemic to this industry because its practices are violent in themselves and because the industry is directly implicated in other violence against women. In addition to the research cited above, other recent studies (e.g. Zeglin 2014; DeKeseredy & Corsianos 2016) confirm that men who consume pornography and the services of prostituted women are more likely to objectify women and girls, sexualise children, and be sexually dominating, aggressive, and violent. This shows demonstrable connections between state regulatory policy, the sex industry, the cultural normalisation of harmful male behaviours and violence, and specific domestic offences such as intimate partner rape and child sexual abuse. When the state neglects to regulate industries which are directly implicated in promoting female subjugation and violence against women and children, the state is also playing a productive role in these harms.

Ideological and epistemic structures and domestic violence

Another way that states are implicated in sexual inequality and domestic violence is through ideological and epistemic structures. As I outlined earlier in this chapter, ideological structural violence against women functions through official patriarchal discourse, perpetuating ways of knowing and understanding the world which centre and privilege men and marginalise and subjugate women. A feminist analysis recognises that the purpose of patriarchal ideology is to reproduce sexual inequality and injustice; it accordingly aims to uncover how this ideology is integrated into daily life, and to identify its symbolic and substantive effects. Patriarchal ideological structures are relevant to domestic violence because they maintain the frameworks through which male superiority and entitlement are constructed as normal and legitimate; where female invisibility, exclusion, or inferiority is assumed; and where male control and abuse become culturally acceptable.

The patriarchal epistemic structures of law exemplify ideological structural violence which directly hinders the recognition of women, their experiences, and domestic violence. Common law systems are ideologically and substantively patriarchal: they are designed by men, about men, and operate in the interests of men. They have developed based upon the presumption that men are law's sole subjects, leading to the broad exclusion of women and their experiences of harm (Henderson 1991; Charlesworth 1995; Otto 2012; Sifris 2014). Law is also based on sexist ontology and epistemology: it is masculine, rational, and material in character, with its central subject the abstract "reasonable man" (Hekman 1999: 13). In fact, law has always conceived of human as a male concept, such that "'human' and 'female' are mutually exclusive by definition; you cannot be a woman and a human being at the same time" (MacKinnon 1994: 6; also 1989; 2006).

Law's model of harm is also masculine. It is based upon the quintessential scenario of male victimisation: a discrete incident of assault causing visible injury, perpetrated in public by an acquaintance or stranger (Chan & Payne 2013). Accordingly, interpersonal crimes tend to be "defined in relation to whether the surface of the body has been violated" (Kelly & Radford 1996: 29). This "legal and cultural story that 'violence' means physical force" (Hunter 2006: 35) has created an exclusionary framework which renders the vast majority of harms against women invisible and undocumentable. Since the most common form of female victimisation – domestic and family violence – takes place in private and is specifically designed not to produce obvious physical injury, what results is a sexist hierarchy of harm where the majority of female victimisation is not recognised or actioned (MacKinnon 1982; Copelon 1994; Subedi 1997; Meyersfeld 2003; Stark 2007; Henry 2011). The experiential and epistemic structures that have shaped law therefore directly contribute to systematic discrimination against women and domestic violence victims in particular, who are categorically constrained in their ability to assert victim claims.

A range of studies across different contexts show that women still face persistent difficulties in having the range of serious harms and dangers associated with domestic violence recognised. The erroneous notion that the home is a haven of safety and security endures in legal discourse and practice, despite the reality that it is the most dangerous place for women (see UN-ODC 2019). Cross-contextually, women also face ongoing challenges when attempting to gain recognition for complex domestic violence victimisation experiences that challenge conventional ideas about crime (Stark 2007; Guggisberg & Fisher 2010; McKenzie et al. 2016; Meyer 2016; Douglas 2019). Particularly when presenting with pain, trauma, or injuries that do not align with traditional legal assumptions about what constitutes actionable violence, women struggle to be seen or heard by law and the state. The lack of recognition of coercive control is a particular way that sexist epistemic structures in law directly hinder appropriate responses to domestic violence. As detailed in previous chapters, coercive control is a distinct form of domestic abuse where perpetrators employ multiple abusive tactics to sustain a regime of power, control, and fear (Stark 2007). It routinely involves psychological, verbal, sexual, economic, and social abuse and can, but does not always, include physical assault. This is why it confronts conventional notions of what constitutes actionable violence.

In Canada, official resistance to recognising coercive controlling domestic abuse is illustrated in the criminal law cases of *R v Craig* (2008 and 2011 in Sheehy 2018). These cases adjudicated Teresa Craig's self-confessed killing of her abusive husband following years of being coercively controlled. The court heard a well-substantiated history of the deceased's abusive regime: he had isolated his wife and son geographically, socially, and financially; forced them to live in abject poverty; regularly brandished weapons, threatened to kill them, and assaulted other people in their presence; and repeatedly de-graded and physically abused the child. Extensive testimony from different witnesses detailed conditions of absolute imprisonment and overwhelming terror which led Teresa to genuinely fear for her and her son's lives. But de-spite a clear, detailed, and substantiated defence narrative of the deceased's coercive control,[2] the court was reluctant to accept its relevance to the de-fendant's lethal violence because it did not involve physical assault or visible injury perpetrated directly against Teresa. The case shows how, in practice, law continues to operate in accordance with masculine epistemic structures which obscure some of the most destructive and dangerous forms of male vi-olence, subjugate women's experiences of victimisation, and deprive women of the opportunity to have their actions appropriately contextualised.

Coercive control is also inadequately recognised or considered in the family law system. Despite its widespread legal codification and centrality to family law, coercive control is widely dismissed as irrelevant to decision-making in relation to child contact and custody. In recognition of the prevalence and major harms of coercive control, in Victoria, Australia, the *Family Violence Protection Act*'s definition of domestic and family violence (State Government of Victoria 2015: 5.1.a) includes behaviour that is psychologically abusive, threatening, coercive, controlling, dominating, and which causes a person to fear for their or others' safety and well-being. Official debate is also under way regarding the criminal codification of coercive control across Australian jurisdictions (Fitz-Gibbon et al. 2020). In the United Kingdom, coercive control is already codified in the *Serious Crimes Act 2015* and encompasses a range of non-physical behaviours such as systematic social isolation, finan-cial abuse, and psychological intimidation (UKCPS 2017). Notwithstanding questions over both the value and risks associated with its specific *criminal* codification (see e.g. Walklate & Fitz-Gibbon 2019), coercive control remains critical to family law practice and to the determination of safe and appropri-ate child custody and parental contact arrangements.

Yet, analyses of judicial practice in family law in the United Kingdom, Australia, and New Zealand reveal the routine dismissal of domestic and family violence when it manifests as coercive control. This was a consistent finding in Coy et al.'s (2015) research with family law subjects in the United Kingdom. One anonymous participant was told that verbal and psychological abuse was not harmful to children and was irrelevant to determining par-enting arrangements. Another anonymous interviewee was admonished by a judge and instructed to "stop using the word violence" when referring to emotional abuse and threats because it was "clearly not" (Anon in Coy et al. 2015: 58). These experiences are echoed in the Australian context. A partic-ipant in Laing's (2017: 1325) research recounted being told that because her ex-partner "appears to be behaving himself, the court is satisfied that he's not really violent". Even though she explained that his abuse was both physical and non-physical and was consistently concealed in the presence of others, she was disbelieved. In New Zealand, Elizabeth (2015) also found that family courts tend to rely on an assault-based model of domestic and family violence rather than the more apt coercive control paradigm.

This cross-contextual evidence points to exclusionary frameworks of harm continuing to operate in both criminal and civil legal practice. The assumption that non-physical violence is not harmful or actionable and that it is irrelevant to the adjudication of domestic crimes or parenting persists, jeopardising the safety of women and children and contradicting legal principles of equality, fairness, and harm prevention. Because these frameworks continue to privilege masculine experience, knowledge, and interests, they in turn structurally discriminate against women and represent a form of epistemic structural violence. Furthermore, since this structural violence directly contributes to obscuring, tolerating, and excusing men's domestic abuse and because it operates via official state channels, I argue that it constitutes domestic violence state crime.

Ideological structural violence state crime can also manifest as institutionalised sexist beliefs that frame and inform law enforcement practice. In Victoria, Australia, research shows that sexist ideologies continue to affect the impartial enforcement of law. The Victorian Equal Opportunity and Human Rights Commission's (VEOHRC 2017: 2–3) review of sex-based discrimination by Victoria Police noted that respect for women was "sorely lacking within the organisation [and its] systems and structures". Across Australian jurisdictions, sexism also plays a direct and persistent role in police responses to domestic violence. In Segrave et al.'s (2018: 105) research, Victorian police openly expressed grossly sexist views of domestic violence victims, with officers broadly characterising women seeking help for alleged victimisation as "a steady procession of imposters, liars and time wasters, presenting … highly suspect claims" (Segrave et al. 2018: 105). Research with victim-survivors also indicates that sexist stereotypes continue to influence law enforcers' perceptions, attitudes, and treatment of men and women when responding to domestic incidents (e.g. Meyer 2011; 2016; Ulbrick & Jago 2018; Douglas 2019). Particularly when women fail to conform to the inherently sexist image of the ideal victim[3] – weak, vulnerable, and compliant with authorities – they tend to be treated as unworthy of state protection by law enforcers. Assumptions about women based on their historical subjugation and their denial of full legal status are still affecting their capacity to assert victim claims and receive state protection from domestic violence.

Sexist ideological constructs are also evident in police responses to women as domestic offenders. United States-based research indicates that police officers tend to perceive female offenders as more unstable, erratic, and volatile than men accused of similar offences (e.g. Miller 2005; Fernandez 2010). Miller (2005: 74) identified a particularly prominent sexist trope drawn on by police: the enigmatic and uncontrollable "crazy woman" who could easily lose control and attack a man with almost superhuman ferocity. This aligns with Roark's (2016: 59) analysis of domestic violence-related arrests in the United States, which suggests that police responses were often premised upon the perception that men are "more responsible" than women. Ongoing investigations in Australia echo these findings. Ulbrick and Jago's (2018) research shows the enduring impact of sexist ideology over police practice which directly impacts the misidentification of women as primary domestic violence aggressors. The study found that misidentification often occurred because police responded positively to male perpetrators portraying themselves as calm and reasonable and their female partner as crazy and dangerous, as was typified by one man's claim – later proven erroneous – that "she's psychotic and I need protection" (1). Cross-contextual scoping conducted for the research study indicated similar misidentification patterns across Australia and globally. Since these gendered narratives reflect those drawn on by male perpetrators to justify their control and abuse of women – for instance, through characterising women as irrational and hysterical – they also contribute to the ideological justification of men's violence.

Similar ideological structural violence can be identified in official narratives in the criminal court system. Through a sexist hierarchy of rationality, women are often attributed negative and stigmatising labels which directly impede their ability to have their voices and experiences of domestic violence recognised. This discursive subjugation of women also functions to obscure and excuse men's violence. One notorious Australian marital rape case which exemplifies the expression of sexist ideology by the judiciary is *R v Donald* (1993 in Kaspiew 1995). This case was heard in a jurisdiction which had officially criminalised intimate partner rape, but in practice, the victim and her pursuit of recognition and justice were treated as illegitimate. Justice Bland's commentary clearly reflected sexist tropes of the dishonest, irrational, and manipulative woman, who was constructed in opposition to the honest, reliable, rational man. The judge communicated outright scepticism of the victim, her testimony and allegations, and extended his pervasive cynicism to all women by asserting that "'No' often means 'Yes'" when it comes to women and sex (Bland in Kaspiew 1995: 367). This commentary dismisses women's capacity to think, feel, or express themselves rationally, accurately, or truthfully; it also characterises women as uniquely suspect because of a perceived innate tendency towards being fickle and deceitful. Similarly, discriminatory assertions about women were expressed in *R v Johns*, another marital rape case heard in the Australian post-criminalisation context (1992 in Hocking 1993). In this case, Justice Bollen specifically – and erroneously – directed the jury to be sceptical of the alleged victim's testimony because she was a woman and was alleging sexual victimisation. He warned them that "experience has taught the judges that … women have manufactured or invented false allegations of rape and sexual assault" (Bollen 1992 in Hocking 1993: 153) and added a dramatic anecdote of the alleged fabrication of rape in an unrelated and irrelevant case.

These examples of judicial commentary illustrate the erroneous stories about women that sustain their subjugation and suppress their claims of domestic victimisation. By officially characterising women as a uniquely irrational, unreliable, and thus suspect category of witness, such comments reinscribe early common law's original framing of women as inferior to men and undeserving of full legal subjectivity (see e.g. Charlesworth 1995; Hekman 1999). In the absence of substantive basis, these assertions constitute powerful and pervasive ideology in the true critical sense: they are empirically unsubstantiated, unjust, and oppressive, yet they masquerade as truth and fact (see Millett 1969; MacKinnon 1982; 1989; Patrick et al. 2008; Shelby 2014; Haslanger 2017). Such discourses reproduce the original sexism of law, demarcating women as undeserving of and ineligible for full equality and just treatment by the state. Despite reforms to domestic violence law, these sexist discourses from state officials continue, reinforcing epistemic structural inequality, subjugating and stigmatising women, and excusing and justifying male abuse.

Ideological structural violence against women also functions in the civil legal system, manifesting through discriminatory narratives of women that, in turn, obscure and perpetuate men's violence. In contrast to the positive notions of men and fathers that I detailed in Chapter 4, women and mothers are consistently painted in a negative and critical light in family law discourse. In Australia, there is a common view amongst family law practitioners that when a family law matter is pending, women often obtain protection orders for tactical rather than genuine reasons (Fehlberg et al. 2015). This is reflected in the experiences of Laing's (2010; 2013) Australian research participants, who reported that the most common assumptions they encountered when interacting with family law authorities were that mothers fabricate intimate partner and child abuse allegations and that attempts to isolate children from their fathers are unjustified (also Flood 2012). Ferguson et al.'s (2018) analysis also suggests that this belief is widespread and deeply ingrained in Australian family law ideology and practice. These authors identify broadly "critical and insensitive" judicial attitudes towards mothers who make allegations against ex-partners, with allegations often perceived as "malicious and intentional fabrications" aimed at limiting paternal access (94).

Conte's (2018) study of Australian family law cases involving allegations of intrafamilial child sex abuse identifies the systematic discrediting of women's and children's testimonies of male violence. In judicial commentary, women were consistently cast as dishonest, deceitful, malicious, manipulative, and mentally unstable, and court deliberations and decisions were premised upon the assumption that allegations of paternal abuse were false and fabricated. The overwhelming majority of children were constructed as being "affected", "influenced", and "coached" by their mother (30–1) and were characterised as "liars and complicit operatives in their mother's scheme" (33). Allegations made by mothers were framed as destructive and harmful to children rather than concerned or protective, and the possibility that they might be based on genuine and well-founded concerns for their children's welfare was rarely acknowledged by any court officials, notably judges.

This sexist hierarchy of veracity and reliability is reflected in family law practice outside of Australia. In the United Kingdom, scepticism of women and their motives remains a powerful facet of pro-contact family law culture. For instance, if children express a view about not wanting paternal contact, it is generally assumed to "have been manipulated by their mothers" (Harne & Radford 2008: 68). In the United States, Nichols' (2013) research shows that independent children's lawyers and judges consistently interpret child abuse allegations as indicative of the alleging mother's ulterior motives or mental health problems rather than of actual abuse (also Gutowski & Goodman 2019). Ferguson et al.'s (2018) international review also indicates the prevalence of similar sexist belief structures in other comparable systems including Canada. They found that it was common for alleging mothers and children to be judged unreliable and to be subjected to interrogation and criticism concerning their honesty, integrity, and mental stability. Overall, evidence points to enduring official ideology which oppresses, stigmatises, and marginalises women and children and impedes the recognition and prevention of men's intimate partner and child abuse.

By systematically relegating women's voices and interests below men's, family law generates discriminatory practices and problematic decisions. Gutowski and Goodman's (2019) research with women survivors of intimate partner abuse involved in family law cases in the United States shows consistent patterns of testimony dismissal along the lines of gender rather than evidence. Even in cases where a man's history of violence had been verified, his testimony was routinely regarded more highly than his ex-partner's. As one mother stated in despair,

Why would they believe someone who has done all these things to me and my children, why would [they] take his word over mine? I don't understand. I feel like even though I was the victim and he was the perpetrator, I really feel like he still has more rights than I do.

(Kelly in Gutowski and Goodman 2019: 10)

Australian studies also show that in cases where a man's violent history had been established and his integrity systematically discredited in court, his testimony was consistently considered more credible than that from a woman with no problematic history (e.g. Patrick et al. 2008; Laing 2010; 2013; 2017; Fehlberg et al. 2015; Kaspiew et al. 2015a; 2015b). This again evidences a persistent gendered hierarchy which undermines the impartial adjudication of law and the detection and prevention of domestic and family violence.

The sexist hierarchy of credibility also aligns with a problematic gendered construction of risk in family law. This risk hierarchy is most obvious in cases involving child abuse allegations where, regardless of the actual risk posed, that emanating from the mother is consistently deemed more serious. This is indicated by Nichols' (2013) research in the United States, where judges were found to be far more inclined to make determinations of false negatives rather than false positives in adjudicating paternal child abuse allegations. This is mirrored in Conte's (2018: 31) Australian study, which concludes that "in constructing the mother as an active saboteur, family consultants and judges seemed to give more emphasis to the risk of emotional abuse perpetrated by the mother [than] the risk of sexual abuse by the father". This is tantamount to ruling that sexual abuse is of less concern than emotional abuse. However, the key variable here is gender, with discriminatory discourses and practices treating risks posed by women as more serious than those posed by men (also see FCA 2014).

Ideological violence continues to structure family law's responses to women and allegations of male abuse in the family. Judicial decision-making still draws on and perpetuates sexist narratives about women as irrational, manipulative, and inherently unstable, which is then used to cast doubt over their claims, reframe protective concerns is evidence of illness or deviance, and damage mothers' relationships with children at the expense of supporting fathers. By not treating paternal abuse allegations as a possible indicator of actual abuse, courts are neglecting their duty to prioritise family violence prevention principles. When family courts contemporarily reproduce inequality in the courtroom through sexist ideological tropes which privilege men's testimony and interests, this directly hinders domestic and family violence detection and prevention and further underscores the structural dimensions of domestic violence.

Conclusion

Structural violence is an insidious form of state criminality. It emerges from policies that are considered normal and neutral but it generates systematic inequality and disadvantage and creates conducive conditions for interpersonal violence. By developing a feminist framework for theorising sex-based structural violence and the interaction between it and domestic violence, I showed how these harms can be understood as state crimes. I then considered specific forms of state structural violence and how they sustain sexual inequality and fuel domestic violence. I looked at socio-economic, industrial, cultural, ideological, and epistemic structures and showed their historical and contemporary impact on producing and reproducing domestic violence.

Addressing harms that emerge from structural violence is a major challenge – they are incredibly tenacious because of their embeddedness in society. Domestic violence is entrenched within and by political, social, economic, industrial, cultural, ideological, and epistemic structures. Therefore, even when contemporary states might officially condemn domestic violence, the powerful structural arrangements and conditions which first enabled it persist. As

MacKinnon (2019: n.p.) argues, "just because something is legally prohibited it doesn't mean it stops. Maybe exceptional acts do, but not pervasive structural practices". This is certainly the case with domestic violence, where the structural violence that originally produced it endures, limiting the impact of targeted violence prevention initiatives. As justice activists continue to highlight, we will only make genuine inroads into preventing interpersonal violence against certain groups when we truly confront the structural harms from which it emerges.

Notes

1 For example, when capitalist states create economic conditions which are systematically oppressive for certain groups whilst systematically advantageous for others, this is understood as state criminality. When mass-scale corporate and industrial harms are officially tolerated and enabled, yet punitive action is taken against minor subsistence-based offending, this is also understood both as criminogenic policy and more broadly as state criminality.
2 The expert witness for the defence was Evan Stark (see 2007), the academic professor and practitioner who pioneered the movement to reconceptualise systematic intimate partner violence regimes through the lens of coercive control.
3 The term 'ideal victim' was coined by critical criminologist Nils Christie (1986), who observed that victim claims are significantly constrained by whether the claimant displays certain stereotyped characteristics and attributes.

References

Amado, Carla & Santos, Sergio & Jose, Jose Sao. 2018. Measuring and decomposing the gender pay gap: A new frontier approach. *European Journal of Operational Research* 271(1). 357–73.

Australian Council of Social Service. 2014. *Poverty in Australia*. (http://www.acoss. org.au/ images/uploads/ACOSS_Poverty_in_Australia_2014.pdf)

Balint, Jennifer & Evans, Julie. 2010. Transitional Justice and Settler States. *Australian and New Zealand Institute of Criminology Critical Criminology Conference*. Sydney: Sydney Law School, University of Sydney.

Balint, Jennifer & Evans, Julie & McMillan, Nesam. 2016. Justice claims in colonial contexts: Commissions of inquiry in historical perspective. *Australian Feminist Law Journal*. June 42(1). 75–96.

Barak, Gregg. 1991. Toward a criminology of state criminality. In Barak, Gregg (ed.), *Crimes by the Capitalist State: An Introduction to State Criminality*, 3–18. New York: State University of New York.

Barak, Gregg. 1994. Crime, criminology, and human rights: Toward an understanding of state criminality. In Barak, Gregg (ed.), *Varieties of Criminology: Readings from a Dynamic Discipline*, 253–68. Westport: Praeger.

Behrendt, Larissa. 2001. Genocide: The distance between law and life. *Aboriginal History* 25. 132–47.

Bernat, Ignasi & Whyte, David. 2017. State-corporate crime and the process of capital accumulation: Mapping a global regime of permission from Galicia to Morecambe Bay. *Critical Criminology* 25(1). 71–86.

Boonzaier, Floretta. 2005. Woman abuse in South Africa: A brief contextual analysis. *Feminism & Psychology* 15. 99–103.

Branigan, Elizabeth. 2007. Who pays in the end? The personal and political implications of financial abuse of women in intimate partner relationships. *Just Policy* 44. 31–6.

Browne, Jennifer & Coffey, Brian & Cook, Kay & Meiklejohn, Sarah & Palermo, Claire. 2018. A guide to policy analysis as a research method. *Health Promotion International* August. 1–13.

Brush, Lisa. 2011. *Poverty, Battered Women, and Work in U.S. Public Policy.* New York: Oxford University Press.

Cameron, Prue. 2014. *Relationship Problems and Money: Women Talk about Financial Abuse.* Melbourne: Women's Information and Referral Exchange.

Caulfield, Susan & Wonders, Nancy. 1993. Personal AND political: Violence against women and the role of the state. In Tunnell, Kenneth (ed.), *Political Crime in Contemporary America: A Critical Approach*, 79–100. New York: Garland Publishing.

Chan, Andy & Payne, Jason. 2013. *Homicide in Australia: 2008–9 to 2009–10 National Homicide Monitoring Program Annual Report.* Canberra: Australian Institute of Criminology.

Chang, Joshua & Connell, Julia & Burgess, John & Travaglione, Antonio. 2014. Gender wage gaps in Australian workplaces: Are policy responses working? *Equality, Diversity and Inclusion: An International Journal* 33(8). 764–75.

Charlesworth, Hilary. 1995. Human rights as men's rights. In Peters, Julie & Wolper, Andrea (eds.), *Women's Rights, Human Rights: International Feminist Perspectives*, 103–13. New York: Routledge.

Christie, Nils. 1986. The ideal victim. In Fattah, Ezzat (ed.), *From Crime Policy to Victim Policy: Reorienting the Justice System*, 17–30. London: Macmillan.

Connell, Raewyn. 2005. The social organisation of masculinity. *Masculinities*, 67–86. 2nd edn. Berkeley: University of California Press.

Conte, Isabella. 2018. *The (In)visible Victim: Characterisations of Child Victims of Intrafamilial Child Sexual Abuse in the Family Court of Australia.* School of Social and Political Sciences, University of Melbourne. (Graduate Thesis.)

Cook, Kay. 2012. Neoliberalism, welfare policy and health: A qualitative metasynthesis of single parents' experience of the transition from welfare to work. *Health* 16(5). 507–30.

Cook, Kay. 2013. Child support compliance and tax return non-filing: A feminist analysis. *Australian Review of Public Affairs.* June 11(2). 43–64.

Cook, Kay. 2015. *Financial Responsibility for Children Following Parental Separation: Welfare-to-work and Child Support Policy Winners and Losers.* Melbourne: Royal Melbourne Institute of Technology Centre for Applied Social Research Symposium.

Cook, Kay & McKenzie, Hayley & Natalier, Kristin. 2015. Mothers' experiences of child support: Qualitative research and opportunities for policy insight. *Journal of Family Studies* 21(1). 57–71.

Copelon, Rhonda. 1994. Recognising the egregious in the everyday: Domestic violence as torture. *Columbia Human Rights Law Review* 2. 291–367.

Coy, Maddy & Scott, Emma & Tweedale, Ruth & Perks, Katherine. 2015. "It's like going through the abuse again": Domestic violence and women and children's (un)safety in private law contact proceedings. *Journal of Social Welfare & Family Law* 37(1). 53–69.

Coy, Madeleine. 2008. The consumer, the consumed and the commodity: Women and sex buyers talk about objectification in prostitution. In Munro, Vanessa & Giusta, Marina (eds.), *Demanding Sex: Critical Reflections on the Regulation of Prostitution*, 181–98. Abingdon: Ashgate.

Curthoys, Ann & Tedeschi, Mark & Balint, Jennifer & Joyce, Daniel. 2018. Forum: The Myall Creek Massacre of 1838: Genocide, war crimes, crimes against humanity? *Law and History* 5(1). 146–68.

De Maio, John & Kaspiew, Rae & Smart, Diana & Dunstan, Jessie & Moore, Sharnee. 2013. *Survey of Recently Separated Parents: A Study of Parents Who Separated Prior to the Implementation of the Family Law Amendment (Family Violence and Other Measures) Act 2011*. Melbourne: Australian Institute of Family Studies.

DeKeseredy, Walter. 1990. Male peer support and woman abuse: The current state of knowledge. *Sociological Focus* 23(2). 129–39.

DeKeseredy, Walter & Corsianos, Marilyn. 2016. *Violence against Women in Pornography*. New York: Routledge.

DeKeseredy, Walter & Schwartz, Martin. 2013. *Male Peer Support and Violence against Women: The history and verification of a theory*. Boston: Northeastern University Press.

DeKeseredy, Walter & Schwartz, Martin & Harris, Bridget & Woodlock, Delanie & Nolan, James & Hall-Sanchez, Amanda. 2019. *Technology-Facilitated Stalking and Unwanted Sexual Messages/Images in a College Campus Community: The Role of Negative Peer Support*. SAGE Open.

Dick, Kirby. 2006. *This Film is Not Yet Rated*. Independent Film Channel.

Dines, Gail. 2010. *Pornland: How Porn Has Hijacked Our Sexuality*. Boston: Beacon Press.

Douglas, Heather. 2019. Policing domestic and family violence. *International Journal for Crime, Justice and Social Democracy* 8(2). 31–49.

Dworkin, Andrea. 1981. *Pornography: Men Possessing Women*. London: Women's Press.

Dworkin, Andrea. 1985. Against the male flood: Censorship, pornography, and equality. *Harvard Women's Law Journal* 8. 1–29.

Eagleton, Terry. 1991. *Ideology: An Introduction*. London: Verso.

Elizabeth, Vivienne. 2015. From domestic violence to coercive control: Towards the recognition of oppressive intimacy in the Family Court. *New Zealand Sociology* 30(2). 26–43.

Enloe, Cynthia. 2000. *Maneuvers: The International Politics of Militarizing Women's Lives*. Berkeley: University of California Press.

Fahmy, Eldin & Williamson, Emma & Pantazis, Christina. 2017. *Evidence and Policy Review: Domestic Violence and Poverty*. Joseph Rowntree Foundation and University of Bristol School for Policy Studies.

Family Court of Australia. 2014. *Tyler v Sullivan, Reasons for Judgement, FCA 178*.

Fehlberg, Belinda & Kaspiew, Rae & Millbank, Jenni & Kelly, Fiona & Behrens, Juliet. 2015. *Australian Family Law: The Contemporary Context*. 2nd edn. Melbourne: Oxford University Press.

Fehlberg, Belinda & Maclean, Mavis. 2009. Child support policy in Australia and the United Kingdom: Changing priorities but a similar tough deal for children. *International Journal of Law, Policy and the Family* 23(1). 1–24.

Ferguson, Claire & Wright, Sarah & Death, Jodi & Burgess, Kylie & Malouff, John. 2018. Allegations of child sexual abuse in parenting disputes: An examination of judicial determinations in the Family Court of Australia. *Journal of Child Custody* 15(2). 93–115.

Fernandez, Marilyn. 2010. *Restorative Justice for Domestic Violence Victims: An Integrated Approach to their Hunger for Healing.* Lanham: Lexington Books.

Fitz-Gibbon, Kate. 2020. *Waiting Decades to Reduce Domestic Abuse Isn't An Option.* Webinar presentation, Australian and New Zealand School of Government (ANZSOG).

Fitz-Gibbon, Kate & Walklate, Sandra & Meyer, Silke. 2020. Australia is not ready to criminalise coercive control - here's why. *The Conversation.* (https://theconversation.com/australia-is-not-ready-to-criminalise-coercive-control-heres-why-146929)

Flood, Michael. 2003. Engaging men: Strategies and dilemma in violence prevention among men. *Women against Violence: An Australian Feminist Journal* 13. 25–32.

Flood, Michael. 2012. Separated fathers and the fathers' rights movement. *Journal of Family Studies* 18(2/3). 235–45.

Foucault, Michel. 1973. *The Birth of the Clinic: An Archaeology of Medical Perception.* London: Tavistock.

Foucault, Michel. 1978. The incitement to discourse. *The History of Sexuality* (vol. 1), 17–35. New York: Pantheon.

Foucault, Michel. 1984. Polemics, politics and problemisations. In Rabinow, Paul (ed.), *The Foucault Reader*, 381–91. New York: Pantheon.

Friedrichs, David. 2010. *Trusted Criminals: White Collar Crime in Contemporary Society.* 4th edn. Belmont: Wadsworth.

Galtung, Johann. 1969. Violence, peace, and peace research. *Journal of Peace Research* 6. 167–91.

Goodmark, Leigh. 2018. *Decriminalizing Domestic Violence: A Balanced Policy Approach to Intimate Partner Violence.* Oakland: University of California Press.

Graham, Mekada & Schiele, Jerome. 2010. Equality-of-oppressions and anti-discriminatory models in social work: Reflections from the USA and UK. *European Journal of Social Work* 13(2). 231–44.

Green, Penny & Ward, Tony. 2000. State crime, human rights and the limits of criminology. *Social Justice* 27(1). 101–15.

Guggisberg, Marika & Fisher, Colleen. 2010. Abused women's double jeopardy interacting with law enforcement on issues of intimate partner violence. *Women Against Violence* 22. 18–27.

Gutowski, Ellen & Goodman, Lisa. 2019. "Like I'm invisible": IPV survivor-mothers' perceptions of seeking child custody through the Family Court system. *Journal of Family Violence* 35. 441–57.

Harne, Lynne & Radford, Jill. 2008. *Tackling Domestic Violence: Theories, Policies and Practice.* Maidenhead: Open University Press.

Haslanger, Sally. 2017. Racism, ideology and social movements. *Res Philosophica* 94(1). 1–22.

Hattery, Angela. 2009. *Intimate Partner Violence.* Lanham: Rowman and Littlefield.

Hattery, Angela & Smith, Earl. 2012. *The Social Dynamics of Family Violence.* Boulder: Westview Press.

Hekman, Susan. 1999. *The Future of Differences: Truth and Method in Feminist Theory.* Cambridge: Polity.

Henderson, Lynne. 1991. Law's patriarchy. *Law & Society Review* 25(2). 411–44.

Henry, Nicola. 2011. *War and Rape: Law, Memory and Justice*. Abingdon: Routledge.

Henry, Nicola. 2015. From reconciliation to transitional justice: The contours of redress politics in established democracies. *International Journal of Transitional Justice*. July 9(2). 199–218.

Hocking, Barbara Ann. 1993. The presumption not in keeping with any times: Judicial re-appraisal of Justice Bollen's comments concerning marital rape. *Australian Feminist Law Journal* 1. 152–8.

Howson, Richard. 2006. A critico-historical analysis of masculinities and family law: Explorations into heterosexuality, breadwinning and aggression. *Challenging Hegemonic Masculinity*, 91–121. London: Routledge.

Hunter, Rosemary. 2006. Law's (masculine) violence: Reshaping jurisprudence. *Law and Critique* 17. 26–46.

Jeffreys, Sheila. 1997. *The Idea of Prostitution*. North Melbourne: Spinifex Press.

Jeffreys, Sheila. 2009. *The Industrial Vagina*. Abingdon: Routledge.

Jeffreys, Sheila. 2010. Brothels without walls: The escort sector as a problem for the legalisation of prostitution. *Social Politics* 17(2). 210–34.

Johnson, Michael. 2008. *A Typology of Domestic Violence: Intimate Terrorism, Violent Resistance, and Situational Couple Violence*. Boston: Northeastern University Press.

Kaspiew, Rae. 1995. Rape lore: Legal narrative and sexual violence. *Melbourne University Law Review* 20(2). 350–82.

Kaspiew, Rae & Carson, Rachel & Coulson, Melissa & Dunstan, Jessie & Moore, Sharnee. 2015a. *Responding to Family Violence: A Survey of Family Law Practices and Experiences*. Melbourne: Australian Institute of Family Studies.

Kaspiew, Rae & Carson, Rachel & Qu, Lixia & Horsfall, Briony & Tayton, Sarah & Moore, Sharnee & Sharnee, Melissa Coulson & Dunstan, Jessie. 2015b. *Court Outcomes Project*. Melbourne: Australian Institute of Family Studies.

Kauzlarich, David & Mullins, Christopher & Matthews, Rick. 2003. A complicity continuum of state crime. *Contemporary Justice Review* 6(3). 241–54.

Kechiche, Abdellatif. 2013. *Blue is the Warmest Colour*. Quat'sous Films.

Kelly, Liz & Radford, Jill. 1996. "Nothing really happened": The invalidation of women's experiences of sexual violence. In Hester, Marianne & Kelly, Liz & Radford, Jill (eds.), *Women, Violence and Male Power: Feminist Activism, Research and Practice*, 19–33. Buckingham: Open University Press.

Kelly, Liz & Sharp, Nicola & Klein, Renate. 2014. *Finding the Costs of Freedom: How Women and Children Rebuild their Lives after Domestic Violence*. London: Solace Women's Legal Aid and Child and Woman Abuse Studies Unit.

Kimmel, Michael. 2010. *Misframing Men: The Politics of Contemporary Masculinities*. New Brunswick: Rutgers University Press.

Kramer, Ronald & Michalowski, Raymond. 1990. *Toward an Integrated Theory of State-Corporate Crime*. Paper presented to American Society of Criminology. Baltimore.

Laing, Lesley. 2010. *No Way to Live: Women's Experiences of Negotiating the Family Law System in the Context of Domestic Violence*. Sydney: University of Sydney.

Laing, Lesley. 2013. *"It's Like This Maze That You Have to Make Your Way Through": Women's Experiences of Seeking a Domestic Violence Protection Order in NSW*. Sydney: University of Sydney.

Laing, Lesley. 2017. Secondary victimization: Domestic violence survivors navigating the family law system. *Violence against Women* 23(11). 1314–35.

Lake, Marilyn. 1996. The inviolable woman: Feminist conceptions of citizenship in Australia, 1900–1945. *Gender & History* 8(2). 197–211.

Leon, Ron & Barowski, Laurie. 2011. MPAA ratings creep. *Journal of Children and Media* 5(1). 53–68.

MacKinnon, Catharine. 1982. Feminism, Marxism, method, and the state: An agenda for theory. *Signs: Journal of Women in Culture & Society* 7(3). 515–44.

MacKinnon, Catharine. 1989. *Toward a Feminist Theory of the State*. Cambridge, MA: Harvard University Press.

MacKinnon, Catharine. 1994. Rape, genocide and women's human rights. *Harvard Women's Law Journal* 17. 5–16.

MacKinnon, Catharine. 2006. *Are Women Human? And Other International Dialogues*. Cambridge, MA: Harvard University Press.

MacKinnon, Catharine. 2011. X-Underrated: Living in a world the pornographers have made. In Tankard Reist, Melinda & Bray, Abigail (eds.), *Big Porn Inc: Exposing the Harms of the Global Pornography Industry*, 9–15. Melbourne: Spinifex.

MacKinnon, Catharine. 2019. *Where #MeToo Came From, and Where It's Going*. (https://www.theatlantic.com/ideas/archive/2019/03/catharine-mackinnon-what-metoo-has-changed/585313/)

Manne, Robert. 2004. Aboriginal child removal and the question of genocide, 1900–1940. In Moses, Dirk (ed.), *Genocide and Settler Society: Frontier Violence and Stolen Indigenous Children in Australian History*, 217–38. New York: Berghahn.

McArthur, Morag & Thomson, Lorraine & Winkworth, Gail. 2013. Jumping through hoops: The cost of compliance on sole parents. *Child and Family Social Work* 18. 159–67.

McKenzie, Mandy & Kirkwood, Deborah & Tyson, Danielle & Naylor, Bronwyn. 2016. *Out of Character? Legal Responses to Intimate Partner Homicides by Men in Victoria 2005–2014*. Melbourne: Domestic Violence Resource Centre Victoria.

Meyer, Silke. 2011. Seeking help for intimate partner violence: Victims' experiences when approaching the criminal justice system for IPV-related support and protection in an Australian jurisdiction. *Feminist Criminology* 6. 268–90.

Meyer, Silke. 2016. Still blaming the victim of intimate partner violence? Women's narratives of victim desistance and redemption when seeking support. *Theoretical Criminology* 20(1). 75–90.

Meyersfeld, Bonita. 2003. Reconceptualising domestic violence in international law. *Albany Law Review* 67. 371–426.

Miller, Susan. 2005. *Victims as Offenders: The Paradox of Women's Violence in Relationships*. New Brunswick: Rutgers University Press.

Millett, Kate. 1969. *Sexual Politics*. London: Virago.

Natalier, Kristin. 2017. Micro-aggressions, single mothers and interactions with government workers: The case of Australia's child support bureaucracy. *Journal of Sociology* 53. 622–36.

Natalier, Kristin. 2018. State facilitated economic abuse: A structural analysis of men deliberately withholding child support. *Feminist Legal Studies* 26(2). 121–40.

Natalier, Kristin & Cook, Kay & Pitman, Torna. 2015. *Single Mother's Experiences with the DHS-CS*. Research report funded by University of Tasmania and Flinders University.

Nichols, Allison. 2013. Toward a child-centred approach to evaluating claims of alienation in high-conflict custody disputes. *Michigan Law Review* 112(4). 663–88.

Oplev, Niels. 2009. *The Girl with the Dragon Tattoo / Men who Hate Women*. Yellow Bird.

Otto, Dianne. 2012. *Feminist Approaches to International Law*. New York: Oxford University Press.

Park, Yoosun. 2015. A curious inconsistency: The discourse of social on the 1922 Married Women's Independent Nationality Act and the intersecting dynamics of race and gender in the laws of immigration and citizenship. *Journal of Women & Social Work* 30(4). 560–79.

Patrick, Rebecca & Cook, Kay & McKenzie, Hayley. 2008. Domestic violence and the exemption from seeking child support: Providing safety or legitimising ongoing poverty and fear. *Social Policy and Administration* 42(7). 749–67.

Patrick, Rebecca & Cook, Kay & Taket, Ann. 2007. Multiple barriers to obtaining child support: Experiences of women leaving violent partners. *Just Policy* 45. 21–9.

Qu, Lixia & Weston, Ruth & Moloney, Lawrie & Kaspiew, Rae & Dunstan, Jessie. 2014. *Post-Separation Parenting, Property and Relationship Dynamics after Five Years*. Canberra: Attorney-General's Department.

Roark, Jennifer. 2016. Predictors of dual arrest for offenders involved in heterosexual domestic violence arrests. *Policing: An International Journal* 39(1). 52–63.

Rothe, Dawn & Mullins, Christopher. 2011. Crimes of the state. In Rothe, Dawn & Mullins, Christopher (eds.), *State Crime: Current Perspectives*, 23–33. New Brunswick: Rutgers University Press.

Royal Commission into Family Violence. 2016. *Report and Recommendations*. Melbourne: State Government of Victoria.

Segrave, Marie & Wilson, Dean & Fitz-Gibbon, Kate. 2018. Policing intimate partner violence in Victoria (Australia): Examining police attitudes and the potential of specialisation. *Australian & New Zealand Journal of Criminology* 51(1). 99–116.

Sheehy, Elizabeth. 2018. Expert evidence on coercive control in support of self-defence: The trial of Teresa Craig. *Criminology & Criminal Justice* 18(1). 100–14.

Shelby, Tommie. 2014. Racism, moralism and social criticism. *Du Bois Review: Social Science Research on Race* 11(1). 57–74.

Short, Damien. 2010. Australia: A continuing genocide? *Journal of Genocide Research* 12(1–2). 45–68.

Sifris, Ronli. 2014. *Reproductive Freedom, Torture, and International Human Rights: Challenging the Masculinisation of Torture*. Abingdon: Routledge.

Stark, Evan. 2007. *Coercive Control: How Men Entrap Women in Personal Life*. New York: Oxford University Press.

State Government of Victoria, Magistrate's Court. 2015. *Family Violence Protection Act 2008*.

Subedi, Surya. 1997. Protection of women against domestic violence: The response of international law. *European Human Rights Law Review* 6. 587–606.

Thompson, Neil. 2001. *Anti-Discriminatory Practice*. 3rd edn. Basingstoke: Palgrave.

True, Jacqui. 2012. *The Political Economy of Violence against Women*. New York: Oxford University Press.

Tyler, Meagan. 2011. *Selling Sex Short: The Pornographic and Sexological Construction of Women's Sexuality in the West*. Online publication. Cambridge: Cambridge Scholars Publishing.

Ulbrick, Madeleine & Jago, Marianne. 2018. *"Officer She's Psychotic and I Need Protection": Police Misidentification of the Primary Aggressor in Family Violence Incidents in Victoria*. Women's Legal Service Victoria.

United Kingdom Crown Prosecution Service. 2017. *Controlling or Coercive Behaviour in an Intimate or Family Relationship in the Serious Crime Act 2015*. (https://www.cps.gov.uk/legal-guidance/controlling-or-coercive-behaviour-intimate-or-family-relationship)

United Nations Office on Drugs and Crime. 2019. *Global Study on Homicide 2019: Gender-related Killing of Women and Girls*. Vienna. (https://www.unodc.org/documents/data-and-analysis/gsh/Booklet_5.pdf)

Uvin, Peter. 1998. *Aiding Violence: The Development Enterprise in Rwanda*. Connecticut: Kumarian Press.

Victorian Equal Opportunity and Human Rights Commission. 2017. *Independent Review into Sex Discrimination and Sexual Harassment, including Predatory Behaviour*. Melbourne: State of Victoria. (Victoria Police Phase 2 Audit.)

Walklate, Sandra & Fitz-Gibbon, Kate. 2019. The criminalisation of coercive control: The power of law? *International Journal for Crime, Justice and Social Democracy* 8(4). 94–108.

Wolfe, Patrick. 2006. Settler colonialism and the elimination of the native. *Journal of Genocide Research* 8(4). 387–409.

Women's Legal Service Victoria. 2018. *Small Claims, Large Battles: Achieving Economic Equality in the Family Law System*. Report by Women's Legal Service Victoria.

Zeglin, Robert. 2014. Participation in prostitution: Associated outcomes within familial relationships. *Sexuality Research and Social Policy* 11(1). 50–62.

Zizek, Slavoj. 2008. *Violence: Six Sideways Reflections*. New York: Picador.

Zuckerman, Elaine. 2014. *The IMF and Gender: A Long Way to Go*. Gender Action Publications. (http://genderaction.org/publications/At-Issue-IMF-Gender.pdf)

Chapter 6

Domestic violence as omissive institutional state crime

This is the first of two chapters which theorise and analyse domestic violence-related state crime specifically via institutions of the nation-state. I look at a spectrum of institutional criminality ranging from passive failures and negligent inaction to direct state violence across these two chapters, but here, I look at the passive end of the spectrum: what I term *omissive institutional state crime*. This refers to demonstrable and systematic institutional neglect, negligence, inaction, and failure which has the impact of overlooking, dismissing, obscuring, enabling, facilitating, extending, or prolonging domestic violence. As with previous Part II chapters, I begin by constructing the feminist state crime theory through which systematic institutional failures in relation to domestic violence constitute state crimes of omission. I then show how this state criminality functions in recent and contemporary practice through legal and social service responses to domestic violence, thereby revealing the complicity of the state institutional apparatus in this problem.

A feminist theory of omissive institutional state crime

State crime and interdisciplinary scholars widely recognise institutions as central to the perpetration of state crimes (e.g. Boraine 2000; Kauzlarich et al. 2003; Stanley 2005; Kolin 2008; Jones 2013). For mass harms to be perpetrated against a particular social group over time there must be extensive "scaffolding and support" by various institutions, both state and non-state (Balint 2012: 168). Balint (2012: 37) further argues that, even when not operating in accordance with explicit directives from authorities, institutional policy, culture, and practice can be understood "as a parallel and hidden structure of the state". In accordance with foundational principles, liberal-democratic states are understood to have basic responsibilities around impartially enforcing and adjudicating law, upholding citizens' equal human rights, and implementing non-discriminatory policies that support these rights. Citizens can therefore reasonably expect official institutions, agencies, and their individual representatives to operate in accordance with human rights

DOI: 10.4324/9781003132370-8

principles and provide the same safety and protections to all, irrespective of class, race, ethnicity, religion, sex, gender, or other identifiers.

Through a state crime lens, omissive state crime therefore refers to systematic institutional failure, neglect, and negligence around these basic responsibilities. When disregard, non-intervention, or inaction by the state results in certain citizens having their fundamental rights violated, the state is understood as omissively complicit in, and to bear responsibility for, these harms (Barak 1991; 2008; Green & Ward 2000; Kauzlarich et al. 2003; Faust & Kauzlarich 2008). Notably, omissive state crimes encompass harms that are the direct outcome of ambiguous inaction against non-state actors as well, such as when the law is not effectively enforced against a certain group that systematically violates another. But although this definition of omissive state crime in principle encompasses violations irrespective of perpetrator or context, it has not been equally applied on the basis of sex or gender, by non-state actors, or in the private sphere. Hinch's (1991: 247) critique of rape law reform in Canada and its ineffectiveness in addressing "the forces of patriarchy" hints at sex-based omissions, yet does not elaborate or conceptualise this as state criminality. McCulloch and Blair's (2012: 178) reference to the "the fallacy of impartial justice" in Australia which has "masked a range of state crimes … [including] the institutionalised failure of the criminal justice system to protect women from male violence" is an important but passing comment and a stark outlier in the field. Broad inattention to omissive institutional state crimes against women in liberal democracies has meant that domestic violence has escaped recognition and integration into state crime thinking.

As feminist international legal scholars have shown, state action and inaction against interpersonal violence occurs along distinct patriarchal lines and with direct and harmful ramifications for women, particularly in the home. For several decades now, states have been identified as "indirectly responsible" for domestic violence when it results from the systematic refusal to intervene and protect women in the private sphere (MacKinnon 1993: 23; also Copelon 1994; Mertus & Goldberg 1994; Romany 1994). This is because state responsibility for domestic violence prevention and protection has been enshrined in human rights law for some time. State obligations to criminalise domestic violence and to actively prevent, protect against, and prosecute it are reiterated in successive binding international documents (e.g. UNGA 1979; 1993; 2003). The United Nations Commission on Human Rights Report (1996: 9, 13) even named states as "complicit" in domestic violence when they systematically fail to protect victims, whilst the Resolution on the Elimination of Domestic Violence against Women (UNGA 2003: n.p.) officially required states "to exercise due diligence" in taking action against this crime. There is thus a decades-long, legally enforceable notion of state responsibility to respond appropriately and decisively against domestic violence. This obligation has been termed 'state bystander responsibility', and when not taken seriously, states are considered to acquiesce to violations that occur as a result of their inaction (Charlesworth 1995; Sullivan 1995; Hakimi 2010).

These domestic violence human rights principles have been invoked and upheld in courts, officially establishing the precedent that states can be held liable for institutional failures to protect women. A notable domestic homicide case which I will soon discuss in further detail – *Lenahan (Gonzales) v. United States* 2011 – was heard in the Inter-American Court of Human Rights. In its Judgement, this court determined that the United States government and its institutions had failed to uphold various rights guaranteed in the American Declaration of Rights: the rights to life, to reasonable protection, and to be able to access appropriate remedies to ensure respect for these rights (IACHR 2011). The Court further found, in line with an earlier ruling in the European Court of Human Rights (see *Opuz v Turkey* 2009), that because domestic violence is overwhelmingly experienced by women, the state's failure to provide protection from this crime constitutes sex-based discrimination. The court also recognised that these institutional failures contribute more broadly to the (re)production of domestic violence and the impunity of perpetrators. These cases have received significant attention in the international legal field[1] and are significant because they confirm that states can be held accountable for upholding their human rights responsibilities and for preventing, protecting against, and remedying domestic violence. Such cases have not previously been discussed in the state crime literature, but I nominate them as examples of omissive institutional state criminality and of sex-based state crimes.

Through this hybrid feminist human rights state crime lens, domestic violence constitutes an omissive institutional state crime. This is because, when state institutions, agencies, and officials are demonstrably negligent in relation to fulfilling key responsibilities, they are complicit in and responsible for harms that result from this negligence. Specifically, when the state institutional apparatus systematically fails to recognise and prevent domestic violence or to prioritise and uphold victims' safety, it is also complicit in the violence itself. Additionally, when state institutions fail to respond appropriately to victim-survivors, they are also responsible for additional harms and suffering caused by these failures. Because domestic violence so disproportionately affects women, state institutional failures in this area also constitute the systematic failure to uphold the rights of a particular social group. In the remainder of this chapter, I unpack how omissive institutional domestic violence state crime plays out through specific recent and contemporary policies and practices.

Domestic violence failures as omissive institutional state crime

Omissive institutional domestic violence state crime occurs via the systematic, repetitive failures and negligence of state institutions in prominent Western liberal democracies. In contexts such as Australia, New Zealand, the United Kingdom, and the United States, there is an expectation that these institutions will operate according to principles of equality and fairness and act decisively to prevent, protect against, and remedy all violence. Yet a feminist state crime analysis of state legal and social service responses to domestic violence shows that these institutions fail to adequately identify, apprehend, understand, and appropriately respond to domestic and family violence; fail to act in accordance with principles of equality, safety, and violence prevention; fail to adequately prosecute and censure perpetrators; fail to deliver safe and just outcomes; and fail to provide basic support and protection to victim-survivors. In fact, state institutions enable and exacerbate domestic abuse through these systemic omissions.

Law enforcement

As gate-keepers of the criminal justice system, police play a significant role in domestic violence response. They are often victims' first point of contact with the system and are therefore instrumental in conveying that a report is valid, worthy of attention, and that allegations will be taken seriously (CIJ 2015). Yet research shows widespread law enforcement failures that exacerbate domestic harms against women. A common form of law enforcement negligence is when police fail to reasonably and adequately identify, assess, and act against domestic violence. Research across Australian jurisdictions shows repeatedly inadequate, inappropriate, and ill-informed police responses to domestic violence incidents (Preston & Gyde 2005; Guggisberg & Fisher 2010; Douglas 2019). A persistent issue is law enforcers' inadequate understanding of domestic violence and their consequent failure to accurately assess harm and risk. Through investigating the experiences of women victims who sought official assistance in Queensland, Australia, Meyer (2011; 2016) found a male-dominated system with minimal understanding of gendered power and domestic violence which often led to inappropriate handling of cases. In Birdsey and Snowball's (2013) research in New South Wales, Australia, the majority of survey respondents chose not to officially report their most recent domestic victimisation, citing poor police understanding of this violence and the inadequacy of prior responses as key to their decision. Victorian research also shows systemic police failure to respond impartially and accurately gather information and evidence when attending domestic violence incidents (Ulbrick & Jago 2018; Reeves 2020). This results in the frequent misidentification of women as primary aggressors, which not only represents law enforcement failure, but has flow-on effects in terms of further jeopardising women's rights and safety.

Research with Australian police officers points to the prevalence and normalisation of negligently misinformed responses to domestic violence. In Victoria, Segrave et al. (2018) found that officers were frequently unresponsive to domestic violence because of the recurrent notion that it was not sufficiently serious to warrant their attention or intervention. An indicative view expressed by one senior constable was that "99 domestics out of 100" are not police matters because they do not involve immediate physical assault (in Segrave et al. 2018: 105). This reveals apparent ignorance of the diverse spectrum of criminal and quasi-criminal domestic violence and the non-physical red flag indicators that are widely used to identify risk of serious, imminent physical harm (see e.g. State Government of Victoria 2019; also Stark 2007). Police also demonstrated little knowledge of coercive control dynamics and the widely documented challenges and risks facing victims. For example, another senior constable stated that "I refuse to regard [a woman seeking help with domestic violence] as a victim when they've got a say in what actually happens to them... You're an adult do it yourself" (Segrave et al. 2018: 105). This shows a concerning level of ignorance of the extreme dangers associated with leaving an abusive partner and of the well-documented need for sensitive and proactive police responses to domestic violence (see e.g. Diemer et al. 2017). These views directly underpin dangerous police apathy and inaction and constitute gross neglect of basic domestic violence knowledge and law enforcement responsibilities.

In the United Kingdom, Hester's (2012) research also reveals ill-informed, inappropriate, and discriminatory police responses to domestic violence. This study of both male- and female-perpetrated partner violence found that police repeatedly failed to accurately assess domestic offending and accurately determine levels of risk, which led to gender-based mishandling of cases. Global studies show that women's domestic violence offending is overwhelmingly less severe than men's and is most often defensive violence against repetitive male abuse (Johnson 1995; Stark 2007; Flood 2012a; Kimmel 2013; Meyer & Frost 2019). Fitting this pattern, in the whole of Hester's study sample, none of the female perpetrators' violence indicated repeated or systematic offending or high risk to their partner. Yet women experienced disproportionate levels of official control, with police arresting them at three times the rate of men. Conversely, the high risk posed by many male offenders elicited relatively lenient police responses. This study shows either negligent police misunderstanding of basic features of domestic violence or the refusal to apply this knowledge to police practice. It also points to systemic problems with applying the law in accordance with principles of impartiality, accuracy, and violence prevention.

Reforms to domestic violence law enforcement policy and practice over the past decade or so have resulted in further discriminatory gendered outcomes. In the United States, mandatory arrest, pro-arrest, and no-drop prosecution policies have had disproportionately negative impacts on women, with harmful consequences for both female victims and offenders, particularly those who are mothers (see e.g. Stark 2007; Fernandez 2010; Durfee 2012). These concerning outcomes have led Goodmark (2018) to question the assumption that increasingly criminalising domestic violence is the right approach. For example, research indicates significant and widening discrepancies in arrest rates between men and women, with women being disproportionately affected in practice. Similar findings in Australia point towards the discriminatory criminalisation of women's defensive responses to male violence and towards police inappropriately siding with and supporting male perpetrators (e.g. Ulbrick & Jago 2018; Reeves 2020). The widespread failure to create non-discriminatory and gender-sensitive law and to impartially enforce it demonstrates systemic failures in state institutional responses to domestic violence, further evidencing institutional domestic violence omissions.

Police omissions in relation to domestic violence are particularly problematic because they erect barriers to victims' future help-seeking. As primary domestic violence responders, the way police treat women who seek their help is critical, as inappropriate police responses can set in chain a series of further harms and injustices (CIJ 2015). This is exemplified by the experiences of an anonymous client of Women's Legal Service Victoria, Australia, who had called police to an incident but was misidentified as the primary aggressor (Ulbrick & Jago 2018). The inaccurate determination of her culpability by police resulted in her being referred to the federal Department of Human Services, who deemed her a safety risk to her infant and arranged for official assessments and intrusive visits to her home. The woman told lawyers that this humiliating and frightening experience led to her to decide never to contact police again, explaining that they "scare me now... I needed to be protected [but] I don't feel like they protected me" (in Ulbrick & Jago 2018: 1). This attitude is commonly expressed by misidentified women: even when they remain at high risk of revictimisation, their negative experiences with law enforcers render them unable or unwilling to seek future assistance. This inhibits their access to the full range of protections to which they are entitled, illustrating how police failures deny women's rights to equal and just treatment, exacerbate harms against them, and heighten their risk of remaining in unsafe situations and being subjected to further violence.

Intersectionally marginalised domestic violence victims are particularly vulnerable to police misidentification and other forms of discriminatory and negligent mistreatment. Ulbrick and Jago's (2018) Victorian research shows that many migrant and refugee women from linguistically diverse backgrounds are not being provided with interpreters when police attend domestic violence incidents (also Douglas 2019). This directly contravenes the relevant Code of Practice for the Investigation of Family Violence (Victoria Police 2014) which requires that police ensure access to interpreters at every stage of the criminal justice process. Without culturally and linguistically appropriate services, these women are severely disadvantaged when it comes to interactions with police (Tucker 2015). For an individual with limited or no English and whose expression of harm and distress might be culturally specific and not easily understood by (majority white, solely English-speaking) police, the already challenging nature of having police attend an incident is significantly exacerbated. Indigenous women victims are also particularly vulnerable to police discrimination. In Australia, Taylor (2018) highlights the high arrest rates of Indigenous women for domestic and family violence offences which are often, as for all women, due to their misidentification as primary aggressors. She also identifies how this problem is further exacerbated by the broad tendency of police to treat minor offending by Indigenous women in a punitive manner. This underscores the persistent treatment of Women of Colour in accordance with oppressive sexist, racist, and ethnocentric patterns. It further illustrates the discriminatory enforcement of the law in relation to women and domestic violence, and evidences state institutional omissions in this area.

Another example of domestic violence law enforcement omissions is the failure to enforce protective orders.[2] As Hunter (2006: 31) argues, the failure of police to enforce a protective order shows that "masculine violence against women … is endorsed and permitted to continue". Specifically, it represents a negligent failure of mandated police responsibilities which places victims at direct risk of further harm. A case from Colorado, United States, which I cited earlier (*Lenahan (Gonzales) v. United States* 2011) demonstrates the devastating consequences of police failing to enforce protective orders. As outlined in the case judgement and legal literature (IACHR 2011; Andrews & Khavinson 2013; Bettinger-Lopez 2013; Cabrera 2015), Jessica Lenahan had obtained a protective order following separation from her abusive husband. After the man violated the order by abducting their three daughters, Ms Lenahan made repeated calls to local police requesting urgent assistance. But despite a statutory requirement that police use every reasonable means to enforce a protective order and despite the existence of a mandatory arrest law for order violations, they took no action at all. They did not lack the resources to respond, as various trivial duties were fulfilled during the time in question including investigating a minor traffic violation and looking for a lost dog; they simply did not treat the case as a priority, revealing a demonstrable lack of interest in domestic violence law enforcement and victim protection. After ten hours, during which Ms Lenahan contacted police nine times, the man murdered all three children. These series of law enforcement failures were deemed by the court to constitute negligent inaction and gross neglect of official responsibilities under constitutional and human rights law; they were also deemed to have directly contributed to the murders. Having already been adjudicated as a case of state responsibility for domestic violence resulting from institutional failures, this case clearly shows domestic and family violence as an omissive institutional state crime.

Another as yet unresolved court case involving police negligence in relation to domestic violence is *Smith [pseudonym] v Victoria* (2018 in VSC 2019), in Australia. The case involves repeated and actionable law enforcement failures which have led to the State of Victoria, for the first time ever, being sued for police negligence and breaches of duties of care in relation to domestic violence. The Supreme Court's judgement summary of the State's request for a summary dismissal of the case (VSC 2019) outlines the plaintiff and her children's allegations that at least eighteen police officers across different regional Victorian towns consistently failed over a nine-year period to protect them or take action against a domestic violence perpetrator. These failures include multiple documented occasions where police did not enforce Family Violence Intervention Orders, resulting in the plaintiffs' repeated victimisation.

For two years prior to the first order, police had attended and documented many incidents of violence by the offender against his partner. These incidents are variously detailed in the Supreme Court's Summary of Judgement and media reports (VSC 2019; Estcourt 2018; Farnsworth 2018). For example, on one occasion during the woman's pregnancy, the man had terrorised her, smashed both the home phone and her mobile phone to prevent her from seeking help, and neighbours had responded to her cries and contacted police. For a year following the birth of one of their children, the man forcibly and repeatedly took the baby from the mother and the home until police intervened. The offender's sister had also reported her own victimisation by her brother to police and conveyed grave concerns about the dangers he posed to others. The woman took out the first of four intervention orders over a period of seven years after her partner went on a two-day drinking spree, wrought havoc in the house, and needed six police officers to subdue him. This first intervention order prohibited the man from assaulting, threatening, contacting her or the children, or being within 100 metres of their home while intoxicated. Yet two violent breaches occurred after police officers who played sport with the perpetrator dropped him at the home after a game while he was intoxicated. The plaintiff alleges that police repeatedly failed to enforce separate intervention order breaches and that these failures caused further assaults on at least six occasions.

This case is based on these law enforcement failures amounting to state negligence, a breach of the victims' human rights, and a breach of state obligations under the *Charter of Human Rights and Responsibilities Act 2006* (Vic) (in VSC 2019: 1). The plaintiff and her legal team argue that there was extensive information and evidence available to police to indicate the grave dangers posed by the offender and that their repeated failure to fulfil their mandated responsibilities constitutes state negligence. The landmark case will consider state liability for domestic violence protection in a new way for Victoria. In the Supreme Court in August 2018, Justice Dixon rejected the State's application for a summary dismissal of the case and refused to strike out the claims alleging a common law duty of care. Describing the case as "fact rich and fact intensive", the judge approved it to proceed to trial (Dixon in VSC 2019). This case does not relate to isolated incidents, individual incompetence, or errant deviant officials; it relates to repeated incidents, an extended time frame, multiple officers, and different regional locations. It shows a pattern of institutional omissions which enabled repeat domestic offending and therefore demonstrates the complicity of official law enforcement and implicates the state in this preventable violence.

Family law

Domestic violence-related ignorance, negligence, and failure through the family law system also constitutes omissive institutional state crime. Across comparable jurisdictions, domestic and family violence is central to the letter and practice of family law since it provides the frameworks for overseeing financial and parenting arrangements for separating couples (Dunford-Jackson 2004; Coy et al. 2015; Harland et al. 2015). In Australia, conservative estimates suggest that over 60% of adult relationship separations involving children have a history of partner violence involving either physical or sexual assault or both, and a substantial further proportion involving other forms of abuse (Qu et al. 2014; Kaspiew et al. 2015b). Coercive controlling relationships in particular often require formal intervention and adjudication and thus tend to be concentrated in family law systems (Fehlberg et al. 2015). Considering the relevance of domestic violence to the majority of separating families, identifying, understanding, and preventing domestic and family violence are critical responsibilities in family law. Yet domestic violence is negligently overlooked, ignored, and misunderstood in family law practice and adjudication, constituting institutional omissions and state complicity in the abuse it enables and exacerbates.

Recent amendments to Australian family law explicitly recognise the centrality of domestic and family violence. In the 2012 Family Violence Amendments to the *Family Law Act* (Commonwealth of Australia 2015), safety is asserted as a key principle and priority; accordingly, family law officials and courts are now legally obligated to recognise, identify, and act upon violence concerns. This includes a stipulated requirement for courts to actively inquire about intimate partner and child abuse (Fehlberg et al. 2015). But in practice, family law officials demonstrably neglect these mandated obligations. De Maio et al.'s (2013: 78) large-scale survey of separated parents found that almost half of parents who disclosed past violence or child safety concerns to family law professionals reported that "nothing happened" in response. Even several years after the introduction of the amendments, a further study found that between 30 and 41% of parents were never asked about domestic or family violence by anyone in the system at any stage (Kaspiew et al. 2015b). The broad neglect of this critical issue by family law administrators, practitioners, and adjudicators – in direct contravention of mandated requirements – directly hinders its detection and prevention, amounting to omissive state institutional complicity in violence that continues, undetected and unaddressed.

Family law officials' failure to identify and act upon safety concerns often arises from negligent ignorance of basic issues which are of crucial relevance to their work. There is an expectation that, in order to fulfil their mandated responsibilities, practitioners and adjudicators understand the fundamental features, dynamics, and common complexities associated with domestic and family violence (Fehlberg et al. 2015). Three particular features of this violence about which basic knowledge and understanding is necessary are coercive control, post-separation violence, and the prevalence and co-occurrence of intimate partner and child abuse. Firstly, it is vital that officials understand that domestic and family violence encompasses a spectrum of harms and that the coercive control regimes that are most often the subject of official adjudication are not necessarily marked by physical assault (Johnson 1995; Stark 2007; Meyer & Frost 2019). Although coercive controlling relationships can be physically violent, what characterises them is a tailored combination of fear-inducing strategies which oppress and intimidate the victim to maintain the perpetrator's dominance. Since this abuse is often invisible and indetectable to outsiders, it requires appropriate professional awareness, along with active and sensitive enquiry with victim-survivors, to be identified (Coy et al. 2015; Elizabeth 2015; Douglas 2018; Rose et al. 2018).

It is also imperative that family law officials know and understand that the end of an abusive intimate relationship rarely signals the cessation of violence. In fact, more often it heralds a period of heightened risk of serious harms to both women and children (Kaye et al. 2003; Phillips & Vandenbroek 2014; Coy et al. 2015; Meyer & Frost 2019). Perpetrators of systematic partner abuse, whose *modus operandi* is dictator-style behaviour designed to dominate, control, coerce, and threaten their partner and family, are particularly unlikely to accept a partner's decision to separate or to engage in reasonable negotiations over financial settlement or child custody (Fehlberg et al. 2015). These types of cases also routinely involve extensive post-separation violence. It is therefore incumbent upon family law – as an institution and a collective of state-ordained professionals with specific mandated responsibilities – to understand coercive control and post-separation abuse, because they are critical to determining safe legal outcomes. Yet these facets of domestic violence are routinely ignored, dismissed, and denied in family law practice and decision-making.

Across the United Kingdom, United States, and Australia, research shows systematic ignorance of coercive control and the high risk of post-separation violence and its exacerbation by mandated communication or contact (Nichols 2013; Kelly et al. 2014; Phillips & Vandenbroek 2014). Coy et al.'s (2015) research with family law subjects in the United Kingdom shows domestic violence survivors frequently confronted with judges' ignorant and erroneous assertions. For instance, one woman recounted being admonished by a judge for "using the word violence" when referring to abuse and threats because it was "clearly not" (58). An interviewee in Laing's (2017: 1325) Australian study was told by a judge that because her ex-husband "appears to be behaving himself, the court is satisfied that he's not really violent". In New Zealand, Elizabeth's (2015) research also shows that family courts lack understanding of the dangers inherent in interactions with an abusive ex-partner. Like many coercive control survivors trying to manage their safety, Amanda (in Elizabeth 2015: 36) requested that the court determine a neutral location for child handovers, but had her request denied by a judge who said that "you have nothing to fear from him now, now that you are separated you have nothing to fear". These negligent failures to recognise and assess the realities of domestic violence and post-separation risk constitute institutional omissions with potentially lethal ramifications for the safety of victim-survivor families.

Another problematic and harmful omission in family law is the negligent failure to adequately recognise intersecting forms of domestic victimisation. It is widely internationally documented that men's violence often involves the co-perpetration of intimate partner and child abuse (Bancroft & Silverman 2004; Rossman et al. 2004; Murray & Powell 2009; UK Women's Aid 2013; Morrison 2015; Laing 2017). In England, Hoyle and Palmer (2014: 198) have suggested that up to two-thirds of cases involving partner violence against a woman also involve direct physical or sexual abuse of children. Although notoriously unreported and undetected, intrafamilial child sexual abuse is prevalent in all societies, with the majority of perpetrators being fathers or other paternal figures (Salter 2017; O'Donohue et al. 2018). Family violence harms also intersect and overlap when accounting for children's indirect victimisation. Child exposure to parental partner violence[3] is widely recognised as a serious harm with significant detrimental impacts on children's health and well-being comparable to those caused by direct abuse and neglect (Dunford-Jackson 2004; Rossman et al. 2004; Sutton 2008; Campo et al. 2014; PHAA 2015; McTavish et al. 2016; Meyer & Frost 2019). The prevalence and impact of this form of victimisation is also leading to its growing recognition as a form of child abuse in itself (see Dunford-Jackson 2004; Commonwealth of Australia 2015).[4]

Yet family law practitioners demonstrate ignorance of these well-documented facts, thereby directly contributing to omissively harmful practice and decision-making. In canvassing a range of family law professionals' views of the recent amendments to Australian family law and their impact, Kaspiew et al. (2015a) found a negligent lack of basic knowledge about child abuse amongst legal professionals. Although many practitioners demonstrated increasing awareness of intimate partner violence, there was widespread obliviousness of intrafamilial child abuse, its prevalence, and the frequent co-occurrence of different forms of family violence. Research suggests that family law practitioners and decision-makers continue to favour erroneous depictions of child abuse as rare, disconnected from, and unrelated to other forms of male violence (Laing 2010; 2017; Conte 2018; Gutowski & Goodman 2019). Consequently, the notion that men can be systematically abusive and violent partners yet safe and appropriate fathers is still widespread in family law systems (see e.g. Harne & Radford 2008; Flood 2012b; Morrison 2015; Coy et al. 2015). This represents, at best, the systemic failure to accurately assess issues at the core of family law work and at worst, the organised concealment of patriarchal violence and direct jeopardising of child safety. Either way, these failures represent institutional omissions and implicate the state legal apparatus in the domestic and family violence harms that they obscure and facilitate.

State social services

Analysing state social service responses to domestic violence also uncovers examples of omissive institutional state crime. In Australia and comparable contexts, the relevant government agencies fail to deliver promised services to address domestic violence victims' basic needs for financial assistance, support, privacy, and safety. These institutional failures include inappropriate and ineffectual institutional design, bureaucratic failures, and policies and practices which not only overlook and ignore domestic violence but actually obstruct victim-survivors' efforts to escape violence and protect themselves. State-based social services are ineffective at responding to domestic violence in systematic, significant, and negligent ways which ultimately hinder and harm victim-survivors.

In Australia, the federal Department of Human Services – and particularly Centrelink and the Child Support Agency[5] – are central to victim-survivors' experiences of domestic violence. This set of institutions, by design, hinders those experiencing domestic violence from acting to protect their own safety and well-being. The Department is marked by inadequate and inconsistent structures and policies which generate a demonstrably user-hostile service for all who attempt to access it (Murphy et al. 2011). Various agencies within the Department have been set up such that, despite operating out of the same or neighbouring government institutions, they are insulated from each other and do not engage in relevant information sharing. For example, while both Centrelink and the Child Support Agency exist under the Department of Human Services umbrella, the employment and income information collected by the former is not used by the latter to calculate child support payments nor to investigate child support avoidance (Natalier et al. 2015; Natalier 2017). Similarly, whilst child support calculations are based on income information provided to the Australian Tax Office, there is no dialogue between the tax office and the Child Support Agency when issues of non-payment or underpayment arise (Cook 2013).

This siloed approach to governance significantly hinders the system's efficiency, consistency, and capacity to enforce policy, which is vital to assisting domestic violence victims. It also forces clients to engage with a maze of multiple bureaucracies where they frequently receive inaccurate, inconsistent, and contradictory information and are required to repeatedly submit duplicate and supplementary paperwork (Murphy et al. 2011). The overwhelming majority of sole parents in McArthur et al.'s (2013) study found navigating the system and its arbitrary requirements extremely difficult, and Murphy et al.'s (2011: 40) participants described attempts to obtain basic entitlements as a "form of [full-time] work in itself". Additionally, the prolonged delays associated with all Department processes and applications often leave vulnerable and victimised clients in limbo and without means of subsistence for significant periods of time. These dysfunctional bureaucracies create significant impediments for those most in need of state assistance, causing many to disengage from the system and miss out on much-needed entitlements.

Domestic violence victim-survivor single parents – the overwhelming majority of whom are women – face unique challenges in dealing with social service institutions. These women have often left relationships isolated, unemployed, or underemployed, and in dire financial straits as a result of long-term economic abuse (Branigan 2007; Natalier 2018). Post-separation financial abuse is also an ongoing reality for many separating mothers, both in Australia and elsewhere (Kelly et al. 2014; Coy et al. 2015; WLSV 2015; 2018; Voth Schrag et al. 2019). For many under-resourced sole parents struggling to care for young children, the emotional and administrative labour required to comply with social service bureaucracies is simply too onerous to manage, particularly when this work may outweigh the financial value of payments such as single-parent payment or child support, which many women end up receiving only partially, temporarily, or not at all (Cameron 2014; Cook et al. 2015).

Underlying many of the problems facing clients is a system which fails to adequately recognise, understand, or respond to domestic violence. According to its own rhetoric, the Australian Department of Human Services *is* well informed and responsive to domestic and family violence and delivers an "effective anti-violence service" (DHS 2016: n.p.). Victim-survivor clients can therefore reasonably expect this institution and its officials to put this rhetoric into practice through adequate basic knowledge and understanding of domestic and family violence, and by assisting victim-survivors to navigate the system and obtain entitlements. But closer review of the Department's Family and Domestic Violence Strategy 2016–19 (DHS 2016) reveals that frontline staff, who are the system gatekeepers and who deal with the bulk of client issues, do not receive substantive education or training in even the most basic domestic and family violence issues nor the critical intersection of these issues with their daily work. Given the centrality of domestic violence in most mothers' transition to sole parenthood, the failure of the Department to centre domestic violence and adequately equip its staff to understand its impact on clients directly underpins the significant difficulties experienced by those seeking assistance. This deficient policy and practice base also relates to further system failures in relation to recognising, protecting, and supporting victim-survivors which I discuss in the next section.

In fact, through failures and omissions, the Australian Department of Human Services' policies and practices are implicated in preventing or delaying women's exit from violent relationships. In recent studies (Cameron 2014; Cook 2015; Cook et al. 2015; Natalier 2017; 2018), women victim-survivors of intimate partner abuse frequently identified the social service system *itself* as a major hindrance to their ability to leave an abusive relationship in a safe and timely manner. This caused some women to significantly delay the separation process and endure extended abuse. Women reported that a prominent reason for this delay was their inability to obtain relevant, appropriate, or consistent information from social service agencies which prevented them from figuring out the practicalities of leaving their partner and surviving independently. Many women described unhelpful and obstructive interactions with the system and its officials which reinforced the fear – first instilled in them by their abuser – that they and their children would end up poor and destitute if they were to leave the relationship (see e.g. Cameron 2014). The inconsistent and contradictory information received from different Department agencies regarding issues like sole-parent payments, work, income thresholds, child support, and taxation led many women to remain with an abusive partner for longer than they intended to (e.g. McArthur et al. 2013; Cameron 2014; Cook 2015; Natalier 2017; 2018). Through presenting institutional barriers and impediments to victim-survivors' help-seeking efforts, this positions state social services as omissively complicit in prolonging abusive relationships and extending domestic violence harms.

Systems abuse as omissive institutional state crime

Another way that state institutions omissively facilitate domestic and family violence is through providing opportunities and tools for perpetrators to engage in protracted post-separation abuse. 'Systems abuse', 'paper abuse', and 'procedural stalking' refer to the many and varied ways that perpetrators use state institutions and systems to extend their regimes of coercive control (see Miller & Smolter 2011; Douglas 2018). Systems abuse has been identified across jurisdictions and all institutions of the legal system, manifesting as various false, malicious, manipulative, and vexatious actions initiated by domestic violence perpetrators that aim to exert power, compel contact, and emotionally and financially burden victims (Douglas & Fell 2020). It can be a "barrage of men's frivolous lawsuits, false reports of child abuse, and other system-related manipulations" (Miller & Smolter 2011: 637); it can also harness law enforcement powers, as occurs when male perpetrators convince police to apply for civil orders against genuine victim-survivors (Reeves 2020).

All forms of systems abuse result in extended psychological, emotional, and financial harms, sometimes for years after a relationship supposedly ends.

In Australia, the court system is frequently used as a vehicle for post-separation systems abuse. A particularly common tactic used by perpetrators is repeated threatened or actual vexatious litigation, which is legal action intended primarily to upset, demoralise, or financially deplete the other party rather than pursue a legitimate claim (Laing 2010; 2017; Douglas 2018). Family law is a key vehicle for this abuse because vexatious litigation commonly relates to financial settlements, child custody and contact, and allegations of child abuse aimed at affecting parenting arrangements. Across different Australian jurisdictions, victim-survivors testify to experiences of intense and protracted legal systems abuse (WLSV 2018). Mary (in Douglas 2018: 89), for example, recounted being forced into court "every six weeks for twelve months" just to obtain one protective order, due to her ex-partner's deliberate obstruction of the process. Many participants in Cameron's (2014) study also described being subjected to continuous cycles of court appearances initiated by their ex-partner, which had devastating impacts on their health and well-being through causing constant stress, anxiety, illness, and economic hardship. For example, Serena explained how her ex-husband was taking her to court for the eighth time, and how

> *he is definitely, blatantly, obviously using the system to abuse me. … It is just a control thing and it is just about breaking me down and he is doing all sorts of things within the system to abuse me* (in Cameron 2014: 35).

Similarly, Cathie recounted ten years of disputes during which her former partner pursued unnecessary actions and regularly threatened to pursue full custody of their son.

Systems abuse is not restricted to the Australian context. In the United Kingdom, Kelly et al. (2014) and Coy et al. (2015) identify parallel patterns and harms, documenting perpetrators' use of court processes to perpetrate post-separation abuse in ways deliberately designed to deplete victim-survivors' emotional and financial resources. Participants in these studies recounted stressful and costly proceedings which caused significant harm to them and their children and sometimes extended over years, resulting in serious psychological ill-health. This sometimes led women to accept parenting and child support arrangements that were unsuitable for them and their children. In New Zealand, Elizabeth (2015) identifies similar patterns, with controlling fathers' aggressive family law pursuits creating costly, traumatic, unnecessary, and long-running disputes with major detrimental impacts on women and children. As in all contexts, these actions were clearly part of the continuation of coercive control.

State financial and social service institutions are another primary – but inadequately recognised – avenue for the perpetration of systems abuse. These institutions provide numerous strategies, opportunities, and tools for per-petrators to psychologically and financially abuse their victims. Australian studies (e.g. Branigan 2004; 2007; Patrick et al. 2007; 2008; Cameron 2014) document several common methods used by perpetrators. Withholding or falsifying income information is widespread and is designed to interfere with an ex-partner's applications and entitlements and abrogate the perpetrator's own payment obligations. Making false reports of tax or social security fraud against an ex-partners is also common and can cause victims' entitlements to be suspended or cancelled while they undergo invasive investigations by au-thorities. But state social services abuse via child support is arguably the most prevalent way that domestic violence perpetrators control and harm their former partner and children.

What I term *child support systems abuse* is extensively documented in Aus-tralia, manifesting as non-custodial or non-primary-carer parents' systematic withholding, manipulation, minimisation, avoidance, and evasion of child support obligations. Research with single mothers who have left abusive partners suggests that this problem is extremely widespread, with study par-ticipants often describing how child support is used as a weapon to purpose-fully harm them and their children (see e.g. Branigan 2007; Cook 2013; 2015; Laing 2013; Cameron 2014; Cook et al. 2015; Natalier et al. 2015; Natalier 2017; 2018). The experiences of the following anonymous interviewee were typical.

> *[My ex-partner] said that he was going to stop the child support payments for a couple of weeks just to teach me a lesson. He said he knew how little money I had and that without the payments I would be unable to pay my rent and I would soon go under. … I explained to him that it would directly affect the children if he didn't pay but he said that he didn't care* (in Laing 2013: 18).

In the United States (e.g. Harris 2015) and the United Kingdom (e.g. Kelly et al. 2014; Coy et al. 2015) also, researchers document similar child support-related economic abuse, noting its significant and long-term impacts on victim-survivors' physical, psychological, and financial health and well-being.

I argue that previous iterations of systems abuse (Douglas 2018; Douglas & Fell 2020; Reeves 2020), paper abuse, and procedural stalking (Miller & Smolter 2011) do not go far enough. It is insufficient to discuss these phe-nomena as extensions of individual domestic offending. I argue that all these manifestations of systems abuse should be understood as *omissive institutional state crimes*. State institutions and systems are clearly being used by perpetra-tors in deliberate, strategic ways in order to continue and expand regimes of coercive control and little is being done to combat this problem. Institutions are systematically failing to recognise post-separation domestic violence, sys-tematically failing to recognise how offenders use various state-sanctioned tools to extend their abuse, and systematically failing to implement measures to counter their active co-optation in harm. Without appropriate and effective deterrence, prevention, or remedial strategies for systems abuse, institutions are effectively functioning as passive, enabling, and tacitly supportive bystanders. In other words, these institutions are complicit by omission in this form of domestic violence.

Specifically, state institutions and officials are complicit in systems abuse through problematic policy and institutional design, bureaucratic failures, negligent ignorance, and through the official avoidance and minimisation of this problem. Based on her considerable experience of systems abuse, Margaret (in Douglas 2018: 90) found the legal apparatus "very archaic" and found that officials were largely ignorant about how the system is used to extend domestic violence. Victims of social service systems abuse also consistently describe actions and advice from officials that indicate ignorance of post-separation violence, financial abuse, and of how perpetrators use systems to extend their offending (see e.g. Branigan 2007; Cameron 2014; Natalier 2017). For example, when Sarah (in Natalier et al. 2015: 32) attempted to explain to officials how her ex-partner was financially abusing her and her children by withholding child support, she was told that it had "nothing to do with collecting money". Institutionalised ignorance directly hinders the identification and prevention of systems abuse and makes it extremely difficult for individuals to counteract their extended victimisation. This further indicates why it is more appropriate to conceptualise systems abuse as an omissive state institutional harm.

Systems abuse is also understood by both victims and perpetrators as officially sanctioned domestic violence. Studies suggest that perpetrators quickly learn how to control and damage their victims' lives through various institutional tools and processes when separation precludes other forms of coercive control; they also rapidly gain experiential awareness that there are few consequences for misusing systems, and experience this as tacit official endorsement for their behaviour (see Elizabeth et al. 2012; Laing 2013; Cameron 2014; Kelly et al. 2014; Cook 2015; Natalier 2018). From a victim-survivor perspective, state institutions do not just fail – they actually align with, enable, and assist abusive men to engage in ongoing psychological, emotional, and financial abuse. For instance, victims have described the child support enforcement vacuum as a form of collusion between their ex-partner and the system in controlling their lives and impeding their economic survival (Patrick et al. 2007; Cameron 2014). They are also acutely aware of the broader oppression inherent in systems abuse. For example, Edna (in Natalier 2018: 129) explained how her abusive ex-partner and other perpetrators could still have "financial power" over their victims specifically because "government departments give them that power". Similar sentiments are expressed by victims of law enforcement systems abuse, who experienced the ease with which their ex-partner manipulated police into discriminating against them as a form of co-oppression by individual perpetrators and state officials (e.g. Guggisberg & Fisher 2010; Hester 2012; Ulbrick & Jago 2018; Reeves 2020).

When state institutions are so easily co-opted in in this way, they should not only be seen as tools of abuse but also as omissive players in and tacit enablers of harm. Moreover, inadequate institutional reform to address these issues communicates the low official priority afforded to addressing these omissions. Given the considerable documentation of systems abuse by researchers, there is a reasonable expectation that state institutions be actively engaged in improving to their capacity to combat this problem and reduce its prevalence and impact. Yet some research findings suggest that it may be intensifying in recent years, as indicated by an increase in the proportion of fathers attempting to illegitimately use family law processes to interfere with maternal custody and contact (see Kaspiew et al. 2015b). This troubling finding – that systems abuse is increasing in prevalence despite its widespread documentation – points to the increasing culpability of state institutions in the problem and highlights that significant work is yet to be done to reform institutions so that they are no longer the "readily available … tool of abuse" (Reeves 2020: 91) that they are at present.

Conclusion

This chapter has detailed the omissive complicity of nation-state institutions in domestic and family violence. Through the feminist state crime lens I developed, this type of omissive state crime occurs when state institutions fail to deliver on either basic human rights standards, liberal–democratic principles, or specific violence protection and prevention responsibilities. These failures implicate the state because they directly contribute to enabling and exacerbating domestic and family violence. I then presented a significant body of evidence to illustrate how these institutional omissions function through contemporary policy and practice. Looking at policing, family law, and state social services, I identified systematic and negligent inaction, ignorant, neglectful, and inappropriate responses, regulatory vacuums, and obstructive policies, all of which contribute to exacerbating and extending domestic violence. I then re-theorised what has previously been termed 'systems abuse'. This systematic, calculated, and repetitive form of domestic violence relies on policy omissions, regulatory vacuums, legal loopholes, and sometimes the specific cooperation of institutional officials; the fact that state institutions have demonstrably failed to recognise, adapt to, prevent, or remedy this abuse positions it as an omissive institutional state crime.

Highlighting these state institutional dimensions of domestic violence forces us to confront that that we are dealing not just with problematic offending individuals and interpersonal violence; we are also dealing with a mass harm that is systemically facilitated by the very apparatus that is meant to prevent and protect against it. Crucially, we need to recognise that despite having officially criminalised and condemned domestic violence, state institutions continue to be seen by offenders and victims as tacitly supportive of domestic violence and directly responsible for perpetrator impunity. This incongruence between the letter of law and policy, political rhetoric, and everyday experiential reality further exposes the need to confront and address the complex scaffolding that underpins and enables this epidemic-scale problem.

Notes

1 See Libal and Parekh (2009), Hakimi (2010), and Andrews and Khavinson (2013) for further discussion of the European case. See Bettinger-Lopez (2008; 2013; et al. 2011), Goldfarb (2008), Meyersfeld (2010), Andrews and Khavinson (2013), and Cabrera (2015) for further discussion of the Inter-American Court of Human Rights case including actions from 2005 onwards.
2 Depending on context, these are variously called protective, protection, intervention, or restraining orders (see Meyer & Frost 2019). They are all civil legal orders which stipulate specific rules for alleged offenders' movements and behaviours in relation to the victim, and are designed to provide some level of victim protection and violence prevention. For example, it is commonly stipulated that an alleged offender may not contact the victim, possess weapons, or be within a certain distance of the victim's home or workplace. To breach a civil order is a criminal offence and police are legally mandated to actively enforce and prosecute breaches.
3 This can include seeing or hearing physical assaults, sexual violations, verbal abuse, threats, or various coercive and controlling violence. It can also include witnessing the impacts of this abuse, such as seeing a parent injured, visibly upset, mentally unwell, or rendering assistance to an affected parent. All these forms of exposure severely constrain children's ability to receive adequate parental care and experience normal development and thus cause significant psychological and emotional impairment (Rossman et al. 2004; Wathen & MacMillan 2013; McTavish et al. 2016).
4 This recent provision contains the caveat that the exposure must cause what is termed 'serious psychological harm', which is problematic because measuring harm, particularly soon after exposure, is impossible. Responses to this type of trauma are often hidden and delayed, with the full impact only apparent much later (O'Brien et al. 2013). I argue that this caveat thus limits the positive features of the amendment and also implies tacit tolerance of some level of domestic and family violence.
5 The Department of Human Services "is responsible for delivering a range of health, social and welfare payments and services through Medicare, Centrelink and Child Support programs for the Australian Government" (DHS 2016: 4). The Child Support Agency is the former name for the agency now officially called the Department of Human Services – Child Support (DHS-CS); however, it continues to be widely known as the Child Support Agency or the CSA amongst users of the system and in most academic and practitioner literature.

References

Andrews, Averil & Khavinson, Jenny. 2013. From international to domestic approaches: Battling domestic violence in the United States. *Family and Intimate Partner Violence Quarterly* Summer. 17–34.

Balint, Jennifer. 2012. *Genocide, State Crime and the Law*. Abingdon: Routledge.

Bancroft, Lundy & Silverman, Jay. 2004. Assessing abusers' risks to children. In Jaffe, Peter & Baker, Linda & Cunningham, Alison (eds.), *Protecting Children from Domestic Violence: Strategies for Community Intervention*, 101–19. New York: The Guildford Press.

Barak, Gregg. 1991. Toward a criminology of state criminality. In Barak, Gregg (ed.), *Crimes by the Capitalist State: An Introduction to State Criminality*, 3–18. New York: State University of New York.

Barak, Gregg. 2008. Towards an integrative study of international crimes and state-corporate criminality: A reciprocal approach to gross human rights violations. In Smeulers, Alette & Haveman, Roelof (eds.), *Supranational Criminology: Towards a Criminology of International Crimes*, 51–74. Antwerp: Intersentia.

Bettinger-Lopez, Caroline. 2008. Human rights at home: Domestic violence as a human rights violation. *Columbia Human Rights Law Review* 40. 19–77.

Bettinger-Lopez, Caroline. 2013. Jessica Lenahan (Gonzales) v United States: Implementation, litigation, and mobilisation strategies. *Journal of Gender, Social Policy and the Law* 21. 207–29.

Bettinger-Lopez, Caroline & Puga, Alma & Contesse, Jorge & Garcia-Rey, Paola & Hortsch, Diana & Kaufman, Risa & Tuszynski, Nicole. 2011. Gender justice in the Americas: A transnational dialogue on sexuality, violence, reproduction and human rights. *University of Miami Law Review*. Spring 65(3). 751–66.

Birdsey, Emma & Snowball, Lucy. 2013. *Reporting Violence to Police: A Survey of Victims attending Domestic Violence Services*. Sydney: New South Wales Bureau of Crime Statistics and Research.

Boraine, Alex. 2000. *A Country Unmasked: Inside South Africa's Truth and Reconciliation Commission*. Oxford: Oxford University Press.

Branigan, Elizabeth. 2004. *His Money or Our Money? Financial Abuse of Women in Intimate Partner Relationships*. Report by the Coburg-Brunswick Community Legal and Financial Counselling Centre Inc.

Branigan, Elizabeth. 2007. Who pays in the end? The personal and political implications of financial abuse of women in intimate partner relationships. *Just Policy* 44. 31–6.

Cabrera, Deborah Mas. 2015. Domestic violence and equal protection of the laws: A look at Town of Castle Rock v Gonzales and Lenahan v United States. *Revista Juridica Universidad De Puerto Rico* 84(2). 321–36.

Cameron, Prue. 2014. *Relationship Problems and Money: Women Talk about Financial Abuse*. Melbourne: Women's Information and Referral Exchange.

Campo, Monica & Kaspiew, Rae & Moore, Sharnee & Tayton, Sarah. 2014. *Children Affected by Domestic and Family Violence: A Review of Domestic and Family Violence Prevention, Early Intervention and Response Services*. Melbourne: Australian Institute of Family Studies.

Centre for Innovative Justice. 2015. *Opportunities for Early Intervention: Bringing Perpetrators of Family Violence into View*. Melbourne: RMIT University.

Charlesworth, Hilary. 1995. Human rights as men's rights. In Peters, Julie & Wolper, Andrea (eds.), *Women's Rights, Human Rights: International Feminist Perspectives*, 103–13. New York: Routledge.

Commonwealth of Australia. 2015. *Family Law Act 1975*. (https://www.comlaw.gov.au/Details/C2015C00552)

Conte, Isabella. 2018. *The (In)visible Victim: Characterisations of Child Victims of Intrafamilial Child Sexual Abuse in the Family Court of Australia.* School of Social and Political Sciences, University of Melbourne. (Graduate Thesis.)

Cook, Kay. 2013. Child support compliance and tax return non-filing: A feminist analysis. *Australian Review of Public Affairs.* June 11(2). 43–64.

Cook, Kay. 2015. *Financial Responsibility for Children Following Parental Separation: Welfare-to-work and Child Support Policy Winners and Losers.* Melbourne: Royal Melbourne Institute of Technology Centre for Applied Social Research Symposium.

Cook, Kay & McKenzie, Hayley & Natalier, Kristin. 2015. Mothers' experiences of child support: Qualitative research and opportunities for policy insight. *Journal of Family Studies* 21(1). 57–71.

Copelon, Rhonda. 1994. Recognising the egregious in the everyday: Domestic violence as torture. *Columbia Human Rights Law Review* 2. 291–367.

Coy, Maddy & Scott, Emma & Tweedale, Ruth & Perks, Katherine. 2015. "It's like going through the abuse again": Domestic violence and women and children's (un)safety in private law contact proceedings. *Journal of Social Welfare & Family Law* 37(1). 53–69.

De Maio, John & Kaspiew, Rae & Smart, Diana & Dunstan, Jessie & Moore, Sharnee. 2013. *Survey of Recently Separated Parents: A Study of Parents Who Separated Prior to the Implementation of the Family Law Amendment (Family Violence and Other Measures) Act 2011.* Melbourne: Australian Institute of Family Studies.

Department of Human Services. 2016. *Family and Domestic Violence Strategy 2016–19.* Australian Federal Government. (http://www.humanservices.gov.au/corporate/publications-and-resources/family-and-domestic-violence-strategy)

Diemer, Kristin & Ross, Stuart & Humphreys, Cathy & Healey, Lucy. 2017. A double-edged sword: Discretion and compulsion in policing domestic violence. *Police Practice & Research* 18(4). 339–51.

Douglas, Heather. 2018. Legal systems abuse and coercive control. *Criminology & Criminal Justice* 18(1). 84–99. (doi:10.1177/1748895817728380)

Douglas, Heather. 2019. Policing domestic and family violence. *International Journal for Crime, Justice and Social Democracy* 8(2). 31–49.

Douglas, Heather & Fell, Emma. 2020. Malicious reports of child maltreatment as coercive control: Mothers and domestic and family violence. *Journal of Family Violence* 35(8). 827–37.

Dunford-Jackson, Billie Lee. 2004. The role of family courts in domestic violence: The US Experience. In Jaffe, Peter & Baker, Linda & Cunningham, Alison (eds.), *Protecting Children from Domestic Violence: Strategies for Community Intervention*, 188–99. New York: Guildford Press.

Durfee, Alesha. 2012. Situational ambiguity and gendered patterns of arrest for intimate partner violence. *Violence against Women* 18(1). 64–84.

Elizabeth, Vivienne. 2015. From domestic violence to coercive control: Towards the recognition of oppressive intimacy in the Family Court. *New Zealand Sociology* 30(2). 26–43.

Elizabeth, Vivienne & Gavey, Nicola & Tolmie, Julie. 2012. "He's just swapped his fists for the system": The governance of gender through custody law. *Gender and Society* 26(2). 239–60.

Estcourt, David. 2018. Woman sues state for failure to protect her from domestic violence. *The Age.* (https://www.theage.com.au/national/victoria/women-sues-

state-for-failure-to-protect-her-from-domestic-violence-20180828-p5009m.
html)

European Court of Human Rights. 2009. *Opuz v Turkey*. (http://www.refworld.
org/docid/4a2f84392.html)

Farnsworth, Sarah. 2018. Woman sues Victoria Police for failing to protect her from
her violent ex-partner. *ABC News*. (https://www.abc.net.au/news/2018-08-28/
woman-sues-police-for-failing-to-protect-her-from-her-partner/10168696)

Faust, Kelly & Kauzlarich, David. 2008. Hurricane Katrina as a state crime of omission. *Critical Criminology* 16(2). 85–103.

Fehlberg, Belinda & Kaspiew, Rae & Millbank, Jenni & Kelly, Fiona & Behrens, Juliet. 2015. *Australian Family Law: The Contemporary Context*. 2nd edn. Melbourne:
Oxford University Press.

Fernandez, Marilyn. 2010. *Restorative Justice for Domestic Violence Victims: An Integrated
Approach to their Hunger for Healing*. Lanham: Lexington Books.

Flood, Michael. 2012a. *He Hits, She Hits: Assessing Debates Regarding Men's and Wom-
en's Experiences of Domestic Violence*. Sydney: Australian Domestic and Family Violence Clearinghouse.

Flood, Michael. 2012b. Separated fathers and the fathers' rights movement. *Journal of
Family Studies* 18(2/3). 235–45.

Goldfarb, Sally. 2008. *The Legal Response to Violence against Women in the United
States of America: Recent Reforms and Continuing Challenges, Expert Paper Prepared
for the United Nations Division for the Advancement of Women*. UN Doc EGM/
GPLVAW/2008/EP.06.

Goodmark, Leigh. 2018. *Decriminalizing Domestic Violence: A Balanced Policy Approach
to Intimate Partner Violence*. Oakland: University of California Press.

Green, Penny & Ward, Tony. 2000. State crime, human rights and the limits of
criminology. *Social Justice* 27(1). 101–15.

Guggisberg, Marika & Fisher, Colleen. 2010. Abused women's double jeopardy interacting with law enforcement on issues of intimate partner violence. *Women
against Violence* 22. 18–27.

Gutowski, Ellen & Goodman, Lisa. 2019. "Like I'm invisible": IPV survivor-mothers'
perceptions of seeking child custody through the Family Court system. *Journal of
Family Violence* 35. 441–57.

Hakimi, Monica. 2010. State bystander responsibility. *The European Journal of International Law* 21(2). 341–85.

Harland, Alexandra & Cooper, Donna & Rathus, Zoe & Alexander, Renata. 2015.
Family Law Principles. 2nd edn. Sydney: Thomson Reuters.

Harne, Lynne & Radford, Jill. 2008. *Tackling Domestic Violence: Theories, Policies and
Practice*. Maidenhead: Open University Press.

Harris, Deborah. 2015. "You just have to look at it as a gift": Low-income single
mothers' experiences of the child support system. *Journal of Poverty* 19(1). 88–108.

Hester, Marianne. 2012. Portrayal of women as intimate partner domestic violence
perpetrators. *Violence against Women* 18. 1067–82.

Hinch, Ronald. 1991. Contradictions, conflicts and dilemmas in Canada's sexual
assault law. In Barak, Gregg (ed.), *Crimes by the Capitalist State: An Introduction to
State Criminality*, 233–52. New York: SUNY.

Hoyle, Carolyn & Palmer, Nicola. 2014. Family justice centres: A model for empowerment? *International Review of Victimology* 20(2). 191–210.

Hunter, Rosemary. 2006. Law's (masculine) violence: Reshaping jurisprudence. *Law and Critique* 17. 26–46.

Inter-American Court of Human Rights. 2011. *Lenahan (Gonzales) v. United States.* (https://www.oas.org/en/iachr/decisions/2011/USPU 12626EN.DOC)

Johnson, Michael. 1995. Patriarchal terrorism and common couple violence: Two forms of violence against women. *Journal of Marriage and the Family* 57. 283–94.

Jones, Adam. 2013. *The Scourge of Genocide: Essays and Reflections.* Abingdon: Routledge.

Kaspiew, Rae & Carson, Rachel & Coulson, Melissa & Dunstan, Jessie & Moore, Sharnee. 2015a. *Responding to Family Violence: A Survey of Family Law Practices and Experiences.* Melbourne: Australian Institute of Family Studies.

Kaspiew, Rae & Carson, Rachel & Dunstan, Jessie & Qu, Lizia & Horsfall, Briony & De Maio, John & Moore, Sharnee & Moloney, Lawrie & Coulson, Melissa & Tayton, Sarah. 2015b. *Evaluation of the 2012 Family Violence Amendments.* Melbourne: Australian Institute of Family Studies.

Kauzlarich, David & Mullins, Christopher & Matthews, Rick. 2003. A complicity continuum of state crime. *Contemporary Justice Review* 6(3). 241–54.

Kaye, Miranda & Stubbs, Julie & Tolmie, Julia. 2003. Domestic violence, separation and parenting: Negotiating safety using legal processes. *Current Issues in Criminal Justice* 15(2). 73–94.

Kelly, Liz & Sharp, Nicola & Klein, Renate. 2014. *Finding the Costs of Freedom: How Women and Children Rebuild their Lives after Domestic Violence.* London: Solace Women's Legal Aid and Child and Woman Abuse Studies Unit.

Kimmel, Michael. 2013. The gender of violence. *The Gendered Society*, 421–52. 5th edn. New York: Oxford University Press.

Kolin, Andrew. 2008. *State Structure and Genocide.* Lanham: University Press of America.

Laing, Lesley. 2010. *No Way to Live: Women's Experiences of Negotiating the Family Law System in the Context of Domestic Violence.* Sydney: University of Sydney.

Laing, Lesley. 2013. *"It's Like This Maze That You Have to Make Your Way Through": Women's Experiences of Seeking a Domestic Violence Protection Order in NSW.* Sydney: University of Sydney.

Laing, Lesley. 2017. Secondary victimization: Domestic violence survivors navigating the family law system. *Violence against Women* 23(11). 1314–35.

Libal, Kathryn & Parekh, Serena. 2009. Reframing violence against women as a human rights violation. *Violence against Women* 15(12). 1477–89.

MacKinnon, Catharine. 1993. On torture: A feminist perspective on human rights. In Mahoney, Kathleen & Mahoney, Paul (eds.), *Human rights in the Twenty-first Century: A Global Challenge*, 21–31. Boston: M. Nijhoff.

McArthur, Morag & Thomson, Lorraine & Winkworth, Gail. 2013. Jumping through hoops: The cost of compliance on sole parents. *Child and Family Social Work* 18. 159–67.

McCulloch, Jude & Blair, Megan. 2012. Law for justice: The history of Community Legal Centres in Australia. In Stanley, Elizabeth & McCulloch, Jude (eds.), *State Crime and Resistance*, 168–82. Hoboken: Taylor and Francis.

McTavish, Jill & MacGregor, Jen & Wathen, Nadine & MacMillan, Harriet. 2016. Children's exposure to intimate partner violence: An overview. *International Review of Psychiatry* 28(5). 504–18.

Mertus, Julie & Goldberg, Pamela. 1994. A perspective on women and international human rights after the Vienna Declaration: The inside / outside construct. *New York University Journal of International Law and Politics* 26. 201–34.

Meyer, Silke. 2011. Seeking help for intimate partner violence: Victims' experiences when approaching the criminal justice system for IPV-related support and protection in an Australian jurisdiction. *Feminist Criminology* 6. 268–90.

Meyer, Silke. 2016. Still blaming the victim of intimate partner violence? Women's narratives of victim desistance and redemption when seeking support. *Theoretical Criminology* 20(1). 75–90.

Meyer, Silke & Frost, Andrew. 2019. *Domestic and Family Violence: A Critical Introduction to Knowledge and Practice.* Abingdon: Routledge.

Meyersfeld, Bonita. 2010. *Domestic Violence and International Law.* Oxford: Hart Publishing.

Miller, Susan & Smolter, Nicole. 2011. Paper abuse: When all else fails, batterers use procedural stalking. *Violence against Women* 17(5). 637–50.

Morrison, Fiona. 2015. All over now? The ongoing relational consequences of domestic abuse through children's contact arrangements. *Child Abuse Review* 24. 274–84.

Murphy, John & Murray, Suellen & Chalmers, Jenny & Martin, Sonia & Marston, Greg. 2011. *Half a Citizen: Life on Welfare in Australia.* Melbourne: Allen and Unwin.

Murray, Suellen & Powell, Anastasia. 2009. What's the problem? Australian public policy constructions of domestic and family violence. *Violence against Women* 15(5). 532–52.

Natalier, Kristin. 2017. Micro-aggressions, single mothers and interactions with government workers: The case of Australia's child support bureaucracy. *Journal of Sociology* 53. 622–36.

Natalier, Kristin. 2018. State facilitated economic abuse: A structural analysis of men deliberately withholding child support. *Feminist Legal Studies* 26(2). 121–40.

Natalier, Kristin & Cook, Kay & Pitman, Torna. 2015. *Single Mother's Experiences with the DHS-CS.* Research report funded by University of Tasmania and Flinders University.

Nichols, Allison. 2013. Toward a child-centred approach to evaluating claims of alienation in high-conflict custody disputes. *Michigan Law Review* 112(4). 663–88.

O'Brien, Kristy & Cohen, Lynne & Pooley, Julie Ann & Taylor, Myra. 2013. Lifting the domestic violence cloak of silence: Resilient women's reflected memories of their childhood experiences of witnessing domestic violence. *Journal of Family Violence* 28. 95–108.

O'Donohue, William & Cummings, Caroline & Willis, Brenan. 2018. The frequency of false allegations of child sexual abuse: A critical review. *Journal of Child Sexual Abuse* 27(5). 459–75.

Patrick, Rebecca & Cook, Kay & McKenzie, Hayley. 2008. Domestic violence and the exemption from seeking child support: Providing safety or legitimising ongoing poverty and fear. *Social Policy and Administration* 42(7). 749–67.

Patrick, Rebecca & Cook, Kay & Taket, Ann. 2007. Multiple barriers to obtaining child support: Experiences of women leaving violent partners. *Just Policy* 45. 21–29.

Phillips, Janet & Vandenbroek, Penny. 2014. *Domestic, Family and Sexual Violence in Australia: An Overview of the Issues.* Australian Parliamentary Library Research Paper.

Preston, Peta & Gyde, Sharon. 2005. *Mistreated and Misunderstood: Young Women and Domestic Violence Negotiating the Justice System*. (Presented at the State Youth Affairs Conference: Working Together for Young People, Brisbane.)

Public Health Association of Australia. 2015. *Submission to the National Children's Commissioner for the Report on the Effects of Family and Domestic Violence on Children*. (https://www.phaa.net.au/documents/item/1180)

Qu, Lixia & Weston, Ruth & Moloney, Lawrie & Kaspiew, Rae & Dunstan, Jessie. 2014. *Post-Separation Parenting, Property and Relationship Dynamics after Five Years*. Canberra: Attorney-General's Department.

Reeves, Ellen. 2020. Family violence, protection orders and systems abuse: Views of legal practitioners. *Current Issues in Criminal Justice* 32(1). 91–110.

Romany, Celia. 1994. State responsibility goes private: A feminist critique of the public / private distinction in international human rights law. In Cook, Rebecca (ed.), *Human Rights of Women: National and International perspectives*, 85–115. Philadelphia: University of Pennsylvania Press.

Rose, Evelyn & Mertens, Charlotte & Balint, Jennifer. 2018. *Addressing Family Violence: Contemporary Best Practice and Community Legal Centres*. Report prepared by the University of Melbourne in collaboration with the Federation of Community Legal Centres.

Rossman, Robbie & Rea, Jacqueline & Graham-Bermann, Sandra & Butterfield, Perry. 2004. Young children exposed to domestic violence: Incidence, assessment, and intervention. In Jaffe, Peter & Baker, Linda & Cunningham, Alison (eds.), *Protecting Children from Domestic Violence: Strategies for Community Intervention*, 30–48. New York: Guildford Press.

Salter, Michael. 2017. Child sexual abuse. In DeKeseredy, Walter & Dragiewicz, Molly (eds.), *Routledge Handbook of Critical Criminology*. London and New York: Routledge.

Segrave, Marie & Wilson, Dean & Fitz-Gibbon, Kate. 2018. Policing intimate partner violence in Victoria (Australia): Examining police attitudes and the potential of specialisation. *Australian & New Zealand Journal of Criminology* 51(1). 99–116.

Stanley, Elizabeth. 2005. Truth commissions and the recognition of state crime. *British Journal of Criminology*. July 45(4). 582–97.

Stark, Evan. 2007. *Coercive Control: How Men Entrap Women in Personal Life*. New York: Oxford University Press.

State Government of Victoria. 2019. *Family Violence Multi Agency Risk Assessment and Management Framework*. (https://www.vic.gov.au/family-violence-multi-agency-risk-assessment-and-management)

Sullivan, Donna. 1995. The public / private distinction in international human rights law. In Peters, Julie & Wolper, Andrea (eds.), *Women's Rights, Human Rights: International Feminist Perspectives*, 126–34. New York: Routledge.

Sutton, Adrian. 2008. A child psychiatry perspective: Children as victims of adult-adult violence. In Keeling, June & Mason, Tom (eds.), *Domestic Violence: A Multi-Professional Approach for Healthcare Practitioners*, 47–56. Berkshire: McGraw-Hill.

Taylor, Louise. 2018. *Domestic Violence, Police Accountability, and Women's Criminalisation*. Public Forum, Royal Melbourne Institute of Technology.

Tucker, Jacqueline. 2015. *Official Witness Statement to Victorian Royal Commission into Family Violence*. Melbourne.

Ulbrick, Madeleine & Jago, Marianne. 2018. *"Officer she's psychotic and I need protection": Police Misidentification of the Primary Aggressor in Family Violence Incidents in Victoria*. Women's Legal Service Victoria.

United Kingdom Women's Aid. 2013. *Domestic Violence Statistics*. (www.womensaid.uk)

United Nations Commission on Human Rights. 1996. *Report of the Special Rapporteur on Violence against Women, its Causes and Consequences*. E/CN.4/1996/53/Add.1

United Nations General Assembly. 1979. *Convention on the Elimination of All Forms of Discrimination against Women*. UN Doc A/RES/34/180.

United Nations General Assembly. 1993. *Declaration on the Elimination of Violence against Women*. UN Doc A/RES/48/104.

United Nations General Assembly. 2003. *Resolution on the Elimination of Domestic Violence against Women*. UN Doc A/RES/58/147.

Victoria Police. 2014. *Code of Practice for the Investigation of Family Violence: Supporting an Integrated Response to Family Violence in Victoria*.

Victorian Supreme Court. 2019. *Summary of Judgment, Smith [pseudonym] v Victoria [2018]*. Vol. VSC 475.

Voth Schrag, Rachel J. & Robinson, Sarah R. & Ravi, Kristen. 2019. Understanding pathways within intimate partner violence: Economic abuse, economic hardship, and mental health. *Journal of Aggression, Maltreatment & Trauma* 28(2). 222–42.

Wathen, Nadine & MacMillan, Harriet. 2013. Children's exposure to intimate partner violence: Impacts and interventions. *Paediatrics & Child Health* 18(8). 419–22.

Women's Legal Service Victoria. 2015. *Economic Abuse and Economic Recovery of Family Violence Victims*. (Official Submission to the Royal Commission into Family Violence.)

Women's Legal Service Victoria. 2018. *Small Claims, Large Battles: Achieving Economic Equality in the Family Law System*. Report by Women's Legal Service Victoria.

Chapter 7

Domestic violence as agentic institutional state crime

This chapter continues the focus on nation-state institutions' complicity in domestic violence but moves beyond the passive inaction and negligent failures that constitute state omissions to consider what I term *agentic institutional state crime*. This is where state institutions and their official representatives play a direct and active role in domestic violence. I begin by constructing a feminist theory of agentic institutional state crime which, like the previous chapter, integrates and extends state crime, human rights, and feminist theory and concepts. I also consider particular ways to conceptualise the agentic when it comes to the state and its institutions, including at the micro, everyday, and experiential levels. Since agentic institutional state crime encompasses a spectrum of active involvement in domestic violence, I then nominate three key points on this spectrum: *productive*, *reconstructive*, and *abusive* agentic institutional state crime, detailing each and explaining its contemporary functioning through the legal and social service apparatus.

A feminist theory of agentic institutional state crime

As with Chapter 6, this lens for understanding the state crime dimensions of domestic violence is premised upon the centrality of institutions to the exercise of state power and the perpetration of state crime (see e.g. Kauzlarich et al. 2003; Green & Ward 2004; Stanley 2005; Rothe & Mullins 2006; Balint 2014). Also like all previous Part II chapters, a feminist perspective is key. Here, I reiterate that state institutions in all of the Western liberal democracies that are the focus of this book are patriarchal in origin, design, interests, and contemporary functioning (see e.g. Radford & Stanko 1996; MacKinnon 1989; Stark 2007; Bumiller 2008). As I have consistently shown, despite being officially premised upon principles of equality, these states have instituted and maintained comprehensive legal, political, cultural, and social systems around sexual and gendered *inequality*. Accordingly, the foundations, values, principles, and practices of all state institutions in these contexts are

DOI: 10.4324/9781003132370-9

fundamentally masculine in character and interest, and consistently function to the detriment of women and children.

I looked in the previous chapter at how state institutions enable and exacerbate domestic violence through omissions. Now, I look at the more active, productive, and directly violent role of state institutions in domestic violence. In state crime studies, there is a common distinction between crimes of omission and commission, with the latter signifying the most proactive, purposeful, and deliberate forms of state involvement in systematic harms (Barak 1991; 1994; Kauzlarich et al. 2003; Green & Ward 2004; Stanley 2007). Here, I nominate these as the *agentic* dimensions of state institutional criminality. At the macro-level, I argue that state institutions play an agentic role in domestic violence through laws and policies that purposefully generate sanctioned opportunities for new domestic and family violence offending or which officially reconstitute domestic violence in a manner that effectively legitimates and decriminalises it, thereby minimising or eliminating perpetrator responsibility.

Further conceptualising the *agentic* when it comes to the state and its institutions poses challenges, since agency is most often an implicitly human attribute. Given the hazards of anthropomorphising a monolithic, abstract entity like a state or institution, I turn to works that have attempted to conceptually deconstruct institutions in order to better understand their composition and machinations and, in turn, the everyday micro-functioning of state crime. Kauzlarich et al. (2003) and Rothe and Mullins (2006) have in fact suggested that the state – and accordingly, state crime – *can* be identified and analysed by conceptualising its institutions *as* actors and agents because state institutions are composed of people entrusted with their daily operation. According to this line of thinking, the state and its institutions are not merely abstract entities because they can be broken down into concrete component human parts. When individual representatives are acting in their official capacity, they can be understood as the state in human agent form. State power, and indeed state oppression and criminality, can therefore be identified by looking at a state institution's 'behaviour' via its official representatives and agents.

This means that, at least to some extent, the state *can* be considered agentic. It also means that some forms of state crime can be identified by examining everyday interactions between state institutional officials and citizens. If the state is composed of multiple human entities who are individually and collectively responsible for administering state power in everyday life, state criminality can play out through the routine, the normalised, and the interpersonal. As sociologists and practitioners have noted in relation to oppression, it is not just an abstract notion, but "is made up of the multiple daily experiences of disadvantage that certain citizens face" (Graham & Schiele 2010: 235). I suggest the same in terms of state criminality: it is not merely abstract, nor does it only occur at the macro-level; it also takes place in everyday life and at the micro-level. State power – and indeed state criminality –

can therefore play out through apparently mundane everyday encounters like the interpersonal exchange between a domestic violence victim-survivor and a frontline official at their local state social service agency.

When an official is the human face of the state, what may otherwise be a casual interaction is at once a formal state encounter. When everyday "speech acts" (Reyes 2011: 783; also Constable 2014) emanate from state officials, they carry the weight of state authority.[1] Aggressive responses, discriminatory views, demeaning comments, and harmful advice from state representatives may thus constitute both state oppression and state complicity in abuse, violence, and trauma. This is why it is important to look to the everyday functioning of governing bodies that make up the nation-state to gain insight into the micro-operation of state crime. Since state encounters tend to express, reinforce, and extend inherent power inequalities, they also function as a more diffuse vehicle of state oppression and criminality. For instance, through a degrading, disempowering, or abusive interaction with a state official, a person who is seeking help for interpersonal victimisation may simultaneously experience devaluation of their personhood, undermining of their citizenship, indifference to their hardships, and even re-victimisation. Researchers have widely documented the poor treatment that already-subjugated and violated citizens routinely receive from state officials, which is often in direct contradiction to institutional policy. Incorporating these insights into state crime thinking helps facilitate conceptualising and identifying the micro-oppressive and micro-abusive dimensions of agentic institutional state crime.

Another important way to think about the agentic in state crime emerges from centring victim-survivor perspectives. As state crime scholars Green and Ward (2000; 2004; Ward & Green 2016; also Stanley 2014; Balint 2019) argue, evolving definitions of state crime must emerge not only from legal or academic frameworks but also from the citizenry itself. Through acts of challenge and resistance, citizens and citizen collectives can identify what they experience and perceive as state victimisation and criminality. Similarly, I argue from a feminist perspective that it is critical to generate new definitions of state crimes against women through privileging the voices and perspectives of interpersonal violence survivors who have also been victimised by patriarchal state institutions. It is for this reason that I draw heavily from qualitative research which centres primary accounts. When domestic violence victim-survivors have clearly experienced – and explicitly identify – the state as an agentic perpetrator of violence, they highlight the importance of understanding and naming these harms *as* state abuse, violence, and criminality.

Agentic productive institutional state crime

This form of agentic state crime occurs when state institutions directly facilitate domestic violence recidivism by creating new opportunities for offending. Family law, family courts, and state social services are particular vehicles for this institutional production of violence.

Through child custody and contact rulings, family courts are directly implicated in creating state-sanctioned opportunities for domestic and family violence perpetrators to reoffend. It is extensively documented across comparable liberal-democratic contexts that family courts routinely endorse unrestricted and unmonitored paternal access to children where there is an established history of violence. Ferguson et al. (2018) cite American data which estimates that, every year, family courts are placing more than 58,000 children in unsupervised care of an abusive parent. Across Australia, the United Kingdom, and the United States, studies show courts' ongoing refusal to consider even serious cases of child abuse as relevant to determining parenting arrangements, and that they continue to consistently rule in favour of father-child contact (Laing 2010; Coy et al. 2015; Fehlberg et al. 2015; Holt 2017; O'Donohue et al. 2018). This institutionalises unsafe parenting arrangements and creates a state-sanctioned framework for further offending against children.

By refusing to take allegations seriously, and in direct contravention of the law's own central safety principles, family courts are placing children in the care of abusive parents and at direct risk of further violence and trauma. Conte's (2018) recent Australian study of custody cases involving paternal child abuse allegations found that the majority of judicial decisions compelled children into contact with their fathers. This was even the case where children had given formal evidence of sexual victimisation by their fathers and clearly expressed a need to cease contact to avoid further victimisation and trauma. In the United Kingdom, research also indicates that forced contact with parents accused of direct child abuse remains common (Kelly et al. 2014; Coy et al. 2015; Holt 2017).

> *Despite histories of violence, despite children refusing contact or expressing terror and distress, despite in some cases injunctions being in place and criminal convictions ... findings here support multiple previous studies' [findings that] unsupervised contact [is] routinely ordered to abusive fathers.*

(Coy et al. 2015: 66)

In cases where there have been clear disclosures of child physical or sexual abuse, when contact induces intense psychological and physical illness, and when contact places children at risk of further abuse, these family court rulings are directly responsible for victims' further suffering and endangerment. These rulings also equate to family courts' effective decriminalisation and endorsement of men's prior violence as they officially enable opportunities for reoffending. This positions the court as the direct orchestrator of any further harms against children that occur during paternal access.

Through endorsing and enforcing abusive fathers' ongoing contact with children, family courts also provide an officially sanctioned framework and frequent opportunities for post-separation partner violence. In Australia, England, Scotland, and the United States, child contact arrangements are confirmed as a primary vehicle for the continuation of men's violence against former partners (Harne & Radford 2008; Morrison 2015; Holt 2017; Thiara & Humphreys 2017). Research shows clear links between contact arrangements and the extension of intimate partner abuse, with child handovers routinely involving verbal abuse, threats, and even physical assault. Of course, children are party to and affected by all such displays of parental violence and are thus indirectly victimised as well, since this exposure constitutes child abuse (Edleson 2004; Wathen & MacMillan 2013; McTavish et al. 2016).

Contact arrangements are also routinely used to exert subtle ex-partner co-ercive control. Kelly et al.'s (2014) study with separated mothers in the United Kingdom identified that child handovers were commonly used by perpe-trators to gain information and represented "a controlling way of knowing exactly what's going on in the woman's life" (Anon in Kelly et al. 2014: 96). Many participants described ex-partners using handover arrangements to strategically control, constrain, or sabotage their work or social life, for instance by being late or not showing up at all specifically when they knew it would interfere with the other parent's commitments.

State-mandated contact between abusive fathers and children also facili-tates the co-optation of children in ex-partner abuse. Numerous studies in different contexts document children being enlisted as detectives, messengers, and proxies for extending perpetrators' monitoring, control, harassment, and verbal abuse of the other parent. Australian researchers have described this as the 'weaponisation' of children in domestic violence (e.g. Meyer & Frost 2019; Fitz-Gibbon 2020; Pfitzner et al. 2020). In the United States, Bancroft and Silverman (2002) document perpetrators compelling children to mon-itor their mother's behaviour, report on her contacts and movements, and relay threats to her. These patterns are echoed in Australia (see e.g. Thiara & Humphreys 2017) and the United Kingdom (see e.g. Holt 2017), with Kelly et al.'s (2014: 97) participant cohort detailing how their children were fre-quently subjected to "mind games [by their father] … just for information" about their mother. Of course, all of these tactics victimise children as well as their primary target, since children are enlisted as collaborators without having the capacity to understand, consent, or indeed to refuse to participate in this abuse.

Contact with an abusive parent can also facilitate children's education as independent perpetrators, as in cases where they are schooled in using ex-plicit derogatory language against their mother. Kelly et al.'s (2014) study documents the common phenomenon of male abusers systematically insult-ing their ex-partner directly to children, which is often repeated when they return to the mother's care. In one example, a woman recounted how, the day after visitation with her father, her daughter "told me 'Mummy you are poisonous' and she didn't even know what poisonous mean[t]" (Anon in Kelly et al. 2014: 96). Meyer and Frost (2019: 78) document parallel patterns in Australia, with many interviewees describing how their former partner instructed and encouraged their children to call them derogatory names. Mc-Kenzie et al.'s (2016) study of intimate partner violence cases in Victoria, Australia, also identifies the use of children as mediums of men's abuse. For example, in *R v McDonald* (2011 in McKenzie et al. 2016: 58, 140), it was documented that during contact visits, the father would compel his children to write offensive notes to their mother labelling her a whore and a slut. These forms of abuse not only sustain intimate partner violence beyond separation; they also constitute child abuse because they subject children to psychological and emotional harms as they are recruited as co-offenders. Since it is family-law-mandated custody and contact arrangements that provide the framework and opportunities for this abuse, children should be understood as *institutionally generated proxies* for their abusive father and the state as the direct and active producer of these harms.

Enforced contact with abusive fathers also implicates the family law system more broadly in domestic and family violence, because it enables abusers to directly coach a new generation of perpetrators. Abuse and violence by children against parents has well-substantiated links with men's intimate partner offending and indicates the strong impact of paternal modelling (Meyer & Frost 2019). Data from the Australian practitioner sector shows that this problem overwhelmingly involves adolescent males abusing their mothers. In Gallagher's (2004) clinical sample, 99% of child perpetrators victimised their mothers and young male perpetrators outnumbered females by six to one, with evidence strongly suggesting that the abuse was modelled on similar treatment of the same target by a father figure. Howard (2011: 6) documented mothers' subjection to "almost identical" verbal abuse by their son and their former partner, with many women particularly disturbed by the parallels between their child's and ex-partner's language and behaviour. A participant in another Australian study, Sandra, described this pattern as "disturbing for me when I recognise it ... sometimes I feel I am [back] living in the relationship with my ex-husband ... It disturbs me enormously" (in Howard & Rottem 2008: 43). Because family courts endorse – and indeed often insist upon – children's ongoing contact with abusive fathers, they are also responsible for the harmful ramifications of this contact. The opportunities for social learning and modelling that court-enforced paternal contact provides directly implicates the state in children's violence, both in their current family situation and into the future, since young male offending against mothers strongly correlates with the future perpetration of intimate partner violence (see Howard 2011). In these ways, family law and the family court are positioned as active producers, commissioners, and brokers of domestic and family violence: clearly agentic and violence-producing roles.

Agentic productive institutional domestic violence state crime also functions through state social service institutions and agencies. In the previous chapter, I discussed the omissive regulatory vacuum in relation to child support in Australia which many perpetrators capitalise on to perpetrate ex-partner financial abuse. But these omissions also cross over into agentic state harms because of how victim-survivors are institutionally coerced into the regulatory vacuum in a manner that can directly precipitate their further victimisation. The problem stems from child support policy and practice omissions and the absence of appropriate regulatory and accountability mechanisms to ensure that parents comply with obligations. In practice, when primary parents are not receiving child support entitlements from the other parent, the Child Support Agency places the onus on them to independently pursue such issues (Cameron 2014; Cook 2015; Natalier 2018). In fact the Agency explicitly advocates that women directly negotiate with or confront their ex-partner, as occurred for Phuong (in Branigan 2007: 35), who was told by officials that if she wanted her entitlements, she would have to "chase" her ex-partner to get them. Holly (in Natalier 2018: 133) found that reporting her ex-partner's physical violence as well as his child support evasion did not change Agency responses and staff maintained that "the onus to prove what [he] is doing is on me".

If clients want child support evasion officially investigated, Agency staff also routinely instruct them to covertly gather information and documentation about their ex-partner's personal and financial affairs in order to instigate and propel non-compliance processes. Gina (in Cameron 2014: 42–3), for instance, was told by staff to "follow it up" and get photos to prove that her ex-partner was working a cash-in-hand job which enabled him to claim no income and avoid paying child support, and said that staff pressured her to "chase him like some kind of stalker". It is not uncommon for women to be told by Agency representatives that if they want an issue pursued, they should hire a private investigator at their own expense (see e.g. Cameron 2014; Natalier et al. 2015; Natalier 2018). Given that single mothers are amongst the most financially disadvantaged groups in society (ACOSS 2014), this suggestion is generally perceived as insulting (Cameron 2014). These various forms of state institutional coercion compel highly vulnerable clients to act on their own to "doggedly investigate and pursue" legitimate entitlements at their own cost and risk (Cook 2015: n.p.).

By actively encouraging victims to engage in these risky activities, the Child Support Agency directly jeopardises the safety and well-being of domestic violence victim-survivor families. This is because, when women are institutionally pressured to pursue non-compliance issues themselves, they are entering into situations that are likely to result in violence that would otherwise not occur (Natalier et al. 2015; Natalier 2018). Confronting a volatile ex-partner with questions and demands, not to mention the intrusive surveillance, monitoring, or the covert information-gathering advocated by some officials, is not only unacceptably risky; it may also be impossible if there is a protective order in place that prohibits contact or proximity. It is widely documented that the most dangerous time for victims of intimate partner violence is during and following separation; it is also common for victims to continue to experience ex-partner abuse for years after leaving (Qu et al. 2014; Fehlberg et al. 2015; PHAA 2015). Many women are genuinely fearful for their and their children's safety in both the immediate and longer term. Based on their experiences of threatened or actual physical violence, victim-survivors know that challenging their ex-partner increases the likelihood of anger and aggression and is also unlikely to achieve any positive outcomes. For Gina (Cameron 2014: 42–3), all that confronting her ex-partner about child support achieved was being "verbally abused by him and hav[ing her] children verbally abused". Pressuring vulnerable women to resolve these issues themselves is not only an insidious form of official victim-blaming; it also represents direct state complicity in any abuse and violence that results from women's actions.

Ultimately, many women decide to abandon pursuing child support altogether in order to avoid contact with an abuser and prioritise safety, with fear of serious assault a major factor in these decisions (Cook 2015). Many women also accurately determine that they would be taking huge risks for negligible to no economic benefit, since assessed child support rates are so low. For example, Phoung (in Branigan 2007: 35) decided to abandon her case since the costs and risks of pursuing her child's father far outweighed the assessed rate of $5 per week. With ludicrous assessed rates like Renee's ex-partner's 33 cents per week based on what he claimed was an annual income of $200 (in Natalier 2018: 133), it is clearly of no benefit to many women to endanger themselves or their children to pursue payments. Findings from other child support systems indicate similar patterns (see e.g. Harris 2005; Patrick et al. 2007; Harris 2015). For instance, in the United Kingdom, around a fifth of parents on the lowest of incomes chose not to even apply for child support payments in the first place because they believed that it would directly endanger them or their children and was not worth it (Patrick et al. 2008; also see Kelly et al. 2014; Coy et al. 2015). When women ultimately decide to avoid or abandon child support cases and forgo financial entitlements, the state is also complicit in the economic losses that accompany these decisions.

Agentic reconstructive institutional state crime

Agentic institutional involvement in domestic violence also plays out through the official discursive reconstruction of men's domestic violence such that it is effectively neutralised or erased. The effective disappearance of men's domestic violence in the official written narratives of police and criminal courts equates to its decriminalisation and is another direct and active way that state institutions are complicit in this problem.

In the Swiss context, Gloor and Meier's (2013) analysis of intimate partner homicide reports reveals systematic agentic discursive reconstruction of men's violence. In accordance with typical patterns of intimate partner homicide (see e.g. Douglas 2012; Reckdenwald et al. 2019), the vast majority of these cases contained clear references to abuse histories. Some reports even referred to prior physical violence and threats of murder and suicide. Police often indicated a clear awareness of repetitive and systematic male abuse yet did not officially document this relevant pattern of offending. Rather, they consistently reconstructed it as irrelevant background rather than vital case evidence. In fact, in not a single case did police identify a pattern of men's abuse nor made links between prior violence and the homicide, even when the offender had made multiple threats of murder. For example, in one case, police mentioned in passing that the man had "threatened to kill his wife and himself if she would separate from him" (73), yet they recast this vital information as unimportant and later disappeared it from the narrative. This led Gloor and Meier (2013: 78) to conclude that "the concept of domestic violence is not present in the reports". By obscuring the well-documented power imbalance, controlling behaviours, and extensive abuse histories that characterise cases of intimate partner homicide, these official accounts discursively erase men's domestic offending.

Another way that these police narratives reconstructed male violence was by discursively disconnecting it from male actors and re-casting it as spontaneous and attributable to outside factors. This had the effect of minimising or removing male culpability. Police frequently employed passive euphemisms and weather metaphors that framed systematic abuse as marital normality and the killings as "a natural force" (76). In one case, the period preceding the homicide was described as a time of "turbulences in the marital sky" (75); in others, it was a time during which "the marriage... was clouding" or "became partly turbid" (75). One clearly abusive history was vaguely indicated by "weathervanes turn[ing] to storm" (75). None of the accounts identified men's responsibility for the incidence of conflict, aggression, abuse, and violence in the relationship; however, some did subtly implicate the woman's behaviour as provocative. When the homicide itself was referenced by police, it was very rarely characterised as a serious crime. Instead, it was most often referred to via vague euphemisms like "the deed" and presented as merely one unfortunate incident amidst "ugly circumstances" (70). These "actorless accounts" (68) isolate lethal violence from its context, erase the concept of male agency and abuse, and indeed often disappear the entire identity of the systematic domestic violence offender. This enables homicidal violence to be reconstructed as an isolated and unfortunate accident rather than the apex of an abusive regime. This systematically minimises male culpability by comprehensively rewriting the domestic violence story.

Courts also play an identifiable agentic reconstructive role in domestic violence through discursively erasing male offending. In criminal courts, prior male abuse is rarely recognised in homicide cases as a pattern of dangerous abusive behaviour or serial criminal offending (Douglas 2012; Wells 2012; Tyson 2013; Sheehy 2018). Examples of judges' sentencing commentary in intimate partner homicide cases offers striking examples of the official discursive disappearance of domestic violence. One example is the intimate partner murder case of *R v Felicite* 2010 (in McKenzie et al 2016: 63–4). This case involved a history of serious and protracted domestic violence which the court reconstructed as innocuous, despite its central relevance to the murder. Ron Felicite had pleaded guilty to murdering his wife Marie Juliette Felicite by repeatedly stabbing her in front of their four-year-old son. During the case, the court heard a documented history of aggressive and threatening behaviour by the defendant for two years preceding the lethal incident. The victim had sought police assistance on several occasions and police had documented the offender's repeated threats to kill her and her son. They had also granted an interim intervention order after one incident involving lethal threats. The court even received as evidence a letter from the defendant to his wife, in which he admitted being "very aggressive" towards her during their relationship (63). The day before the murder, Marie Juliette had sought police assistance and reported that her husband had threatened her with a knife; yet later, in the presence of her husband, she altered this account. The following day, Ron stabbed her twelve times in the neck after an argument about her wanting to separate.

But despite this extensive and substantiated history of violence, the sentencing judge recast it as unproblematic and benign. His sentencing commentary (see McKenzie et al. 2016: 64) noted the defendant's "passive, caring nature" and reconstructed his prior violence as "verbal conflicts" in the relationship. In addressing the defendant directly, the judge said that "there is no suggestion that you were ever violent to your wife before this event", emphasised the defendants' "concern for immediate and extended family" and his work ethic, and even framed the homicide as an unfortunate incident for which the defendant might deserve official compassion. In this and many other cases analysed by McKenzie et al., courts routinely favoured narratives of men's lethal violence as isolated and out of character and their histories as admirable and unproblematic. By dismissing and erasing evidence of repetitive abuse, these narratives reveal courts' direct and demonstrable complicity in domestic violence, their reconstruction of the past in order to mitigate male culpability, and active judicial support and protection for perpetrators.

Agentic abusive institutional state crime

This refers to the most direct and active form of agentic state institutional harms against domestic violence victims. Here, I consider what has already been identified as secondary victimisation or revictimisation but reframe it as state criminality. This is because it involves varying degrees of institutional oppression, aggression, and abuse against victim-survivors that not only replicates and reinforces domestic abuse; it also represents official participation in it. For some women, this is also experienced as a discrete and unique form of state victimisation and violence which needs to be recognised and named as such.

Feminist researchers have already documented and theorised domestic violence victim-survivors' experiences with state institutions as revictimisation. Mills (1996; 1999) offers an incisive early analysis of how states harm domestic abuse victims, identifying that "policy solutions replicate the very violence the state seeks to eradicate" and that "a dynamic between the state and the battered woman emerges that distinctly mimics the very dynamic in the battering relationship" (1999: 585). Bumiller (2008: 97) also observes in the United States that when female victims of male violence are "thrust into new relationships within the public sphere ... they experience brutalities that mimic the violence they hoped to leave behind". Contemporarily, researchers continue to identify that for many victims, engaging with the legal system feels like going through "a second round of victimisation" (Fitz-Gibbon 2020: n.p.). Because institutions routinely hinder and harm rather than help, thus exacerbating the original experience of suffering, many survivors experience "a continuation of the violence and abuse that they were subjected to by their current or ex-partners" (Guggisberg & Fisher 2010: 25).

But conceptualising this as revictimisation or secondary victimisation does not go far enough. To more accurately and adequately understand and depict these harms, and notably the *experience* of these harms, I nominate reconceptualising them as a form of state crime. As the following collection of evidence and first-hand accounts highlight, revictimisation is not just the result of poorly designed, inadequately esourced institutions manned by ill-informed and insensitive officials who disregard traumatic experience and inadvertently reproduce it, as has been previously suggested. Nor is it merely retraumatising because criminal and civil justice processes are inherently – and indeed specifically designed to be – challenging, confronting, and adversarial. Rather, these experiences are actually unique, distinctive, and independent harms that not only *reflect* and *compound* previous experiences of victimisation – they actually constitute original experiences of micro-oppression, micro-aggression, and even gross abuse and violence. Survivors explicitly identify the state functioning as a criminal actor and agent in their accounts, which points to these as experiences of state crime.

Directly oppressive, aggressive, and abusive experiences are common in domestic violence survivors' accounts of contact with legal institutions in Western liberal-democratic contexts. Exemplifying the experiences of numerous participants in Australian studies, one woman categorically described "the entire legal system oppressive" of victims (in Cameron 2014: 32; also see e.g. Preston & Gyde 2005; Laing 2010; 2017). In the United States, Bumiller's (2008) research with survivors uncovers widespread aggressive and abusive treatment by state officials across the legal system, with law enforcement officers a common source of verbal and psychological abuse. In one cited example, police on a routine street patrol not only witnessed the woman being assaulted by her partner and failed to intervene, but later that day ridiculed the woman about her victimisation. This shows police not only neglecting their mandated responsibilities and being passively complicit bystanders to domestic violence – it shows them being active supporters and agents of abuse. When police directly participate in exacerbating domestic violence, their actions have an amplified impact because their status as state institutional representatives endows them with unique power and authority. The victim in this case, along with others in Bumiller's study, described the profound sense of injustice and betrayal when official state representatives were the source of abuse, rather than just a regular individual citizen. This experience is echoed in survivor accounts across diverse contexts and demonstrates the value in understanding these harms not just as secondary victimisation but also as a form of state criminality.

The family court is a particularly common source of oppression and abuse for domestic violence victims, positioning this state institution as a participant in and direct perpetrator of harm. In Gutowski and Goodman's (2019) qualitative research with women involved in the United States family law system, participants specifically described re-experiencing coercive controlling victimisation. Many women recounted having their personality criticised and their mental stability questioned during court proceedings, just as their former partner had done when psychologically abusing them. Daniella (in Gutowski & Goodman 2019: 7), for example, was demeaned by the family court judge, branded "abnormal", and labelled as someone who responded in an "abnormal way to normal stimuli" rather than acknowledged as a trauma survivor. Olivia (in Gutowski & Goodman 2019: 11) also reflected on the disempowering parallels between her ex-partner's psychological abuse and her family court experiences, describing the sense that she was "invisible" and her "words had no weight". Laing's (2017) Australian research also shows that many women engaging with the family law system experience the same silencing, controlling, and undermining treatment that their ex-partner had subjected them to. This is echoed by Steph (in Coy et al. 2015: 60), who described how going through the United Kingdom's family court system was "like going through the abuse again … That abuse that I suffered in my marriage … it's been the same thing in the legal system". Aligning with Bumiller's (2008) findings, women in these studies identify the particularly significant impact of being harmed by a powerful state institution rather than just an abusive individual. Olivia (in Gutowski & Goodman 2019: 11) aptly described the sense of profound betrayal when she was "victimised by the very same system that is supposed to protect me".

The state social service system is another common institutional avenue through which agentic abusive domestic violence state crime operates. In Australia and the United States, researchers identify the persistently dismissive, disenfranchising, and sometimes degrading and abusive treatment that subjugated citizens receive from state social service officials (Harris 2005;

Murphy et al. 2011; Cook et al. 2015). Often in direct contradiction with principles and practices enshrined in institutional policy, this treatment consistently confirms vulnerable citizens' stigmatisation and oppresses them at the micro-level of interpersonal interaction. Single mothers are particular targets. Natalier's (2017: 622) research reveals frequent "micro-aggressions" against single mothers by social service officials via demeaning attitudes, derogatory language, verbal harassment, and generally disrespectful, oppressive, and aggressive behaviour. Other research reflects these findings, showing how state agents routinely approach single mothers with criticism and contempt, communicating the underlying belief that they are morally irresponsible, blameworthy, and undeserving of state support (Bumiller 2008; McArthur et al. 2013; Harris 2015).

In Australia, the everyday interface between single mother domestic violence survivors and the Child Support Agency is a particular source of harm. Studies indicate that the pervasive negativity expressed by Agency officials towards mothers seeking help with child support issues follows systematic discriminatory patterns and is underpinned by strong sexist undercurrents (e.g. Branigan 2007; Cameron 2014; Cook 2015; Natalier et al. 2015; Natalier 2017; 2018). When attempting to communicate about child support issues such as their ex-partner's payment evasion, women in these studies routinely faced derision, contempt, criticism, and victim-blaming. They also experienced Agency representatives' annoyance with their enquiries, and the labelling of any expectations regarding accurate assessments or consistent payments as unrealistic and presumptuous. Both Australian and United States researchers identify pervasive attitudes within social service systems that women should be grateful for any child support payments, no matter how paltry, partial, or irregular (Harris 2005; Harris 2015; Natalier 2018). In line with the prevailing societal belief that single mothers receive lucrative payments to the detriment of fathers, Natalier et al. (2015) found that some officials considered women greedy for seeking child support and actively discouraged them from using the system to pursue claims. For instance, Wendy was told by staff to "count yourself lucky" because she received a few irregular, partial payments from her ex-partner (25), and Ida was repeatedly told by different Agency representatives that "you'll never get what you want … you should just give up" (42).

Cross-contextually, women describe consistent parallels between their experiences of intimate partner abuse and their oppressive and abusive interactions with state social services. A common refrain is the stark similarities between social service institutions' intense surveillance and regulation of their personal affairs and intimate partner coercive control. Serena (in Cameron 2014: 44), for example, described the sense of invasion and violation that characterised her experiences with Australian agencies. She was coerced into providing unnecessary personal details to the Federal Department of Human Services which made her "feel laid out [and] absolutely raped". She was then subjected to invasive interrogation and criticism over the micro-details of her life, including being "questioned over everything [and having] a Child Support person say 'You shouldn't have a cat [because you] shouldn't be spending money on cat food'". Jasmine (in Branigan 2007: 34–5) suggested that getting out of an abusive relationship and entering the world of interactions with state-based social services equated to "exchanging one abuser for a whole system". Like many other participants who spoke of state bureaucracies directly contributing to, and even perpetrating abuse, Jasmine asserted that "it is the systems that abuse you too … All the government institutions assist in the abuse of women". In the United States also, Vicki (in Bumiller 2008: 123) confirmed this pervasive experience of state harm:

> *You become a battered woman and then [try] to get assistance or any help from any social service agency … you get battered by them too, you get battered by a society and a system … it's very traumatic because it's like, I feel like I am just being beat in the head … over and over and over again.*

As Patrick et al. (2008) and Bumiller (2008) put it, these women have merely replaced one coercive and violent relationship with another.

For a woman already accustomed to the denigration, control, and micro-management of an abusive relationship, experiencing invasive, oppressive, controlling, aggressive, and abusive treatment by the state and its agents has an amplified effect. By reinforcing the disempowering experience of intimate partner abuse, Natalier et al. (2015: 33) argue that these institutional practices "exacerbate the intimidating, manipulating, monitoring, denying, destroying and deceiving behaviours that constitute coercive control". Many psychologically abusive relationships involve specific attacks on victims' womanhood, motherhood, and parenting capacity (see e.g. Evans 2006; Stark 2007; McKenzie et al. 2016; Meyer & Frost 2019); therefore, being subjected to similar interrogation and criticism by state agents powerfully resonates for these women. State institutional abuse also functions as both practical and symbolic reinforcement of abusive former partners' ongoing control over their lives and a reminder of the stigmatisation and precarity of single motherhood (Natalier 2017; 2018).

When state institutions directly oppress and abuse domestic violence victims, this compounds and augments the experience of interpersonal abuse. However, this is not just an experience of secondary victimisation. I argue that when state institutions, agencies, and officials treat victims in oppressive, aggressive, and abusive ways, they are at once *participating* in domestic violence and *perpetrating* agentic state abuse. In different contexts, women's accounts of their victimisation by the state are framed in explicitly active, agentic, and criminal terms that denote these experiences *as* direct state violence. Women do not just recount state failures, systemic oversights, or even harmful or abusive treatment that exacerbates their previous interpersonal victimisation. Rather, they use explicit action verbs and animated metaphors to describe these experiences of state harm. They describe being "raped", "abused", "battered", and "beat in the head" by the state, its institutions, and systems (see e.g. Branigan 2007; Bumiller 2008; Cameron 2014; Natalier 2017; Gutowski & Goodman 2019). This testimony shows the state apparatus functioning as more than just a reflection or extension of previous victimisation; according to these accounts, the state is distinctly experienced *as* an agentic perpetrator. In fact, when participants' concerns are "centred on indignities perpetrated by the system rather than the individual men who battered them" (Bumiller 2008: 109), it highlights that abuse emanating from state institutions is not supplementary or peripheral, but *central* to, and arguably *more* significant than interpersonal domestic victimisation.

In accordance with a survivor-centred approach to defining state crime, we need to consider and incorporate these accounts of harm that explicitly label the state as actor and agent. As state crime authors have suggested, definitions of state crime should constantly evolve to incorporate bottom-up as well as top-down perspectives (e.g. Ward & Green 2016; Balint 2019). Accordingly, we need to specifically include the *experiential* dimensions of the harmful state encounters that domestic violence survivors testify to. Since the theme of state institutions *as* perpetrators resonates with survivors across a range of contexts, I argue that it is important to identify and name these state institutions and their officials as active participants in domestic violence, as agents of harm, and the oppression and abuse as state institutional criminality. This also has important implications for responding to the harm, as I further explore in the final chapter.

I now turn to the most direct manifestations of agentic abusive state institutional criminality and consider how the family court apparatus can function as direct perpetrator of state violence against intimate partner and child abuse survivors. First, through the lens of a particular Australian case, I explore the notion of the family court as the site, vehicle, and perpetrator of direct intimate coercive control and unmediated state institutional violence against a mother and child who alleged domestic victimisation. Based on an analysis of the court's Reasons for Judgement and direct testimonial excerpts, I argue that the family court and judge actually *constructed* and *enacted* an intimate abusive relationship with the mother victim-survivor and perpetrated direct institutional coercion and abuse against her and, by extension, the child.

Tyler v Sullivan (FCA 2014) was a child custody case where both parents were seeking sole custody of their son. The mother alleged paternal sexual abuse of the child many years prior, when he was aged two and three, and argued that he would be at ongoing risk if placed in his father's unsupervised care. The father's legal team made no allegations of physical or sexual abuse by the mother but argued that her allegations were entirely fabricated and that she was psychiatrically ill and an emotional risk to the child. The mother's case was based on extensive, detailed, and cogent evidence indicating genuine and well-founded concerns that paternal abuse had occurred. She presented details of many conversations and interactions with her son during which he confided specific scenarios involving sexual abuse by his father. Testimony from multiple professionals including childcare workers documented sudden and significant verbal and behavioural developmental delays and indications of significant psychological disturbance in the boy which correlated precisely with the alleged abuse in terms of timing and likely impact. The mother could not provide physical evidence of the abuse, as is commonly the case, and evidence from child protection interviews with the child were inconclusive, given the boy's young age and limited verbal skills at the time. However, he had referred in officially documented child protection interviews to his father causing him "hurties", to being "very sore", and to not liking his father (FCA 2014: 56–7).

Yet, despite strong indicators of the mother's intelligence, rationality, and reliability, and her account being supported by an expert witness with extensive academic and practitioner knowledge of child abuse, the court dismissed her arguments, deemed both her and the child psychiatrically ill, and ruled in favour of the father. The judge accepted arguments from psychiatrists on the father's legal team that the child's significant psychological and developmental abnormalities, which emerged at precisely the time the mother alleged abuse occurred, were spontaneous "Early Onset Psychiatric Disorder" (160) and dismissed the relevance of exploring causal or precipitating factors for the boy's dramatic regression. In assessing Ms Sullivan, the judge accepted and directly cited testimony from one of the father's psychiatric witnesses, who had asserted without consultation or diagnostic assessment that "the mother meets the criteria for diagnosis of the Psychotic Illness 'Delusional Disorder' because she holds with absolute conviction her belief that her son had been sexually abused by his father" (Dr R in FCA 2014: 129–30). Chiefly because of her belief and her refusal to engage in an abstract legal game of hypotheticals during questioning, Ms Sullivan was pathologised by psychiatry and the law. Justice Watts concluded his comprehensive medicalisation of her by definitively stating that "I have found that the mother has a mental illness. It needs to be treated. It cannot be treated until the mother concedes she could have been wrong" (187). Taking this stigmatisation process even further, the judge deemed her a serious psychological risk to the child because she was seen to have coached and manipulated her son based on so-called false allegations. Confirming Conte's (2018: 31) conclusion that family courts tend to "give more emphasis to the risk of emotional abuse perpetrated by the mother [than] the risk of sexual abuse by the father", in this case, the father was awarded full custody and parental responsibility and the mother was prohibited from any face-to-face contact with her child.

I argue that the court in this case actively discriminated against and abused Ms Sullivan in several ways. First, the judge uniquely allocated doubt and scepticism to her based on the sexist framing of women as innately predisposed to irrationality, instability, mental illness, and manipulative and harmful behaviours. This was then used as the basis for dismissing her claims, stigmatising her, essentially erasing her status as a mother, and removing her child from her care. I argue that Ms Sullivan – both an unacknowledged victim of coercive controlling domestic violence and a mother attempting to protect her son from a perceived risk of paternal sex abuse – was not only oppressed by law; the court actually constructed and enacted an intimate coercive controlling relationship with her in which she was comprehensively silenced, gaslit, stigmatised, and ultimately disenfranchised and censured.

The foundations for this coercive controlling relationship pre-dated case proceedings, commencing with the inequality between the under-resourced, self-represented individual woman and her powerful and well-equipped adversaries: a superiorly resourced male ex-partner backed by a legal team including psychiatric 'experts', and ultimately also the male judge who sided with this team. In terms of financial and gendered power (although notably not intellectual capacity), this woman was no match for those who ended up thoroughly oppressing her. Like a coercive controlling intimate relationship, the inherent power imbalance between the individual and the court meant that the court's capacity to interpret information, make decisions, and coerce and control, was absolute. Also like in an intimate partnership from which a victim cannot escape due to the perpetrator's power over her, Ms Sullivan was compelled into intense, repeated, and oppressive contact with the family law system because she had dared to raise allegations of male violence. Like so many other mothers seeking to protect their children from a perceived risk of abuse, she had already experienced protracted legal proceedings, had suffered chronic stress-induced illness, and had experienced the system as repeatedly unreceptive to her concerns for her son's safety and welfare (see FCA 2014).

During the case itself, this unreceptive dynamic continued, with the court not only being hostile to Ms Sullivan and her case but also adopting psychological abuse tactics like those used by domestic violence perpetrators. Like an intimate coercive controlling partner, the judge and the court interrogated and demeaned her, scrutinised her every decision and action relating to her son's care, accused her of dishonesty, questioned her sanity, gaslit her, and labelled her psychiatrically ill. Also like a coercive controlling relationship, Ms Sullivan was subjected to particularly harsh treatment when she confronted dominant notions of appropriately deferent female behaviour, as occurred when she challenged the psychiatrists' understanding of child abuse and questioned the court's authority. As she herself incisively argued in court:

> this court has itself behaved in a coercive and controlling manner. It is my concern that Family Court judges involved in this case are behaving abusively towards me and my son and identifying with [the father] and [therefore] support the further perpetration of abuse.

(Sullivan in FCA 2014: 158)

The judge's and court's treatment of this woman all fit within a coercive control analysis and constitute direct state institutional domestic abuse, and thus state crime.

This kind of harsh treatment may be considered routine in an adversarial system; however, the Family Court of Australia's 'Less Adversarial' approach in such disputes should have guarded against this. This approach was put in place specifically for remedying the problematic power dynamics inherent in many family law parenting disputes. It recognises "particular difficulties ... in family disputes ... where there are allegations of family violence or more subtle imbalances of power" by allowing judges a more active and inquisitory role whilst upholding the fundamental importance of "an impartial publicly accountable and independent judiciary" (Harrison 2007: 6, 30). But *Tyler v Sullivan* did not appear to be conducted according to these principles because the judge neglected to maintain impartiality and independence. He not only allowed the father's legal team to pursue an aggressive adversarial approach but supported this approach, sided with this team, and indeed participated in it. The judge also specifically ignored his mandated responsibility to carefully consider all forms of domestic and family violence in assessing the case. Ignoring official definitions of domestic violence recognised in family law, he summarily dismissed Ms Sullivan's account of her ex-partner's controlling, coercive, economic, and psychological abuse by declaring that "I do not find that [any] of these actions amount to acts of family violence" (in FCA 2014: 176).

The family court's position as a diminutive state in this scenario also strengthens the notion of state institutional coercive control. What I mean here is that the family court can be understood as a microcosm of the wider patriarchal state, with the judge positioned as the micro-sovereign and the parents as the immediate legal subjects. This therefore sets up an intimate familial micro-state relationship between the parties and the court. However, it is a situation where the court is expected to play the role of neutral arbiter, not hostile adversary. Therefore, when the judge sided with the father and his team to intimidate, coerce, control, oppress, abuse, and ultimately pathologise and cast out the mother by prohibiting her from a face-to-face relationship with her son, the woman was coercively controlled by not just her ex-partner but also the court and the state. This shows the court functioning as agentic perpetrator of direct state crime in the form of coercive controlling intimate abuse. In this situation, the court *is*, to all intents and purposes, the woman's intimate partner abuser. What is distinct here is that the coercion, abuse, and violence not only *resembles* intimate abuse – it actually *constitutes* it.

I now turn to a final manifestation of agentic abusive state institutional crime: when institutions and their representatives perpetrate direct, unmediated, and unmitigated physical, sexual, and psychological violence against women and children. This is a direct, agentic, and undiluted form of state crime which also occurs through the family law apparatus. Earlier, I considered family courts' agentic productive role in domestic and family violence through unsafe parenting determinations. I showed how these decisions pro-duce and facilitate further offending and why states are complicit in abuse that occurs under these conditions.[2] But states also play a more direct and abu-sive role when the family law apparatus directly perpetrates violence against children. Two ways this occurs is through coercive, violent, and trauma-inducing enforcement of harmful child contact rulings, and through trau-matic 'treatment' programs imposed on children who refuse paternal contact.

In Australia, the United Kingdom, and the United States, state-managed child contact centres sometimes enforce family court judgements in coercive, manipulative, and even directly psychologically and physically violent ways. I argue that this constitutes direct agentic state violence against children and their primary carers and must be recognised as state institutional criminality. Laing's (2010) research in New South Wales, Australia, documents examples of direct state violence of this nature. This study details several cases where children were forced into contact with fathers who had perpetrated serious physical, sexual, and emotional abuse against them. In one example, even though there was a protective order in place for the child, she was forced to spend hours at a time with her father at a supervised contact centre. The mother was legally compelled to leave her daughter there and on one doc-umented occasion, when the child cried and refused to interact with her father, staff reprimanded and bullied her into playing with him by telling her she had no choice. The child was so distressed by the time her mother returned that she was sobbing and soiling herself. Here, the family court and the state facility which enforces its rulings not only aid and abet an alleged offender – they perpetrate direct state violence against a self-identified victim: an already-traumatised child. This disturbing case is not isolated; rather, it is reflected in other documented victim experiences in America and the United Kingdom (see e.g. Parker et al. 2012; Kelly et al. 2014; Coy et al. 2015). When child victims are coerced, manipulated, and terrorised into unhealthy and possibly abusive parental contact, this shows these state institutions func-tioning *as* abuser. The active involvement of state officials in directly violat-ing children's rights and integrity and using harassment and bullying to force traumatic contact with an alleged offender constitutes direct child abuse and should be understood as state criminality.

This state violence against children also directly victimises mothers. When they are forced to compel their child to comply with a contact ruling which the child actively resists, mothers face an impossible and traumatic quandary. They first risk being regarded by their child as a harmful agent and even a participant in their distress. They are then vicariously traumatised by seeing their child's profound suffering, in which they have participated. Further, as the primary carer of the child, they must deal with the everyday ramifications of this serious and repeated trauma. Mothers in this situation experience the patriarchal state's profoundly oppressive effects through repeatedly having to conform to harmful institutional decisions that wreak ongoing havoc in their own and their children's lives. This reveals the state functioning as an active supporter of patriarchal power as it advocates for and violently enforces paternal interests without regard for children's basic rights, safety, and well-being, nor for those of their primary caregiver. When the state assures the patriarchal fantasy of necessary fatherhood in these coercive and violent ways, it brings the notion of domestic and family violence as a patriarchal state crime into stark focus.

Another way that family law directly violates child victims of family violence is through court-ordered 'reunification therapy'. This recent trend in the United States, critiqued by Kleinman (2017), involves direct state coercion, violence, trauma, and even torture, through forcibly implemented measures designed to compel children into ongoing contact with alleged abusers. These family-court-ordered treatment programs are being recommended and utilised across the country in cases involving an estranged parent and child, where the child does not want to re-engage with that parent and includes cases where children allege physical, sexual, and psychological victimisation. Given that the most common estrangement dynamic involves a child and their father, the trend can be understood within wider patriarchal narratives in family law which privilege paternal figures without regard for their suitability as parents (see Harne & Radford 2008; Flood 2012; Alderson et al. 2013; Morrison 2015; Holt 2017).

These court-mandated programs contravene basic human rights, child rights, violence prevention principles, and exemplify agentic abuse of victims. This occurs in a number of ways. First, courts harm victims by systematically disbelieving and discrediting their testimony and by making rulings that directly contradict their expressed needs. Rather than consider the likelihood that allegations of direct paternal abuse have substance and that children exposed to parental partner violence are genuinely traumatised and fearful of the offending parent (see Ferguson et al. 2018), 'reunification therapy' assumes that children need "deprogramming" (Kleinman 2017: 296) because they are affected by 'Parental Alienation Syndrome'. This widely discredited pseudo-scientific theory is premised upon the denial of children's feelings, memories, and experiences. It assumes that a child who does not want to see their father is either mentally ill, recalcitrant, or has been deceived and manipulated by their mother; it does not recognise the validity of children's perspectives (see Clemente & Padilla-Racero 2021).

Parental Alienation Syndrome dominated proceedings in a case in Michigan and led to the imposition of not just reunification therapy but also juvenile detention for the three Tsimhoni siblings, aged nine, ten, and fourteen. According to court transcripts obtained by the media (see Carrero 2015; Loudon 2015; Staff 2015), when fourteen-year-old Liam Tsimhoni apologised if he had broken any court rules but added that "I do not apologise for not talking to [my father] … because he's violent. I saw him hit my mom", Judge Gorcyca admonished Liam for being "a defiant, contemptuous young man" and labelled him "mentally messed up" and "brainwashed". She added that "your father is a great man", and then threatened:

> I'll tell you this, you don't have a nice lunch with your dad and make this up to your dad, you're going to come back here … and I'm going to have the Deputies take you to Children's Village (a juvenile detention centre). You're not even going to be with your brother. You won't be in the same cell. I'll put in there (the directive), 'Stay away from your brother.'
>
> (Gorcyca in Staff 2015: n.p.)

She then additionally threatened that all three children would remain jailed until they were eighteen, and specifically intimidated Liam's nine-year-old sister by saying "Do you like going to the bathroom in front of people?" (Gorcyca in Staff 2015: n.p.). This sexualised psychological abuse directly threatens a child's privacy, safety, and integrity and constitutes direct state institutional violence. However, despite the intimidation and threats, the children did indeed refuse to have lunch with their father and were all sent to juvenile detention where they were forcibly separated from each other and where they remained for several weeks.

In addition to compulsory intensive psychological programs and the enforced resumption of contact with the estranged parent, court-ordered 'reunification therapy' can also involve forced separation from the parent the children want to be with. For the Tsimhoni children, court-mandated 'alienation treatment' involved forced separation from their mother for 90 days while they received 'therapy' and began seeing their father again (Brasier 2015; Carrero 2015; Loudon 2015). In this and similar cases, this all occurs without the children's consent, via state coercion, and involves the use of extreme psychological and physical violence against children as they are deprived of their basic rights to liberty, freedom, and age-appropriate autonomy. Kleinman (2017: 296) argues that these programs, along with the compulsion involved and the unwanted and possibly dangerous parental contact they enforce, are "tantamount to torture". This positions the family court in the United States not only as a complicit actor and enabler of violence, but as an abusive agent that violates children's rights and forces them to endure significant trauma. I argue that this constitutes direct state institutional participation in and perpetration of direct violence against children, as children are violently compelled to comply with the father's and the patriarchal state's directives.

Conclusion

This chapter has shown state institutions and officials functioning as domestic violence agents when they directly and actively produce domestic violence, reconstruct it so as to erase or decriminalise it, participate in it, or

independently abuse women and children who actually need help following victimisation. When, through institutions, the state functions as a direct
agent of abuse, this has unique and significant effects. In liberal democracies,
there is an expectation that institutions will be neutral authorities, operating
on the basis of equality and justice and assisting citizens whose rights have
been violated by others. Therefore, when victim-survivors experience abuse
not just from another citizen but from a state institution, it is a heightened
experience of harm and injustice. In fact, intimate partner violence survivors
consistently describe victimisation by the state, its institutions, and officials,
as *more* traumatic and damaging than their original domestic victimisation.
When agentic abusive state crime involves direct coercive control of women
or direct psychological and physical violation of child victims, this transforms
the notion of domestic and family violence-related state crime into a particularly harsh reality.

As this and the previous chapter highlight, confronting the state institutional dimensions of domestic violence is of urgent concern if we are to more
comprehensively address it as the complex problem it is. Domestic violence
is clearly not just criminal offending by the odd errant man. For a harm
to be perpetrated on such a mass scale and with such consistent gendered
patterns requires extensive historical, contemporary, structural, institutional,
and cultural scaffolding. It also involves the passive and active involvement
of state institutions and their officials. As all Part II chapters have shown, the
apparent resistance of domestic violence to a range of contemporary interventions makes more sense if we understand its multi-faceted interpersonal,
micro-state, structural, institutional, historical, contemporary, overt, subtle,
direct, and indirect dimensions. Next, in Part III, I bring these ideas together
into a cohesive whole before considering what a more holistic approach to
domestic violence justice might look like.

Notes

1   The influence of state officials' everyday conduct and utterances cannot be over-
    stated. In fact, Fehlberg et al. (2015) have argued in the context of family law that
    the attitudes and opinions of system professionals have such a significant impact
    on the overall functioning of the system that they may be more influential than
    legal and policy frameworks themselves. This highlights the power and produc-
    tive capacity of everyday institutional practices and micro-interactions and the
    importance of analysing informal as well as formal encounters with the state.
2   Even officially supervised visitation does not eliminate the risk of further violence.
    Parker et al. (2012) cite a survey of Canadian supervision centres which found that
    direct abuse was not uncommon, even in these highly controlled settings.

References

Alderson, Susan & Westmarland, Nicole & Kelly, Liz. 2013. The need for account-
    ability to, and support for, children of men on domestic violence perpetrator pro-
    grammes. *Child Abuse Review* 22. 182–93.

Australian Council of Social Service. 2014. *Poverty in Australia.* (http://www.acoss.
org.au/ images/uploads/ACOSS_Poverty_in_Australia_2014.pdf)

Balint, Jennifer. 2014. Transitional justice and state crime. *Macquarie Law Journal* 13.
147–63.

Balint, Jennifer. 2019. Prosecuting and partnering for social change: Law, social
movements, and Australia's mandatory detention for refugees and asylum seekers.
In Sarat, Austin (ed.), *Studies in Law, Politics and Society*, 169–89. Emerald Group
Publishing Limited.

Bancroft, Lundy & Silverman, Jay. 2002. *The Batterer as Parent: Addressing the Impact
of Domestic Violence on Family Dynamics.* Thousand Oaks: Sage.

Barak, Gregg. 1991. Toward a criminology of state criminality. In Barak, Gregg
(ed.), *Crimes by the Capitalist State: An Introduction to State Criminality*, 3–18. New
York: State University of New York.

Barak, Gregg. 1994. Crime, criminology, and human rights: Toward an understanding of state criminality. In Barak, Gregg (ed.), *Varieties of Criminology: Readings from
a Dynamic Discipline*, 253–68. Westport: Praeger.

Branigan, Elizabeth. 2007. Who pays in the end? The personal and political implications of financial abuse of women in intimate partner relationships. *Just Policy*
44. 31–6.

Brasier, L.L. 2015. Children who refused lunch with dad reunite with him. *USA Today.*
(https://www.usatoday.com/story/news/nation/2015/09/10/parental-alienation-
case-michigan-reunited/71992150/)

Bumiller, Kristin. 2008. *In an Abusive State: How Neoliberalism Appropriated the Feminist Movement against Sexual Violence.* Durham: Duke University Press.

Cameron, Prue. 2014. *Relationship Problems and Money: Women Talk about Financial
Abuse.* Melbourne: Women's Information and Referral Exchange.

Carrero, Jacquellena. 2015. Michigan Judge Orders Siblings to Juvenile Center
for Refusing to Have Lunch with Father. *NBC News.* (https://www.nbcnews.
com/news/us-news/judge-orders-siblings-juvenile-center-refusing-see-dad-
n389456?cid=sm_fb)

Clemente, Miguel & Padilla-Racero, Dolores. 2021. Obey the justice system or protect children? The moral dilemma posed by false parental alienation syndrome.
Children and Youth Services Review 120(105728). 1–11.

Constable, Marianne. 2014. *Our Word is Our Bond: How Legal Speech Acts.* Stanford:
Stanford University Press.

Conte, Isabella. 2018. *The (In)visible Victim: Characterisations of Child Victims of Intrafamilial Child Sexual Abuse in the Family Court of Australia.* School of Social and
Political Sciences, University of Melbourne. (Graduate Thesis.)

Cook, Kay. 2015. *Financial Responsibility for Children Following Parental Separa-
tion: Welfare-to-work and Child Support Policy Winners and Losers.* Melbourne:
Royal Melbourne Institute of Technology Centre for Applied Social Research
Symposium.

Cook, Kay & McKenzie, Hayley & Natalier, Kristin. 2015. Mothers' experiences of
child support: Qualitative research and opportunities for policy insight. *Journal of
Family Studies* 21(1). 57–71.

Coy, Maddy & Scott, Emma & Tweedale, Ruth & Perks, Katherine. 2015. "It's like
going through the abuse again": Domestic violence and women and children's
(un)safety in private law contact proceedings. *Journal of Social Welfare & Family Law*
37(1). 53–69.

Douglas, Heather. 2012. A consideration of the merits of specialised homicide offences and defences for battered women. *Australian and New Zealand Journal of Criminology.* December 45(3). 367–82.

Edleson, Jeffrey. 2004. Should childhood exposure to adult domestic violence be defined as child maltreatment under the law? In Jaffe, Peter & Baker, Linda & Cunningham, Alison (eds.), *Protecting Children from Domestic Violence: Strategies for Community Intervention*, 8–29. New York: The Guildford Press.

Evans, Patricia. 2006. *The Verbally Abusive Man: Can he change? A Woman's Guide to Deciding Whether to Stay or Go.* New York: Adams Media.

Family Court of Australia. 2014. *Tyler v Sullivan, Reasons for Judgement, FCA 178.*

Fehlberg, Belinda & Kaspiew, Rae & Millbank, Jenni & Kelly, Fiona & Behrens, Juliet. 2015. *Australian Family Law: The Contemporary Context.* 2nd edn. Melbourne: Oxford University Press.

Ferguson, Claire & Wright, Sarah & Death, Jodi & Burgess, Kylie & Malouff, John. 2018. Allegations of child sexual abuse in parenting disputes: An examination of judicial determinations in the Family Court of Australia. *Journal of Child Custody* 15(2). 93–115.

Fitz-Gibbon, Kate. 2020. *Waiting Decades to Reduce Domestic Abuse Isn't an Option.* Australian and New Zealand School of Government (ANZSOG). (https://www.anzsog.edu.au/resource-library/news-media/waiting-decades-to-reduce-domestic-abuse-isnt-an-option)

Flood, Michael. 2012. Separated fathers and the fathers' rights movement. *Journal of Family Studies* 18(2/3). 235–45.

Gallagher, Eddie. 2004. Parents victimised by their children. *Australian and New Zealand Journal of Family Therapy* 25(1). 1–12.

Gloor, Daniela & Meier, Hanna. 2013. "Clouds darkening the blue marital sky": How language in police reports (re)constructs intimate partner homicides. In Klein, Renate (ed.), *Framing Sexual and Domestic Violence through Language*, 57–86. New York: Palgrave Macmillan.

Graham, Mekada & Schiele, Jerome. 2010. Equality-of-oppressions and anti-discriminatory models in social work: Reflections from the USA and UK. *European Journal of Social Work* 13(2). 231–44.

Green, Penny & Ward, Tony. 2000. State crime, human rights and the limits of criminology. *Social Justice* 27(1). 101–15.

Green, Penny & Ward, Tony. 2004. *State Crime: Governments, Violence and Corruption.* London: Pluto Press.

Guggisberg, Marika & Fisher, Colleen. 2010. Abused women's double jeopardy interacting with law enforcement on issues of intimate partner violence. *Women against Violence* 22. 18–27.

Gutowski, Ellen & Goodman, Lisa. 2019. "Like I'm invisible": IPV survivor-mothers' perceptions of seeking child custody through the Family Court system. *Journal of Family Violence* 35. 441–57.

Harne, Lynne & Radford, Jill. 2008. *Tackling Domestic Violence: Theories, Policies and Practice.* Maidenhead: Open University Press.

Harris, Deborah. 2015. "You just have to look at it as a gift": Low-income single mothers' experiences of the child support system. *Journal of Poverty* 19(1). 88–108.

Harris, Nonie. 2005. *The Effects of Ideological Decision-making on the Materiality of Women's Lives: A Comparative Study of Child Care Subsidy Policies and Services in Australia and California*. James Cook University, Australia. Networked Digital Library of Theses & Dissertations.

Harrison, Margaret. 2007. *Finding a Better way: A Bold Departure from the Traditional Common Law Approach to the Conduct of Legal Proceedings*. Canberra: Family Court of Australia.

Holt, Stephanie. 2017. Domestic violence and the paradox of post-separation mothering. *British Journal of Social Work* 47. 2049–67.

Howard, Jo. 2011. *Adolescent Violence in the Home: The Missing Link in Family Violence Prevention and Response*. Stakeholder Paper 11, Australian Domestic and Family Violence Clearinghouse.

Howard, Jo & Rottem, Naomi. 2008. *It All Starts at Home: Male Adolescent Violence to Mothers*. Inner South Community Health Service Inc., Child Abuse Research Australia, and Monash University.

Kauzlarich, David & Mullins, Christopher & Matthews, Rick. 2003. A complicity continuum of state crime. *Contemporary Justice Review* 6(3). 241–54.

Kelly, Liz & Sharp, Nicola & Klein, Renate. 2014. *Finding the Costs of Freedom: How Women and Children Rebuild their Lives after Domestic Violence*. London: Solace Women's Legal Aid and Child and Woman Abuse Studies Unit.

Kleinman, Toby. 2017. Family court ordered 'reunification therapy': Junk science in the guise of helping parent/child relationships? *Journal of Child Custody* 14(4). 295–300.

Laing, Lesley. 2010. *No Way to Live: Women's Experiences of Negotiating the Family Law System in the Context of Domestic Violence*. Sydney: University of Sydney.

Laing, Lesley. 2017. Secondary victimization: Domestic violence survivors navigating the family law system. *Violence against Women* 23(11). 1314–35.

Loudon, Hope. 2015. Tsimhoni children placed in father's custody after controversial court-ordered "therapy." *Huffington Post*. (https://www.huffpost.com/entry/tsimhoni-children-placed-_b_8119428)

MacKinnon, Catharine. 1989. *Toward a Feminist Theory of the State*. Cambridge, Massachusetts: Harvard University Press.

McArthur, Morag & Thomson, Lorraine & Winkworth, Gail. 2013. Jumping through hoops: The cost of compliance on sole parents. *Child and Family Social Work* 18. 159–67.

McKenzie, Mandy & Kirkwood, Deborah & Tyson, Danielle & Naylor, Bronwyn. 2016. *Out of Character? Legal Responses to Intimate Partner Homicides by Men in Victoria 2005–2014*. Melbourne: Domestic Violence Resource Centre Victoria.

McTavish, Jill & MacGregor, Jen & Wathen, Nadine & MacMillan, Harriet. 2016. Children's exposure to intimate partner violence: An overview. *International Review of Psychiatry* 28(5). 504–18.

Meyer, Silke & Frost, Andrew. 2019. *Domestic and Family Violence: A Critical Introduction to Knowledge and Practice*. Abingdon: Routledge.

Mills, Linda. 1996. On the other side of silence: Affective lawyering for intimate abuse. *Cornell Law Review* 81. 1225–63.

Mills, Linda. 1999. Killing her softly: Intimate abuse and the violence of state intervention. *Harvard Law Review* 113(2). 550–613.

Morrison, Fiona. 2015. All over now? The ongoing relational consequences of domestic abuse through children's contact arrangements. *Child Abuse Review* 24. 274–84.

Murphy, John & Murray, Suellen & Chalmers, Jenny & Martin, Sonia & Marston, Greg. 2011. *Half a Citizen: Life on Welfare in Australia*. Melbourne: Allen and Unwin.

Natalier, Kristin. 2017. Micro-aggressions, single mothers and interactions with government workers: The case of Australia's child support bureaucracy. *Journal of Sociology* 53. 622–36.

Natalier, Kristin. 2018. State facilitated economic abuse: A structural analysis of men deliberately withholding child support. *Feminist Legal Studies* 26(2). 121–40.

Natalier, Kristin & Cook, Kay & Pitman, Torna. 2015. *Single Mother's Experiences with the DHS-CS*. Research report funded by University of Tasmania and Flinders University.

O'Donohue, William & Cummings, Caroline & Willis, Brenan. 2018. The frequency of false allegations of child sexual abuse: A critical review. *Journal of Child Sexual Abuse* 27(5). 459–75.

Parker, Tracee & Rogers, Kellie & Collins, Meghan & Edleson, Jeffery. 2012. Danger zone: Battered mothers and their families in supervised visitation. In Renzetti, Claire & Edleson, Jeffery & Bergen, Raquel (eds.), *Companion Reader on Violence against Women*, 349–58. Thousand Oaks: SAGE.

Patrick, Rebecca & Cook, Kay & McKenzie, Hayley. 2008. Domestic violence and the exemption from seeking child support: Providing safety or legitimising ongoing poverty and fear. *Social Policy and Administration* 42(7). 749–67.

Patrick, Rebecca & Cook, Kay & Taket, Ann. 2007. Multiple barriers to obtaining child support: Experiences of women leaving violent partners. *Just Policy* 45. 21–29.

Pfitzner, Naomi & Fitz-Gibbon, Kate & Meyer, Silke & True, Jacqui. 2020. *Responding to Queensland's 'Shadow Pandemic' During the Period of COVID-19 Restrictions: Practitioner Views on the Nature of and Responses to Violence against Women*. Australia: Monash Gender and Family Violence Prevention Centre, Monash University.

Preston, Peta & Gyde, Sharon. 2005. *Mistreated and Misunderstood: Young Women and Domestic Violence Negotiating the Justice System*. (Presented at the State Youth Affairs Conference: Working Together for Young People, Brisbane.)

Public Health Association of Australia. 2015. *Submission to the National Children's Commissioner for the Report on the Effects of Family and Domestic Violence on Children*. (https://www.phaa.net.au/documents/item/1180)

Qu, Lixia & Weston, Ruth & Moloney, Lawrie & Kaspiew, Rae & Dunstan, Jessie. 2014. *Post-Separation Parenting, Property and Relationship Dynamics after Five Years*. Canberra: Attorney-General's Department.

Radford, Jill & Stanko, Elizabeth. 1996. Violence against women and children: The contradictions of crime control under patriarchy. In Hester, Marianne & Kelly, Liz & Radford, Jill (eds.), *Women, Violence and Male Power: Feminist Activism, Research and Practice*, 65–80. Buckingham: Open University Press.

Reckdenwald, Amy & Szalewski, Alec & Yohros, Alexis. 2019. Place, injury patterns, and female-victim intimate partner homicide. *Violence against Women* 25(6). 654–76.

Reyes, Antonio. 2011. Strategies of legitimisation in political discourse: From words to actions. *Discourse and Society* 22(6). 781–801.

Rothe, Dawn & Mullins, Christopher. 2006. *Symbolic Gestures and the Generation of Global Social Control: The International Criminal Court*. Lexington: Lanham.

Sheehy, Elizabeth. 2018. Expert evidence on coercive control in support of self-defence: The trial of Teresa Craig. *Criminology & Criminal Justice* 18(1). 100–14.

Staff, Toi. 2015. Israeli–American kids freed after weeks in juvie for refusing to talk to father. *The Times of Israel*. (https://www.timesofisrael.com/israeli-american-kids-jailed-for-refusing-to-talk-to-father-released/)

Stanley, Elizabeth. 2005. Truth commissions and the recognition of state crime. *British Journal of Criminology*. July 45(4). 582–97.

Stanley, Elizabeth. 2007. Towards a criminology for human rights. In Barton, Alana & Corteen, Karen & Scott, David & Whyte, David (eds.), *Expanding the Criminological Imagination: Critical Readings in Criminology*, 168–97. Cullompton: Willan.

Stanley, Elizabeth. 2014. The victimisation of children in state-run homes in New Zealand. In Rothe, Dawn & Kauzlarich, David (eds.), *Towards a Victimology of State Crime*, 46–65. London: Routledge.

Stark, Evan. 2007. *Coercive Control: How Men Entrap Women in Personal Life*. New York: Oxford University Press.

Thiara, Ravi K. & Humphreys, Cathy. 2017. Absent presence: The ongoing impact of men's violence on the mother–child relationship. *Child & Family Social Work* 22(1). 137–45.

Tyson, Danielle. 2013. *Sex, Culpability and the Defence of Provocation*. London: Routledge.

Ward, Tony & Green, Penny. 2016. Law, the state, and the dialectics of state crime. *Critical Criminology* 24(2). 217–30.

Wathen, Nadine & MacMillan, Harriet. 2013. Children's exposure to intimate partner violence: Impacts and interventions. *Paediatrics & Child Health* 18(8). 419–22.

Wells, Elisabeth. 2012. "But most of all, they fought together": Judicial attributions for sentences in convicting battered women who kill. *Psychology of Women Quarterly* 36(3). 350–64.

Part III

Theorising and addressing domestic violence as state crime

Chapter 8

A typological theory of domestic violence as state crime

Throughout Part II, I detailed five stand-alone lenses through which to conceptualise domestic violence as a state crime; now, I bring these together to create an overarching feminist typological theory. With a diagram as a visual and conceptual aid, I reiterate the contributions of each part of this typology, explain the relationships between them, and elaborate on how they cohere as a patriarchal state crime phenomenon. I then consider some case examples through this typological lens: identifying each type of domestic violence state criminality in the case and how it functioned, and looking at how the types reinforced the others. Finally, I discuss a concept which emerged from analysing domestic violence as a multi-faceted patriarchal state crime: the *domestic violence experience*. By highlighting the seamless spectrum of interpersonal, institutional, and structural harms that together constitute a holistic victimisation experience, I argue that this concept more accurately depicts many victim-survivors' experiential reality; it also helps shed light on the reluctance of some women to disclose interpersonal victimisation and seek help, particularly from the state.

A typology of domestic violence as state crime

The diagram on the following page depicts the five types of domestic violence state criminality I outlined in Part II and how they cohere to theorise domestic violence as a *patriarchal state crime*. At the centre of the model sits *state crime against humanity*, which I detailed in Chapter 3. This establishes domestic violence as a crime of extreme gravity and international significance, with clear patterns that show it functioning as a symptom and tool of individual and collective patriarchal power, control, and violence. This way of understanding domestic violence state criminality highlights the interplay between the personal and political dimensions of the harm which position it as simultaneously a crime against individual women and against women as a subjugated group, and thus with political underpinnings (see e.g. Russell & Radford 1992; Caulfield & Wonders 1993; MacKinnon 1994; Stark 2007). This state crime type is located at the heart of the model because the official

DOI: 10.4324/9781003132370-11

A typology of domestic violence as state crime

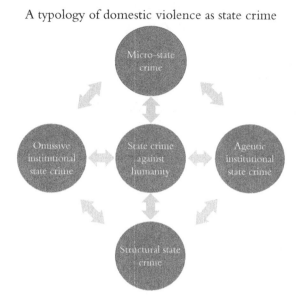

authorisation of patriarchal political power is central to, and generative of, the exercise of power through structural avenues, public and private institutions, and individual masculine violence.

At the top of the model sits *micro-state crime*, the framework detailed in Chapter 4. This refers to a way of understanding the family as a diminutive state and the family patriarch as sovereign, which accordingly positions domestic violence as a state crime. This state crime type is situated directly above the patriarchal political centre of the typology because it is the political authorisation of masculine power and control that provides the justificatory frameworks for men's violence in the family. It is also located at the head of the model to depict the chief expression and experience of domestic violence in everyday life. This position in the typology also represents how other forms of institutionalised sexism and violence flow from the sexual domination of women and girls in the private sphere and through intimate interpersonal relationships (see e.g. Barry 1979; Russell 1982). It emphasises the far-reaching effects of patriarchal power within the family and highlights the value in better understanding this primary manifestation of women's subjugation and its relationship to other forms of sex- and gender-based violence.

Structural state crime, the subject of Chapter 5, refers to the state-created structures and structural conditions which produce society-wide sexual inequality and which symbolically and substantively underpin, justify, and support domestic violence. Socio-economic, industrial, cultural, ideological, and epistemic modes of structural power are several examples I considered. In this state crime typology, structural state crime sits at the base and undergirds the whole model because it provides the material and ideological conditions for domestic violence to occur. The position of structural state crime in the model also emphasises how patriarchal structural violence underpins the political and institutional types of domestic violence state crime.

On the horizontal axes are the state crime types emanating from institutions of the nation-state that were addressed in Chapters 6 and 7. On the left, *omissive institutional state crime* refers to systematic state inaction, oversights, failures, neglect, and negligence in relation to domestic and family violence. On the right, *agentic institutional state crime* refers to active, direct, productive, reconstructive, participatory, and abusive forms of institutional involvement in domestic and family violence. Visually and conceptually, the way these two types of institutional state crime flow upwards and outwards from a base of structural state crime represents how structures continuously feed into and support institutional harms (see e.g. Barak 1994; Zizek 2008). The fact that these arrows also point from the institutional back to the structural also shows how institutional state harms simultaneously support and sustain structural inequalities.

As a whole, this model illuminates how political, structural, macro-state and micro-state harms function in concert to mutually reinforce different levels of patriarchal power. In the diagram, the inter-connectedness of all parts is indicated by the arrows throughout, with their bi-directionality emphasising how, in practice, all types of domestic violence state crime intersect and fortify each other. In Chapter 4, I extended feminist scholarship on the despotic and terrorist dynamics of coercive controlling domestic violence (see e.g. Taylor Mill 1869; Cobbe 1878; Graham 1994; Marcus 1994; Johnson 1995; Stark 2007; Hayes & Jeffries 2016) and characterised these as totalitarian regimes of private-sphere patriarchal power. Now, I nominate the term *patriarchal totalitarianism* to describe domestic violence harms on a grander scale: the interlocking convergence of the different modes of public- and private-sphere patriarchal power in this domestic violence state crime typology which creates an overarching process of patriarchal totalitarianism.

This model offers a new iteration of state crime through both an expanded and inter-connected notion of state criminality. It emphasises the structural foundations of all state crime and indicates the identifiable thread of connection between interpersonal, micro-institutional, macro-institutional, and structural violence. It also depicts the complex web of intersecting harms that constitute a state crime phenomenon and helps show how state crimes can play out through a "strategic field" of power networks and "broad alliances" of loosely associated institutions and actors (Lasslett 2012: 127). Although I developed it to conceptualise the state crime dimensions of domestic and family violence, the model also offers value for identifying, theorising, and labelling other systematic harms in which the state is implicated. For organised sex-based harms with intersecting socio-economic, cultural, familial, and multi-faceted institutional dimensions – such as human trafficking or forced marriage – it could be particularly useful. Certain elements of the model could also contribute to innovation in analysing and understanding state crimes as diverse as slavery, genocide, mass incarceration, famine, and climate change. In particular, the model can help map complex historical and contemporary state crimes which cannot necessarily be identified at a particular point in time or as a single policy, incident, or isolated action (see Wolfe 1994; Balint et al. 2014; Henry 2015). Analysing and critiquing these complex unfolding state crimes, as I have aimed to do with domestic violence, is best done when seeing them as a mutually supportive set of structures, institutions, policies, practices, and ideologies, which interact with cultural and interpersonal power.

An integrated model through case examples

At the very outset of this book, I opened with an account of Hannah Clarke's domestic murder by her ex-husband Rowan Baxter and the facets of this case that pointed towards state criminality. Viewed through the typological lens I now present, these state dimensions are clarified. Firstly, this case was not just an isolated murder of a woman and her children but also part of a pattern of male control and abuse that is repeated in intimate relationships around the world every day. The murders also reflect the wider collective annihilation of women not conforming to standards of patriarchal dominance and control and reveals them as state crimes against humanity. The case also exemplifies domestic violence as micro-state crime. Rowan had constructed the archetypal micro-state dictatorship at home, insisting on total control over the marriage and family and ruling via threats and terror. He used specific strategies to dehumanise his wife and destroy her personhood, and when she showed her strength by separating from him, he deemed her punishable by death for challenging his sovereignty.

Also like countless other women across the world who are murdered by male (ex-)partners, Hannah's abuse was underpinned by socio-economic, cultural, and ideological structural violence. Rowan's unrelenting financial, sexual, and psychological violation of his wife was largely normalised and directly contributed to obscuring his offending and the lethal risks he posed. This shows how patriarchal structures of power and inequality intersect with domestic violence and position it as a structural state crime. State institutions also directly contributed to these murders, both through official action and inaction. Even though Hannah had done precisely what authorities advocate – speaking up and seeking official support and protection – state institutions failed her and her children. The murders were perpetrated *when* a protective order was in place, *after* Rowan had already violated the order and assaulted Hannah, and *as* she awaited a court hearing. This underscores how domestic violence continues to be perpetrated through state institutional omissions. And, finally, in a gross expression of overt victim-blaming and active participation in justificatory narratives for men's violence, senior police reframed these horrific crimes and communicated official alignment with and support for the perpetrator, thereby demonstrating agentic reconstruction of the crimes.

Through another case example, adjudicated in the criminal court system in Victoria, Australia, domestic violence can also be illuminated as a state crime through this feminist typological lens. The 2013 intimate partner murder of Cathy McPhee by her husband Stephen along with the subsequent trial, sentencing, and sentence appeal, reveals all facets of domestic violence state criminality. Through McKenzie et al.'s (2016) analysis of case transcripts of the murder trial and its ensuing sentence appeal case (*R v McPhee* [2013] VSC 581 and *McPhee v R* [2014] VSCA 156 in McKenzie et al. 2016), domestic violence is clearly identifiable as a structural state crime, omissive and agentic institutional state crime, micro-state crime, state crime against humanity, and collective and political state crime. The case also further shows how these intricate state crime parts function together as a cohesive machine of patriarchal harm.

At the initial murder trial, the court heard the history and circumstances preceding and surrounding Stephen McPhee stabbing his wife Cathy McPhee to death. Multiple witnesses including family, friends, and a marital psychologist testified to the defendant's history of controlling, obsessive, jealous, and aggressive behaviour towards his wife, which culminated in him stabbing her to death when she told him she no longer loved him and rejected his attempt to kiss her. After Stephen McPhee was convicted of murder in the Victorian Supreme Court, the initial sentencing judge accepted the defence narrative that the lethal violence was aberrant and exceptional, citing this as mitigating when imposing a murder sentence of moderate length. The defence then appealed this sentence as manifestly excessive and won, with the joint judgement of the appeal court citing the defendant's "unblemished history" as grounds for a reduced sentence and adding that the murder "not only fit within the lowest category of seriousness of the offence of murder, but at the lower end of that category" (Redlich & Priest in McKenzie et al. 2016: 71).

The case highlights how domestic violence is a structural state crime in several ways. Firstly, structures of sexual inequality underpinned the whole case. The intimate relationship within which the murder was committed was marked by substantive and symbolic gendered inequality. Case evidence points to strong gendered roles and behaviours structuring the couple's relationship and to Stephen's industrially and ideologically defined hegemonic masculinity and his objectification of women, since earlier in the relationship, Cathy had expressed concerns about his excessive consumption of alcohol and pornography and his possessive and jealous behaviours. The highly gendered way in which evidence was received and interpreted in the courtroom also reveals sexist ideological and epistemic structures at play. The case narrative accepted by the court was based on a masculine model of harm whereby only injurious physical violence was considered relevant to the homicide. Given that Stephen's prior violence had not caused visible physical injuries to Cathy, it was readily dismissed as irrelevant, even though it involved demonstrable and substantiated aggression, abuse, and threats.

Judicial conduct and commentary also illustrate both omissive and agentic forms of institutional state crime. Omissions were clearly demonstrated through judges' failure to appropriately and impartially consider all available evidence in their decision-making and through the discriminatory manner in which evidence was treated in court. There was extensive documentation of Stephen's problematic behaviour including manipulating, monitoring, stalking, verbally abusing, intimidating, and aggressing against Cathy; threatening self-harm and suicide; and making threats made while brandishing a knife. Yet this information was systematically dismissed by the initial sentencing judge who stated that the defendant's lethal conduct was "totally out of character ... and ... inexplicable" (in McKenzie et al. 2016: 70). By failing to recognise or acknowledge this relevant history, the judges treated evidence in a discriminatory manner, were negligent in their curation of the case, and engaged in omissive decision-making.

The judges and court also played an agentic role by actively siding with the defendant and facilitating his teams' reconstruction of facts in order to minimise culpability. Through reconstituting the past such that "the marriage was not marked by violence" (in McKenzie et al. 2016: 70), the initial trial judge actively supported the defence's case narrative, effectively erasing the defendant's history of abuse and disappearing the aggravating features of his offending. In this way, the court acted as the defendant's supporter and advocate rather than a neutral arbiter and actively participated in inventing an unblemished history for Stephen McPhee. This enabled his lethal violence to be downgraded to a first-time offence and significantly mitigated his culpability. In so doing, the court actively produced the effective decriminalisation of prior domestic violence.

Trial evidence also indicates domestic violence as a micro-state crime, since the intimate relationship within which the murder was perpetrated typified a regime of systematic patriarchal violence. Stephen's obsessive, possessive, jealous, aggressive, and threatening behaviour towards Cathy throughout their marriage indicates a coercive controlling dynamic in which he took on the role of sovereign, designated his wife as subject, and perceived this to entitle him to impose his will over her. Stephen thoroughly fulfilled a conventionally masculine gender role through maintaining patriarchal order, controlling his wife, constraining her capacity for autonomy, and demanding her submission throughout their relationship. These behaviours are hallmarks of the proprietary ideology that is central to micro-state regimes: the notion that a woman is a man's personal and sexual property rather than an autonomous human being, and accordingly, that violence is a legitimate expression and tool of patriarchal dominion. The fact that Stephen murdered Cathy in the context of her attempting to separate shows his denial of her independent rights or decision-making capacity in their relationship, and his motivation to destroy her if she did not conform to his wishes. In addition, the court provided official institutional support for this micro-state ideology and the defendant's abusive reign. By failing to recognise or problematise the defendant's controlling and dictatorial behaviour, the court normalised male control and tacitly endorsed abusive methods of maintaining micro-state power.

Finally, the case also illustrates domestic violence as a state crime against humanity because the victim was murdered in the context of countless similar domestic crimes against women around the world every day. As data from the United Nations Office on Drugs and Crime (2019) shows, every year, more than 30,000 women are intentionally killed by a current or former male intimate partner and tens of thousands more are killed by other family members. In Australia alone, despite a tiny population, an average of one woman every week is killed in this way (Walklate et al. 2019). Cathy McPhee represented the unlucky Australian woman in that particular week of January 2013, and her murder was one part of this pattern of mass private-sphere violence against women. These continuities expose these crimes not just as individual or interpersonal crimes, but as distinctly collective and political crimes with state dimensions, since they target women because of their sex and inferior status.

The domestic violence state crime experience

Another contribution of this feminist typological model is that it helps illuminate how diverse domestic violence harms are experienced by women, how the experiential whole is far greater than the sum of its parts, and how this impacts women's help-seeking attitudes and behaviours. Feminists have long theorised men's violence against women as a continuum of harm that pervades everyday and everynight life across contexts and settings (Enloe 1983; Kelly 1988; 2010; Russell & Radford 1992). MacKinnon (1994: 5) has described women's experiences everywhere as akin to a "state of everyday hostilities".

Specifically in relation to domestic violence, I nominate an expanded and extended conceptualisation of women's victimisation experience to include domestic violence harms at diverse sites, from diverse sources, and over extended time periods. The typology of domestic violence state crime helps to depict this holistic experience of multiple forms of domestic violence-related victimisation: interpersonal, micro-state, structural, institutional, historical, contemporary, overt, subtle, direct, and indirect. Like in an abusive relationship, where a crude sum of single incidents of physical or sexual violence cannot capture the cumulative and pervasive effect of relentless and reinforcing forms of coercion and abuse (see Stark 2007), domestic violence as state crime is a multi-faceted, cumulative, and all-encompassing experience. When women are harmed at many sites, in many spaces, by many different actors, and over time, these multiple harms combine to produce an exponentially impactful, ongoing, and uncontained experience of victimisation.

For an individual victim-survivor, the experience of domestic violence as state crime predates her existence through a long history of state-created structural and institutional arrangements that ensured men's superior status in all spheres (see MacKinnon 1989; Harne & Radford 2008). This oppressive history often manifests through tenacious state-reified institutional practices and cultural traditions that entrench women's subordination in the public sphere, the social sphere, labour and employment, families, and intimate relationships (see e.g. Brush 2011; Cook 2012; Goodmark 2018). An individual woman may experience this via its contemporary cultural expression: assumptions about her male partner's primary authority in the family, or limiting ideas about her own value hinging upon her role as partner or parent rather than autonomous individual (see Hattery 2009).

Her specific experience of intimate partner violence may begin gradually and imperceptibly: behaviours that initially appeared loving, caring, and concerned become increasingly protective, possessive, and suspicious, and eventually morph into obsessive, jealous, threatening, abusive, and violent control (see Stark 2007; Hayes & Jeffries 2016). Emanating from initial violations by a supposedly trusted individual who has abused their unique power (see McQuigg 2011), the woman's domestic violence experience can then expand and extend to encompass multiple encounters with various others as she attempts to seek help, through unofficial and official channels.

This domestic violence experience may grow to include counterproductive and disempowering interactions with police, hostile encounters with social service agents, futile attempts to receive financial and other entitlements from the state, traumatic and costly criminal and civil legal proceedings, persistent state-facilitated victimisation by the original perpetrator, and ongoing struggles to receive recognition, and secure personal safety and security (see Meyer 2016; Natalier 2017; Goodmark 2019). For some women, this experience also extends to being compelled into protracted coercive and abusive relationships with state institutions, where the state tacitly allows and even actively endorses perpetrators' ongoing influence and continued harms (see Elizabeth 2015; Conte 2018; Gutowski & Goodman 2019). Sometimes, state institutions themselves take on the role of intimate abuser and directly violate and traumatise victims (see Kleinman 2017; Laing 2017). These wide-ranging oppressive experiences often culminate in debilitating chronic health issues and lifetimes of hardship, disadvantage, and suffering (see Guggisberg 2018; Voth Schrag et al. 2019).

This spectrum of harm should not be regarded as separate or distinct from the original interpersonal domestic violence victimisation. As its seamless extension, these diverse forms of structural and institutional state oppression, aggression, abuse, and violence constitute a part of victim-survivors' whole domestic violence experience. They also contribute to a cohesive harmful phenomenon that is far greater than the sum of its parts. As previously discussed, it is a common refrain amongst domestic violence victim-survivors that harms emanating from official channels – and particularly from state institutions and their agents – have a greater impact than violence from any individual perpetrator, due to the heightened sense of injustice and betrayal associated with being failed by a state authority (Bumiller 2008; Cameron 2014; Gutowski & Goodman 2019). When state oppression and abuse complements and compounds interpersonal victimisation, and is even experienced as new violence separate from the original victimisation, it highlights that domestic violence is better understood as a cohesive network of patriarchal harms and an overarching experience of interpersonal, institutional, and structural state crime victimisation.

Understanding the all-encompassing domestic violence experience also helps shed light on many women's reluctance to disclose their victimisation and to engage with state institutions and systems. Simply put, it is because such efforts are often the origin of significant further (and even new) harms. If, during previous attempts to speak up or seek help, women have experienced individuals, organisations, and indeed state authorities, institutions, and agents as unhelpful and even harmful, they are unlikely to repeat these attempts (CIJ 2015). This is not only based on individuals' first-hand experiences. Through personal contacts, informal support networks, community knowledges, and collective memories, women also come to know, feel, and recall others' experiences of systemic and institutional harms. This can naturally create reticence – and even fear – of disclosing or seeking help from authorities. Particularly for Indigenous women in Australia and other colonial contexts, state violence is indelibly etched into personal and collective memories (Auguste 2009; Balint et al. 2014; Curthoys et al. 2018). State authorities are therefore widely perceived as something to be avoided rather than sought out, even when facing severe interpersonal victimisation (Blagg et al. 2015; Cunneen & Tauri 2016). Indeed, for all women, when the state and the system are an integral *part of* their individual and collective experience of violence, this presents a major barrier to speaking up, seeking help, and securing safety from domestic and family violence. Surely this needs to be reflected in the way we understand, name, and address the problem.

Conclusion

This chapter has contributed broadly to the expansion of state crime theory and specifically to theorising domestic violence through a holistic state crime framework. The typological theory I presented depicts the state crime dimensions of domestic violence and the many synchronous and mutually reinforcing way that states – historically, contemporarily, indirectly, directly, passively, actively, and through private and public institutions – produce and reproduce domestic violence. Through the lens of two real-life case examples,

I identified how all these state crime types can function in a mutually supportive way. I then put forward the concept of the *domestic violence experience*. This concept more accurately captures the spectrum of interpersonal, structural, and institutional harms that constitute women's experiences of domestic violence-related victimisation. I hope that these models provide what new frameworks can: "the capacity to challenge existing social relationships and power structures" (Merry 2006: 180). Now, working from this fresh platform for understanding domestic violence, victimisation, and the role of the state, I turn in the following and final chapter to consider what it means for alternative avenues of domestic violence response.

References

Auguste, Isabelle. 2009. On the significance of saying sorry: Politics of memory and Aboriginal reconciliation in Australia. *Coolabah* 3. 43–50.

Balint, Jennifer & Evans, Julie & McMillan, Nesam. 2014. Rethinking transitional justice, redressing Indigenous harm: A new conceptual approach. *The International Journal of Transitional Justice* 8. 194–216.

Barak, Gregg. 1994. Crime, criminology, and human rights: Toward an understanding of state criminality. In Barak, Gregg (ed.), *Varieties of Criminology: Readings from a Dynamic Discipline*, 253–68. Westport: Praeger.

Barry, Kathleen. 1979. *Female Sexual Slavery*. New York: New York University Press.

Blagg, Harry & Bluett-Boyd, Nicole & Williams, Emma. 2015. *Innovative Models in Addressing Violence against Indigenous Women*. Sydney: Australia's National Research Organisation for Women's Safety (ANROWS).

Brush, Lisa. 2011. *Poverty, Battered Women, and Work in U.S. Public Policy*. New York: Oxford University Press.

Bumiller, Kristin. 2008. *In an Abusive State: How Neoliberalism Appropriated the Feminist Movement against Sexual Violence*. Durham: Duke University Press.

Cameron, Prue. 2014. *Relationship Problems and Money: Women Talk about Financial Abuse*. Melbourne: Women's Information and Referral Exchange.

Caulfield, Susan & Wonders, Nancy. 1993. Personal AND political: Violence against women and the role of the state. In Tunnell, Kenneth (ed.), *Political Crime in Contemporary America: A Critical Approach*, 79–100. New York: Garland Publishing.

Centre for Innovative Justice. 2015. *Opportunities for Early Intervention: Bringing Perpetrators of Family Violence into View*. Melbourne: RMIT University.

Cobbe, Frances Power. 1878. Wife torture in England. In Radford, Jill & Russell, Diana (eds.), *Femicide: The Politics of Woman Killing*, 46–52. Buckingham: Open University Press.

Conte, Isabella. 2018. *The (In)visible Victim: Characterisations of Child Victims of Intrafamilial Child Sexual Abuse in the Family Court of Australia*. School of Social and Political Sciences, University of Melbourne. (Graduate Thesis.)

Cook, Kay. 2012. Neoliberalism, welfare policy and health: A qualitative metasynthesis of single parents' experience of the transition from welfare to work. *Health* 16(5). 507–30.

Cunneen, Chris & Tauri, Juan. 2016. Understanding the impact of colonialism. *Indigenous Criminology*, 45–66. Bristol: Policy Press.

Curthoys, Ann & Tedeschi, Mark & Balint, Jennifer & Joyce, Daniel. 2018. Forum: The Myall Creek Massacre of 1838: Genocide, war crimes, crimes against humanity? *Law and History* 5(1). 146–68.

Elizabeth, Vivienne. 2015. From domestic violence to coercive control: Towards the recognition of oppressive intimacy in the Family Court. *New Zealand Sociology* 30(2). 26–43.

Enloe, Cynthia. 1983. *Does Khaki Become You: The Militarisation of Women's Lives.* London: Pluto.

Goodmark, Leigh. 2018. *Decriminalizing Domestic Violence: A Balanced Policy Approach to Intimate Partner Violence.* Oakland: University of California Press.

Goodmark, Leigh. 2019. *Punishment, Protection or Prevention? The Role of the Law in Domestic and Family Violence.* Webinar presentation, Australia's National Research Organisation for Women's Safety (ANROWS).

Graham, Dee. 1994. *Loving to Survive: Sexual Terror, Men's Violence, and Women's Lives.* New York: New York University Press.

Guggisberg, Marika. 2018. The impact of violence against women and girls: A life span analysis. In Guggisberg, Marika & Hendricksen, Jessamy (eds.), *Violence against Women in the 21st Century: Challenges and Future Directions,* ch 1. New York: Nova Science Publishers.

Gutowski, Ellen & Goodman, Lisa. 2019. "Like I'm invisible": IPV survivor-mothers' perceptions of seeking child custody through the Family Court system. *Journal of Family Violence* 35. 441–57.

Harne, Lynne & Radford, Jill. 2008. *Tackling Domestic Violence: Theories, Policies and Practice.* Maidenhead: Open University Press.

Hattery, Angela. 2009. *Intimate Partner Violence.* Lanham: Rowman and Littlefield.

Hayes, Sharon & Jeffries, Samantha. 2016. Romantic terrorism? An auto-ethnographic analysis of gendered psychological and emotional tactics in domestic violence. *Journal of Research in Gender Studies* 6(2). 38–61.

Henry, Nicola. 2015. From reconciliation to transitional justice: The contours of redress politics in established democracies. *International Journal of Transitional Justice.* July 9(2). 199–218.

Johnson, Michael. 1995. Patriarchal terrorism and common couple violence: Two forms of violence against women. *Journal of Marriage and the Family* 57. 283–94.

Kelly, Liz. 1988. *Surviving Sexual Violence.* Cambridge: Polity.

Kelly, Liz. 2010. The everyday / everynightness of rape: Is it different in war? In Sjoberg, Laura & Via, Sandra (eds.), *Gender, War, and Militarism: Feminist Perspectives,* 114–23. Santa Barbara: Praeger Security International.

Kleinman, Toby. 2017. Family court ordered 'reunification therapy': Junk science in the guise of helping parent/child relationships? *Journal of Child Custody* 14(4). 295–300.

Laing, Lesley. 2017. Secondary victimization: Domestic violence survivors navigating the family law system. *Violence against Women* 23(11). 1314–35.

Lasslett, Kristian. 2012. Power, struggle and state crime: Researching through resistance. *State Crime Journal.* Spring 1(1). 126–48.

MacKinnon, Catharine. 1989. *Toward a Feminist Theory of the State.* Cambridge, MA: Harvard University Press.

MacKinnon, Catharine. 1994. Rape, genocide and women's human rights. *Harvard Women's Law Journal* 17. 5–16.

Marcus, Isabel. 1994. Reframing 'domestic violence': Terrorism in the home. In Fineman, Martha & Mykituik, Roxanne (eds.), *The Public Nature of Private Violence: The Discovery of Domestic Violence*, 11–35. New York: Routledge.

McKenzie, Mandy & Kirkwood, Deborah & Tyson, Danielle & Naylor, Bronwyn. 2016. *Out of Character? Legal Responses to Intimate Partner Homicides by Men in Victoria 2005–2014.* Melbourne: Domestic Violence Resource Centre Victoria.

McQuigg, Ronagh. 2011. *International Human Rights Law and Domestic Violence: The Effectiveness of International Human Rights Law.* London: Routledge.

Merry, Sally Engle. 2006. Localizing human rights and rights consciousness. *Human Rights and Gender Violence: Translating International Law into Local Justice.* Chicago: University of Chicago Press.

Meyer, Silke. 2016. Still blaming the victim of intimate partner violence? Women's narratives of victim desistance and redemption when seeking support. *Theoretical Criminology* 20(1). 75–90.

Natalier, Kristin. 2017. Micro-aggressions, single mothers and interactions with government workers: The case of Australia's child support bureaucracy. *Journal of Sociology* 53. 622–36.

Russell, Diana. 1982. *Rape in Marriage.* New York: Macmillan.

Russell, Diana & Radford, Jill (eds.). 1992. *Femicide: The Politics of Woman Killing.* Buckingham: Open University Press.

Stark, Evan. 2007. *Coercive Control: How Men Entrap Women in Personal Life.* New York: Oxford University Press.

Taylor Mill, Harriet. 1869. Enfranchisement of women. In Rossi, Alice (ed.), *Essays on Sex Equality by John Stuart Mill and Harriet Taylor Mill*, 89–122. Chicago: University of Chicago Press.

United Nations Office on Drugs and Crime. 2019. *Global Study on Homicide 2019: Gender-related Killing of Women and Girls.* Vienna. (https://www.unodc.org/documents/data-and-analysis/gsh/Booklet_5.pdf)

Voth Schrag, Rachel J. & Robinson, Sarah R. & Ravi, Kristen. 2019. Understanding pathways within intimate partner violence: Economic abuse, economic hardship, and mental health. *Journal of Aggression, Maltreatment & Trauma* 28(2). 222–42.

Walklate, Sandra & McCulloch, Jude & Fitz-Gibbon, Kate & Maher, JaneMaree. 2019. Criminology, gender and security in the Australian context: Making women's lives matter. *Theoretical Criminology* 23(1). 60–77.

Wolfe, Patrick. 1994. Nation and miscegenation: Discursive continuity in the post-Mabo era. *Social Analysis* 36. 93–131.

Zizek, Slavoj. 2008. *Violence: Six Sideways Reflections.* New York: Picador.

Chapter 9

Responding to domestic violence as state crime

We are standing at a crossroads. Despite the millions of dollars being poured into domestic violence response strategies across the liberal-democratic world, women are still being controlled, abused, violated, traumatised, and murdered by the men closest to them. Of course, we must continue to invest in improving existing response systems – in particular, listening to survivors and frontline practitioners and delivering on the specific protections and resources they ask for. We need also to sharpen and augment our legal, cultural, social, and educational toolkit for combatting this problem on many levels. But we may also need a profound rethink of what is missing from current approaches. Throughout this book, I have highlighted the institutional, structural, and state dimensions of domestic violence and argued for its conceptualisation as a state crime. Now, I argue that we need to confront the state's role in this problem because it directly underpins gaps in our present response repertoire.

This is also a significant historical moment. Amidst a global pandemic, we are seeing increased rates and diversified forms of domestic violence against women (Boserup et al. 2020; Boxall et al. 2020; Pfitzner et al. 2020; Women's Aid 2020). It is also the age of social media, #YesAllWomen, #MeToo, Black Lives Matter, and unprecedented international activism against racism, sexism, structural injustice, and other group-based harms. Activists are highlighting that the mass-scale violence experienced by oppressed groups cannot be addressed merely by confronting individuals and attitudes – it must involve systematically interrogating and dismantling the systems, institutions, and structures that have produced and endorsed the subjugation and violation of these groups (Dunn 2020). In relation to violence against women, activist voices are compelling the wider society to confront the disturbing reality that women's everyday lives are shaped by violence, that victims are still being blamed for their victimisation, that men still evade responsibility, and that these injustices are being institutionally (re)produced.

Earlier this year, Australian protesters converged upon capital cities to demand justice for women. This action followed a series of rape allegations within the highest echelons of politics which underscored women's constant

DOI: 10.4324/9781003132370-12

vulnerability to violence from men and proved that speaking up and seeking help remains a risky and harmful business (Hitch 2021). Protesters were also specifically demanding proper investigation of rape allegations against our country's Attorney-General; to decry the media's unethical attacks upon the integrity and sanity of the complainant, Katharine Thornton; and to demand justice in her absence, since she tragically took her own life after numerous futile attempts to communicate with authorities about her allegations (Gartry 2021). In London, women and their supporters gathered in Clapham Common to mourn and protest the murder of yet another woman, Sarah Everard; this time the accused a police officer (BBC News 2021). Worldwide, women have been gathering to demand wholesale societal transformation that will enable them to exercise the most basic right that has thus far eluded them: to be safe at home, at work, in public, and when going about their everyday and everynight lives (see Kelly 2010).

Yet, contemporary thinking – not only in politics and policy but also in academia – tends to avoid the deeper dimensions of these problems. Domestic violence remedy and prevention are dominated by individualised, responsibilising discourses that target individuals and culture narrowly defined as attitudes, thereby perpetuating broad neglect of the institutional, structural, and state dimensions of the problem. Across Australia, there is a tendency to focus on singular victims and offenders: on the one hand, a medicalised approach prioritises victims' immediate health needs, whilst a criminal justice approach centres offender accountability and management (Meyer 2011; Yates 2020). In my local Australian jurisdiction, the recent Royal Commission into Family Violence (2016) approached prevention by focussing on individual perpetrator accountability, men's behaviour change, broader attitude education, and improving existing response systems. Despite identifying that domestic violence "is deeply rooted in power imbalances" and "social and economic exclusion", the Commission targets "attitudes towards women" and frames these as effective "primary prevention strategies" (RCFV 2016: 2, 3, 11). Attitudes and norms are disconnected from their historical, political, and material origins; institutional policies and practices that actively (re) produce the sexist culture from which harmful attitudes develop are also overlooked. By framing attitude-change education as an adequate remedy for sexual inequality and domestic violence, this narrative obscures and distracts from the deeper origins of sexism and violence in the family, from state-level institutional and structural complicity, and the need for a broader understanding of accountability, redress, and prevention.

Elsewhere, domestic violence responses are similarly limited. In the United Kingdom, although recent policies identify sexual inequality as the foundation of domestic violence, specific initiatives tend to focus on individual remedy and prevention (Groves & Thomas 2014). In the United States, responses are dominated by an individual model of harm which approaches prevention through a family conflict lens, promoting respect and non-violence in relationships; remedy is generally handled through aggressive and often counterproductive criminal justice sanctions (Goodmark 2018). In international programs also, individuals and attitudes are targeted but the structural, institutional, and substantive dimensions of violence against women are generally neglected (Salter 2016). This produces a superficial and palatable focus on attitude change, allowing patriarchal structures to remain unchallenged (also Mertens & Pardy 2017; Rose et al. 2018). Indeed, across diverse contexts, responses to domestic and other violence against women do not adequately reach the heart and the history of this issue: the patriarchal state-created and state-maintained structures and institutions that create and sustain sexual inequality, which ideologically legitimate men's violence against women, and which effectively decriminalise it through contemporary policy and practice.

Addressing domestic violence as a state crime

Identifying domestic violence as a state crime indicates a fundamentally different approach. By challenging the discourse of the state as neutral and external to the harm and instead centring it as active creator, facilitator, contributor, and participant, this framework highlights the need to diversify beyond an individual, cultural, and technical response framework. It calls for a broader range of accountability, remedial, and preventative responses that address multiple dimensions of responsibility. There are unique justice needs that arise from recognising a harm as collective and political, and from recognising that both state and non-state structures and institutions have played, and still play, a central role in its perpetration and prevalence. If we recognise these dimensions of domestic violence, they must be matched with a corresponding response framework that can address these unique needs. This is where transitional justice – the dominant framework for addressing state crimes – is useful.

What I put forward in the remainder of this chapter is a *domestic violence state crime justice toolkit* inspired by Cohen's (1995) phasic justice approach to addressing state crimes. The initiatives I propose target the state crime dimensions of domestic violence rather than just its individual, interpersonal, and cultural dimensions, therefore representing a suite of responses with the potential to complement our current repertoire. The initiatives consider important sequential stages of recognition, remedy, and prevention that are necessary for addressing mass collective violence in which states are implicated. The relevant justice phases drawn from Cohen's work are knowledge and truth, accountability and justice (encompassing apology and atonement), expiation, reconciliation, and reconstruction. These phases are connected and to some extent sequential, since many cannot occur without prior steps having first being addressed. For instance, without full and accurate collective knowledge about the state's role in a harm, there can be no corresponding apology or accountability, and reconstructive and transformative efforts will also be hampered. The toolkit elements I put forward therefore aim to generate an accurate account of the state's role in domestic violence, gain official acknowledgement of this, address multiple levels of accountability, cultivate individual and collective victim healing, and work towards substantive and transformative institutional and structural change.

Survivor tribunal

A survivor tribunal would be an important starting point in a justice process for addressing the state crime dimensions of domestic violence. In Cohen's (1995) phasic justice model, knowledge and truth are vital first steps in pursuing justice for state crimes because they provide the foundation for all subsequent initiatives. Because survivor tribunals are primarily platforms for centring survivor voices and perspectives, they help facilitate a clear and accurate account of mass, group-based harms and the role of various individuals, collectives, organisations, institutions, and state entities. This helps to counter omissive and partial narratives that impede progress towards recognition and justice. As part of transitional justice processes in the aftermath of systematic conflict-related violations, women's tribunals in particular have enabled survivors to voice their experiences and contribute to accounts of state criminality, unencumbered by government control or oversight (Henry 2013; Clark 2016; Dolgopol 2018; Simm 2018).

A domestic violence survivor tribunal could similarly contribute. Rather than being organised and administered by the state, this tribunal would be an independent body, yet still hold symbolic, institutional, and narrative power just like the many different types of "legal and political-legal" transitional justice bodies (Balint 2014: 147). The institution's initial objectives would be to foster survivors' individual and collective well-being and to provide an official discursive space for them to speak their truth and have it officially documented. Subsequently, tribunal authorities would be tasked with producing a thorough, substantiated account of domestic violence and the webs of complicity that implicate the state. Like other women's tribunals, they would have the capacity to investigate and adjudicate state responsibility and to challenge state power. Also like other tribunals, the tribunal could "implant itself in the institutional memory" and "provide a basis for prevention … through … the systematic and accurate accounting … of responsibility" (Balint 2012: 205). By publicly exposing the state's complicity in and responsibility for domestic violence, the tribunal could then open up possibilities for other justice initiatives.

Specific tribunal processes could involve gathering survivor testimony, along with a substantive research and practitioner evidence base, of the state's role in domestic violence. The authoritative, testimony-driven narrative developed by the tribunal could then constitute an official bottom-up account of domestic violence as a state crime. This can be likened to other processes of civil-society-defined state crime where, through acts of challenge and resistance, citizen collectives demand recognition and remedy for what they have experienced or perceive as systematic injustice and state-based harms (see Green & Ward 2004; McCulloch & Blair 2012; Stanley 2014; Ward & Green 2016; Balint 2019). Like other women's tribunals, a domestic violence survivor tribunal would enable a critical redefining of the harm through a feminist approach which privileges the voices of survivors (see Otto 2017). This feminist, survivor-centred approach to justice recognises that "women are not only a source of information, but agents and interpreters of history" (Zajović in Clark 2016: 68; also Durbach & Geddes 2017). It also recognises their insider expertise on the justice needs of the society. By enabling individual and collective survivors to bring together their experiential knowledge about how and why domestic violence is a state crime and what might need to be done about it, the tribunal's account could transform the way the problem is understood and approached.

Several further justice aims could be addressed by a survivor tribunal, the first being opportunities for acknowledgement and healing. This type of forum can provide survivors with a critical level of recognition. Survivor-centred processes can offer personal catharsis, support, individual and collective validation, community-building, and even profound personal restoration and reconciliation for some people (Boraine 2000; Moon 2008; Rose 2015). In cases where the state does not acknowledge its role in the harms under investigation, a tribunal can still offer a form of recognition and justice. Although it should never be presumed that "just revealing is healing" for trauma victims (Henry 2009: 124; also Hesford 2004; Schaffer & Smith 2004; Dawes 2007), testifying in a formal setting can be valuable. Victims of collective harms consistently express the basic desire for their suffering to be heard, acknowledged, and documented in some official manner (Porter 2007; Henry 2011; Simm 2018), and domestic violence victims are no different (see e.g. Fernandez 2010; Burgess-Proctor 2015; Goodmark 2018). A survivor tribunal could offer such a platform by enabling survivors not only to narrate their victimisation but also "to become cognisant of their own resilience and fortitude" (Clark 2016: 71).

A survivor-centred tribunal could also contribute towards restorative justice aims. A key principle of restorative justice is the centrality of the victim. In conventional criminal justice processes, domestic violence victim-survivors often find the emphasis on perpetrator accountability alienating, since it can result in the disregard or neglect of their perspectives and needs (Fernandez 2010). Hence, recently, the value and utility of certain aspects of restorative justice for domestic violence are increasingly being recognised, albeit in specific circumstances and with caution, given the risks of reproducing the abusive dynamic between victim and offender in traditional group conferencing-style forums (NCRVAWC 2009; Goodmark 2018; State Government of Victoria 2020). However, what is unique about a restorative justice through the survivor tribunal I propose is the focus on collective as well as individual restoration. Characterising domestic violence as a state crime, particularly through the crimes against humanity lens, highlights its group dimensions and its broad, pervasive impact. Since domestic and other sex-based violence constitutes mass persecution because it is directed at women "precisely because they are women" (True 2012: 9), justice responses need to recognise its fundamentally disempowering effects, both individually and collectively. By firmly centring victim-survivors and their experiences and curating a supportive community in which they can voice and process these experiences, a tribunal could contribute to women's sense of recognition and agency, thereby promoting multi-faceted personal and group restoration.

In addition to fostering individual and collective restoration, a domestic violence survivor tribunal could also contribute towards redistributive justice. This is because having hidden experiences of violence and trauma officially documented and generating an official "repository of information" about group and state harms (Dolgopol 2018: 93) can function as a form of symbolic and discursive redress. As well as enabling survivors to speak and testify to their experiences, a repository of survivor memory and information gained through a domestic violence survivor tribunal could significantly expand the knowledge and truth base from which we are currently operating. It could promote public understanding about domestic violence; its connections with political, institutional, structural, and state power; and how it is perpetuated through official policy, practice, and ideology.

The tribunal could also address expiative dimensions of the phasic justice process. Expiation is conceptualised by Cohen (1995: 37) as a process of societal "purification" and "making amends for previous sins"; I also suggest that it is inextricably linked to justice, accountability, redistribution, reconciliation, and reconstruction. Broadly, a survivor tribunal could provide an avenue for challenging both partial and harmful narratives of domestic violence, its perpetrators, and victims. Specifically, it could redress the "odious narratives" of domestic violence that are so prevalent in legal and other official institutional settings (Cummins 2016: n.p.). As I documented in earlier chapters, these narratives continue to systematically normalise, minimise, and legitimise male control and abuse; they also systematically subjugate, stigmatise, and blame women for their victimisation. In relation to the adjudication of intimate partner homicide in particular, courts have produced outrageous stories about women which frame them as responsible for provoking men's lethal violence (Tyson 2011; 2013; McKenzie et al. 2016). Cummins (2016: n.p.) argues that these narratives are "nothing short of character assassination" as they deliberately remove responsibility from perpetrators and reallocate it to victims.

Specifically, the survivor tribunal could offer the opportunity to re-narrate such cases from a victim-survivor perspective, thereby representing a form of discursive expiative redress. In Cohen's (1995: 3) iteration of the expiative process, rituals which "cleanse the identities of those who were unfairly blamed" are important for individual and collective state crime justice. They can involve "simple public declarations" which help to clear people's sullied names and reputations, thereby enabling "'freeze-dried' stigmas [to] be unfrozen: an invaluable way of making reparation to living victims as well as their surviving families and friends" (38). The re-narration of cases I advocate resonates with the Feminist Judgements Project. This global project involves scholars, lawyers, and activists rewriting legal case judgements from a feminist perspective, with the aim of challenging harmful official narratives and providing updated interpretations and determinations (Douglas et al. 2014; Hodson & Lavers 2019). As well as providing discursive justice to individual survivors and the surviving loved ones of those deceased, the re-narration of domestic violence cases through a survivor tribunal could contribute to a more accurate and complete historical record of these crimes and the contexts in which they occurred. Challenging authoritative narratives like those produced by the legal system can have a real impact on shifting discursive power and providing remedy for injustice (Cohen 1995; Dunn 2020). The official publication and promotion of these revised case narratives, along with ongoing funding for the production of Feminist Judgements, would be a valuable strategy for integrating these knowledges into the public consciousness. It should be sustained at least until these perspectives have penetrated the collective judicial mind, mainstream legal practice, and popular discourse.

Institutional accountability

Another element in a domestic violence state crime justice toolkit is a specific framework and process for addressing institutional accountability. What I propose draws on the South African Truth and Reconciliation Commission's institutional hearings (SATRC 1998) and Balint's (2012: 167–72) civic liability model. Institutional accountability primarily addresses Cohen's (1995) accountability and justice phase, but it also contributes towards the society's reconstructive and preventative needs. The actual investigative process for pursuing institutional accountability for domestic violence could take place during a specific set of hearings within the survivor tribunal I just outlined.

Institutional accountability begins with the recognition that society-wide group-based violations are underpinned by extensive institutional scaffolding. Therefore, a critical part of justice for state crimes is to identify the institutional architecture that enabled the subjugation and violation of a group to be perpetrated *en masse* and with impunity. The initial task of institutional accountability is to investigate and identify precisely how institutions have been involved in producing and reproducing systematic collective discrimination and injustice, and also how institutions have directly or indirectly enabled specific group-based violations. Investigations can point to specific institutional policies and practices that oppress the victim group, heighten their vulnerability to violence, or justify harms against them; they might also identify specific connections between institutional policy and practice and the legitimation or enabling of perpetrators' crimes. Investigations can also clarify various types and levels of institutional involvement, ranging from knowledge, passive complicity, and ideological support; they can also explicitly name and attribute responsibility for more direct and active ways that institutions and their agents have participated in and perpetrated harms. The process untangles and clarifies the webs of complicity that enabled the harm to be perpetrated on such a scale and with impunity. In relation to domestic violence, mapping the web of complicity would necessarily involve a detailed accounting for the state institutions and the spectrum of tacit and active complicity I have identified in this book. Additionally, like the South African Truth and Reconciliation's institutional hearings (see SATRC 1998; Rose 2015), investigations could look at other institutions – both state and non-state, such as religious bodies, media, or medicine – which have also played an identifiable role in ideologically or materially supporting domestic violence and its perpetrators.

An institutional accountability process necessarily involves holding to account both institutions as organisations, and institutions as composed of individuals. As with all mass harms, institutional officials like individual police, lawyers, and judges are "drawn into the regime" and become part of the machinery of harm (Cohen 1995: 42). In relation to domestic violence, police, as legal system gatekeepers, have played a key role in denying and dismissing domestic violence, obstructing its prosecution, shielding perpetrators, and blaming victims (Meyer 2011; Birdsey & Snowball 2013; Ulbrick & Jago 2018). In the medical system, general practitioners and emergency room doctors have been instrumental in obscuring and concealing men's domestic violence and perpetuating the harmful justificatory narratives that keep women subjugated and silent (Stark & Flitcraft 1996; Bacchus et al. 2010; Tower et al. 2011; Ramsay et al. 2012; Sifris 2014). When individual and collective actors have deliberately and strategically ignored, obscured, normalised, minimised, tolerated, and enabled domestic violence through both action and inaction, institutional accountability processes need to address their complicity in the harms too.

Mapping institutional accountability can be understood as a deconstructive process and a necessary precursor to institutional and societal reconstruction. This is because when systematic harms have become embedded within a society, reconstructive efforts can only begin once complex webs of complicity have been untangled. Systematically identifying the various parts of this web of complicity and mapping their intersecting relationships is critical if we are to reverse the conditions under which the harms were perpetrated and prevent their recurrence (Cohen 1995). The key aim here is obtaining transparency and clarity around institutional involvement, which can then become a roadmap for specific accountability measures and a policy strategy for guarding against the re-establishment of this harmful architecture. Institutional accountability is not just about obtaining information or establishing a narrative; it is about generating outcomes. If institutions are to become truly "transformative", they must "alter the conditions that enabled, and continue to underlie, this violence, and to prevent its repetition" (Durbach 2016: 366). The deconstructive process of institutional accountability must therefore be used to direct practical and meaningful action towards creating a transformed future.

Official acknowledgement and apology

Holding a survivor tribunal and institutional accountability processes could pave the way for the vital next step towards holistic domestic violence justice: an official admission and apology from the state for its role. Whilst testifying in official fora like tribunals can help fulfil other justice aims, it does not diminish most survivors' fundamental desire for the state to admit to, and preferably apologise for, its part in their victimisation and suffering (Kévork-ian 2011; Balint 2012; Dolgopol 2018; Simm 2018). Through Cohen's (1995) phasic justice framework, state apologies can contribute towards addressing truth, acknowledgement, accountability, and potentially atonement. As Auguste (2009) outlines in relation to the Australian Prime Minister's apology to the 'Stolen Generations' (see Rudd 2008) – generations of Indigenous children forcibly removed from their families by state authorities – a successful state apology contains three immediate elements: acknowledgement of the harm, explanation of what is being apologised for, and genuine expression of remorse.

A successful apology by the state for its role in domestic violence would necessarily fulfil all these elements, and specific content for the apology could be generated from the survivor tribunal's account of the state's role. Since this account would have incorporated survivor and expert testimony, various evidence, and the detailed findings of institutional accountability hearings, it would provide comprehensive insights into what should be addressed in an apology. A formal acknowledgement of precisely how the state – through structures, institutions, and officials – has contributed to producing and re-producing domestic violence could represent a significant turning point for victim-survivors and the whole society. It would help complexify the current focus on individual perpetrators and attitudes and rebalance attention towards the broader factors that have played, and continue to play, a demonstrable role in producing and reproducing domestic violence.

A full and accurate apology, accompanied by genuine remorse and clear intentions to atone for and repair these harms, might also fulfil the symbolic requirements for qualifying as a foundational historical moment. According to Balint (2001: 133), these moments can occur when a significant symbolic event offers a potential collective turning point, a "break from the past", and the "basis for the transformation of state and society". By bringing "cathartic relief" and "critical recognition for many victims and survivors", these moments can also contribute to individual and group healing (Balint 2012: 204). A clear official statement of state and institutional responsibility for domestic violence harms could signal the beginning of addressing some women's personal and collective needs for acknowledgement, accountability, cleansing, expiation, and healing. However, deeper transformation is also needed if the society is to significantly reduce and successfully prevent ongoing injustice and violence.

Reparative, substantive, and transformative justice

If domestic violence is understood as a state crime, it follows that states have a fundamental obligation to substantively repair the harms caused by domestic violence and transform the context which produced them. This final element in the justice toolkit addresses individual, collective, and society-wide needs for justice, atonement, and reconstruction (see Cohen 1995). The idea of substantive repair is crucial to genuine atonement for mass harms against groups and requires concerted, substantive, and sustained attempts to return, repair, or compensate for what was done to, or taken from, victims. In Tatz's (1985: 70) words, it must involve "giving back that which can be given … restoration of that which can be restored … [and] recompense for that which can neither be given back nor restored".

Most Western jurisdictions have provisions for individual financial compensation for domestic violence crimes; however, this does not adequately address victims' circumstances and needs. Schemes are generally restrictive and poorly suited to the diverse range of harms and impacts of domestic violence. For instance, the Victorian Victims of Crime Assistance Tribunal (see VOCAT 2016) only considers applications concerning criminal offences which were promptly reported to police, which are punishable by imprisonment, and which involve assault, injury, or threat of injury. Assistance is also not available for any suffering or expenses indirectly incurred by victimisation or experienced over an extended period of time. These requirements automatically disqualify most victims, considering the vast spectrum of invisible and non-injurious harms involved with domestic violence and the spectrum of long-term problems it causes (see e.g. Flood 2015; Guggisberg 2018). Such schemes do not adequately address domestic violence victims' rights and needs for compensation, and certainly fail to consider the more pervasive dimensions and impacts of domestic violence.

The concept of legacy and responsibility for domestic violence is important here. If states are complicit in a harm, it follows that they have a fundamental responsibility for the legacy of this harm (Stanley 2014). This is more complex than merely seeking to repair direct trauma caused by specific violations; it also requires efforts to address the lost opportunities suffered by victims which affect all facets of life, across the lifespan, and even inter-generationally. Recognising domestic violence as a patriarchal state crime implies that women be recognised as a victim collective deserving of state compensation for immediate victimisation, proximate victimisation, and for the pervasive impact of domestic atrocities on all women. Collective restitution for domestic violence would highlight and target the group-based nature of the harm and could take the form of social and economic policies aimed at substantively improving conditions for women, just as similar policies in post-apartheid South African aimed to help "compensate [Peoples of Colour] for centuries of injustice", oppression, and victimisation (Cohen 1995: 24).

A restitutive approach to domestic violence justice and prevention also necessarily includes efforts to transform sexist structures and redress women's disadvantage in everyday life. Sexism, sex-based injustice, and sex-based violence involve more than just bad men and bad attitudes; they involve unfair distribution of goods and resources (Haslanger 2017). Problems which have arisen from inequality, like domestic violence, are intractable problems, and because they are "part of the society that generates them, any resolution brings with it a call for changes in that society" (Brown et al. 2010: 4). This is why justice efforts must include specific action to disrupt the unequal structures through which domestic violence emerges, along with tangible strategies to address persistent imbalances in symbolic and substantive power. It is imperative that these initiatives are premised upon a multi-faceted and structurally grounded understanding of domestic violence. As an outgrowth of women's inequality, domestic violence must be understood not as a singular physical assault or violent event but as a systematic harm and a pervasive experience of oppression and abuse that occurs within the context of women's structural subordination (Stark 2007; Coy et al. 2015; Rose et al. 2018). Crucially, this approach recognises that domestic violence impacts all aspects of everyday life and that prevention must address diverse issues including housing, health, education, employment, business, financial services, taxation, social security, citizenship, residency, child custody, and childcare.

Substantive initiatives are indeed the only way to address the underlying conditions that produce systematic group-based injustice and violence. Such measures are also helpful for drawing a line in the sand and ending the tacit approval of continued group-based oppression and victimisation (Durbach & Geddes 2017). Targeted substantive justice initiatives need to address the multiple ways in which women experience inequality, subjugation, and discrimination which, in turn underpin their vulnerability to domestic violence. Socio-economic measures must be central to any such approach because women can best avoid, prevent, resist, and safely escape abusive situations when materially independent. In advocating approaching domestic violence as an economic problem, Goodmark (2018) emphasises the need to address structural economic factors in prevention strategies. For example, substantive change is needed to economic policies that leave millions of women across the liberal-democratic world struggling to secure stable employment, earn a reasonable income, or to be remunerated comparably to their male counterparts. There also needs to be a greater focus on economic abuse awareness and prevention because this invisible form of domestic violence can comprehensively and pervasively undermine women's capacity to survive and thrive independently (Cameron 2014; WLSV 2015). Broad, concerted efforts towards substantive redress are critical to the reconstructive and transformative justice process because it is the only way to affect the structures of privilege and subordination that produced violence in the first place (Laplante 2009; Muvingi 2009).

If domestic violence is understood as a patriarchal state crime and approached through a transformative remedial lens, this will inevitably involve affirmative action and similar policies for actively redressing the systematic imbalances that have led to men's symbolic and substantive dominance in all spheres. Although some may claim that men are being unfairly disadvantaged by such policies, we cannot simply approach this problem with ordinary equality measures. This would be to deny that systematic discrimination was what first enabled male privilege and dominance and what normalised masculine abuse and violence. It would also be to deny that systematic measures are required to reverse these injustices and to erroneously imply that the problem can be fixed by treating women as if they are the same as men. Additionally, Tatz (1985) suggests that this type of opposition has a deeper and more insidious meaning. In the context of populist criticism of socio-economic provisions specifically for Indigenous Peoples in Australia, Tatz argues that when it is claimed

> that advantages cannot be offered to Aborigines that are not offered to all… this is to deny, negate, forget and forgive all past treatment of the Aboriginal minority: worse, perhaps, it is to imply that **nothing ever happened**.
>
> (171; emphasis original)

Applying this logic to women's subjugation and domestic victimisation, failing to provide unique provisions for women equates to the denial of sex-based harms and the denial that domestic violence has systematically impacted women as a group. Transformative redress for domestic violence must maintain a determined focus on addressing the substantive sexual inequality that underpins all violence against women and actively engaging in the uncompromising pursuit of concrete and materially significant measures that level the playing field in all aspects of life. This will help rebalance sexual and gendered power in the domestic and public spheres and provide individual and collective women with the strongest basis for living genuinely autonomous, self-determining, self-sustaining, and safe lives.

Feminism, domestic violence, and state crime: Closing comments

If feminist research "must be predicated on both theoretical premise and practical commitment: its purpose being to understand women's oppression in order to change it" (Kelly 1988: 4), I hope to have met this challenge. My aim is for this book to have both a theoretical and substantive impact over the way that domestic violence is understood and approached: specifically, by enhancing its recognition as a severe, global, sex-based harm, reframing it in a manner that more accurately depicts the architecture of state complicity around it, cultivating a multi-level understanding of responsibility, and promoting a more comprehensive framework for responding to the problem. I also aim to spearhead a new feminist state crime criminology that better incorporates women's unique voices and experiences of harm – not just in war and conflict but also in liberal-democratic societies and in the private sphere. Just as anti-capitalist Marxist and anti-racist decolonial perspectives have been successfully integrated into the field (e.g. Barak 1991; Cohen 1995; Cunneen 2008; Balint & Evans 2010; Henry 2015; Bernat & Whyte 2017), it is time for anti-sexist feminist perspectives to take their rightful place.

I also hope that my work has highlighted the enduring value of radical feminist theory and methods for understanding and approaching contemporary social problems. The creative and innovative insights and modes of thinking employed by revolutionary women of different generations including Taylor Mill (1869), Barry (1979), and MacKinnon (1982; 1993; 2011) are still very much needed. The social and political sciences – and notably criminology – are too often constrained by orthodoxy, repetition, and a lack of imagination. I hope to be part of a conceptual and theoretical criminology that is more adventurous and dynamic: traversing boundaries, integrating knowledges, attempting intellectual leaps, taking risks, and offering the potential for genuine innovation and value. Indeed, understanding and addressing the 'wicked problems' (Rittel & Webber 1973; Lazarus 2009; Lawrence 2010) of the present day – like domestic violence – calls for flexible, open, imaginative, problem-driven approaches that "draw on all our intellectual resources, valuing the contribution of all the academic disciplines as well as other ways in which we construct our knowledge" (Brown et al. 2010: 4; also Owens 2016). This means working in a transdisciplinary manner and not only extending disciplinary frontiers but also challenging dichotomies of theory-practice, academic-practitioner, generalist-specialist, and layperson-expert.

Doing this research has confirmed my conviction that being feminist means "belie[ving] in the possibility of a better future, if not in utopia" (Ahmed et al. 2000: 6). With domestic violence, incremental steps towards utopia would include formal acknowledgement of the state's complicity in this harm, a range of comprehensive accountability and justice measures aimed at recognition, individual and collective healing, and adequate symbolic and material support for victim-survivors. It would also involve genuine and remorseful official recognition of the patriarchal histories, structures, institutions, ideologies, policies, and practices that so unjustly privilege men and so pervasively harm women; this recognition would be accompanied by concerted efforts to transform these injustices. We would be working towards reconstructing a state apparatus which is more democratic and representative of the diversity of its constituents, and state officials would be better equipped with accurate knowledge of social problems as well as the motivation and capacity to address abuse, violence, and injustice wherever it appears. And at the micro-level of this society would be people living in whatever independent or collective arrangements they choose, unconstrained by gross structural inequality, substantive disadvantage, oppressive cultural expectations, or interpersonal coercion and abuse. This would be the beginning of a generation where individual and collective women can fully realise their basic right to safety and security, both in and outside of the home.

References

Ahmed, Sarah & Kilby, Jane & Lury, Celia & McNeil, Maureen & Skeggs, Beverly. 2000. Thinking through feminism. *Transformations: Thinking Through Feminism*, 1–24. London: Routledge.

Auguste, Isabelle. 2009. On the significance of saying sorry: Politics of memory and Aboriginal reconciliation in Australia. *Coolabah* 3. 43–50.

Bacchus, Loraine & Bewley, Susan & Vitolas, Carlos Torres & Aston, Gillian & Jordan, Peter & Murray, Susan. 2010. Evaluation of a domestic violence intervention in the maternity and sexual health services of a UK hospital. *Reproductive Health Matters* 18(36). 147–57.

Balint, Jennifer. 2001. Law's constitutive possibilities: Reconstruction and reconciliation in the wake of genocide and state crime. In Christodoulidis, Emilios & Veitch, Scott (eds.), *Lethe's Law: Justice, Law and Ethics in Reconciliation*, 129–49. Oxford: Hart Publishing.

Balint, Jennifer. 2012. *Genocide, State Crime and the Law*. Abingdon: Routledge.

Balint, Jennifer. 2014. Transitional justice and state crime. *Macquarie Law Journal* 13. 147–63.

Balint, Jennifer. 2019. Prosecuting and partnering for social change: Law, social movements, and Australia's mandatory detention for refugees and asylum seekers. In Sarat, Austin (ed.), *Studies in Law, Politics and Society*, 169–89. Emerald Group Publishing Limited.

Balint, Jennifer & Evans, Julie. 2010. Transitional Justice and Settler States. *Australian and New Zealand Institute of Criminology Critical Criminology Conference*. Sydney Law School, University of Sydney.

Barak, Gregg. 1991. Toward a criminology of state criminality. In Barak, Gregg (ed.), *Crimes by the Capitalist State: An Introduction to State Criminality*, 3–18. New York: State University of New York.

Barry, Kathleen. 1979. *Female Sexual Slavery*. New York: New York University Press.

BBC News. 2021. *Sarah Everard: How a Woman's Death Sparked a Nation's Soul-Searching.* (https://www.bbc.com/news/uk-56384600)

Bernat, Ignasi & Whyte, David. 2017. State-corporate crime and the process of capital accumulation: Mapping a global regime of permission from Galicia to Morecambe Bay. *Critical Criminology* 25(1). 71–86.

Birdsey, Emma & Snowball, Lucy. 2013. *Reporting Violence to Police: A Survey of Victims attending Domestic Violence Services.* Sydney: New South Wales Bureau of Crime Statistics and Research.

Boraine, Alex. 2000. *A Country Unmasked: Inside South Africa's Truth and Reconciliation Commission.* Oxford: Oxford University Press.

Boserup, Brad & McKenney, Mark & Elkbuli, Adel. 2020. Alarming trends in US domestic violence during the COVID-19 pandemic. *The American Journal of Emergency Medicine* 38(12). 2753–55.

Boxall, Hayley & Morgan, Anthony & Brown, Rick. 2020. *The Prevalence of Domestic Violence among Women during the COVID-19 Pandemic.* Canberra: Australian Institute of Criminology.

Brown, Valerie & Deane, Peter & Harris, John & Russell, Jacqueline. 2010. Towards a just and sustainable future. In Brown, Valerie & Harris, John & Russell, Jacqueline (eds.), *Tackling Wicked Problems through the Transdisciplinary Imagination*, 1–15. London: Earthscan.

Burgess-Proctor, Amanda. 2015. Methodological and ethical issues in feminist research with abused women: Reflections on participants' vulnerability and empowerment. *Women's Studies International Forum* 48. 124–34.

Cameron, Prue. 2014. *Relationship Problems and Money: Women Talk about Financial Abuse.* Melbourne: Women's Information and Referral Exchange.

Clark, Janine. 2016. Transitional justice as recognition: An analysis of the Women's Court in Sarajevo. *International Journal of Transitional Justice* 10(1). 67–87.

Cohen, Stanley. 1995. State crimes of previous regimes: Knowledge, accountability, and the policing of the past. *Law and Social Inquiry* 20. 7–50.

Coy, Maddy & Scott, Emma & Tweedale, Ruth & Perks, Katherine. 2015. "It's like going through the abuse again": Domestic violence and women and children's (un)safety in private law contact proceedings. *Journal of Social Welfare & Family Law* 37(1). 53–69.

Cummins, Phillip. 2016. *How is Family Violence Recognised in Legal Responses to Intimate Partner Homicides?* Melbourne: Domestic Violence Resource Centre Victoria Public Forum.

Cunneen, Chris. 2008. State crime, the colonial question and Indigenous Peoples. In Smeulers, Alette & Haveman, Roelof (eds.), *Supranational Criminology: Towards a Criminology of International Crimes*, 159–79. Antwerp: Intersentia.

Dawes, James. 2007. *That the World May Know: Bearing Witness to Atrocity.* Cambridge, Massachusetts: Harvard University Press.

Dolgopol, Ustinia. 2018. The Tokyo Women's Tribunal. In Byrnes, Andrew & Simm, Gabrielle (eds.), *Peoples' Tribunals and International Law*, 84–106. Cambridge: Cambridge University Press.

Douglas, Heather & Bartlett, Francesca & Luker, Trish & Hunter, Rosemary. 2014. *Australian Feminist Judgements: Writing and Rewriting Law.* Oxford: Hart Publishing.

Dunn, Kaela. 2020. Lessons from #Metoo and #Blacklivesmatter: Changing narratives in the courtroom. *Boston University Law Review* 100(6). 2367–410.

Durbach, Andrea. 2016. Towards reparative transformation: Revisiting the impact of violence against women in a post-TRC South Africa. *International Journal of Transitional Justice* 10(3). 366–87.

Durbach, Andrea & Geddes, Lucy. 2017. "To shape our own lives and our own world": Exploring women's hearings as reparative mechanisms for victims of sexual violence post-conflict. *International Journal of Human Rights* 21(9). 1261–80.

Fernandez, Marilyn. 2010. *Restorative Justice for Domestic Violence Victims: An Integrated Approach to their Hunger for Healing.* Lanham: Lexington Books.

Flood, Michael. 2015. *Official Witness Statement to the Victorian Royal Commission into Family Violence.* Melbourne.

Gartry, Laura. 2021. Christian Porter rape accuser requested Skype interview with police. *ABC News.* (https://www.abc.net.au/news/2021-04-08/christian-porter-rape-accuser-sought-police-interview/13293494)

Goodmark, Leigh. 2018. *Decriminalizing Domestic Violence: A Balanced Policy Approach to Intimate Partner Violence.* Oakland: University of California Press.

Green, Penny & Ward, Tony. 2004. *State Crime: Governments, Violence and Corruption.* London: Pluto Press.

Groves, Nicola & Thomas, Terry. 2014. *Domestic Violence and Criminal Justice.* London: Routledge.

Guggisberg, Marika. 2018. The impact of violence against women and girls: A life span analysis. In Guggisberg, Marika & Hendricksen, Jessamy (eds.), *Violence against Women in the 21st Century: Challenges and Future Directions*, ch 1. New York: Nova Science Publishers.

Haslanger, Sally. 2017. Racism, ideology and social movements. *Res Philosophica* 94(1). 1–22.

Henry, Nicola. 2009. Witness to rape: The limits and potentials of international war crimes trials for victims of wartime sexual atrocity. *International Journal of Transitional Justice* 3. 114–34.

Henry, Nicola. 2011. *War and Rape: Law, Memory and Justice.* Abingdon: Routledge.

Henry, Nicola. 2013. Memory of an injustice: The 'Comfort Women' and the legacy of the Tokyo Trial. *Asian Studies Review* 37(3). 362–80.

Henry, Nicola. 2015. From reconciliation to transitional justice: The contours of redress politics in established democracies. *International Journal of Transitional Justice.* July 9(2). 199–218.

Hesford, Wendy. 2004. Documenting violations: Rhetorical witnessing and the spectacle of distant suffering. *Biography* 27(1). 104–44.

Hitch, Georgia. 2021. Brittany Higgins tells women's March 4 Justice rally in Canberra "the system is broken." *ABC News.* (https://www.abc.net.au/news/2021-03-15/brittany-higgins-national-womens-march-canberra-parliament-house/13248604)

Hodson, Loveday & Lavers, Troy (eds.). 2019. *Feminist Judgments in International Law.* Oxford: Hart Publishing.

Kelly, Liz. 1988. *Surviving Sexual Violence.* Cambridge: Polity.

Kelly, Liz. 2010. The everyday / everynightness of rape: Is it different in war? In Sjoberg, Laura & Via, Sandra (eds.), *Gender, War, and Militarism: Feminist Perspectives*, 114–23. Santa Barbara: Praeger Security International.

Kévorkian, Raymond. 2011. *The Armenian Genocide: A Complete History.* London: I.B.Tauris & Co.

Laplante, Lisa. 2009. Transitional justice and peace-building: Diagnosing and addressing the socio-economic roots of violence through a human rights framework. *International Journal of Transitional Justice* 2. 331–55.

Lawrence, Roderick. 2010. Beyond disciplinary confinement to imaginative transdisciplinarity. In Brown, Valerie & Harris, John & Russell, Jacqueline (eds.), *Tackling Wicked Problems Through the Transdisciplinary Imagination*, 16–30. London: Earthscan.

Lazarus, Richard. 2009. Super wicked problems and climate change: Restraining the present to liberate the future. *Cornell Law Review.* 94(5). 1153–234.

MacKinnon, Catharine. 1982. Feminism, Marxism, method, and the state: An agenda for theory. *Signs: Journal of Women in Culture & Society* 7(3). 515–44.

MacKinnon, Catharine. 1993. On torture: A feminist perspective on human rights. In Mahoney, Kathleen & Mahoney, Paul (eds.), *Human rights in the Twenty-first Century: A Global Challenge*, 21–31. Boston: M. Nijhoff.

MacKinnon, Catharine. 2011. X-Underrated: Living in a world the pornographers have made. In Reist, Tankard & Melinda & Bray, Abigail (eds.), *Big Porn Inc: Exposing the Harms of the Global Pornography Industry*, 9–15. Melbourne: Spinifex.

McCulloch, Jude & Blair, Megan. 2012. Law for justice: The history of Community Legal Centres in Australia. In Stanley, Elizabeth & McCulloch, Jude (eds.), *State Crime and Resistance*, 168–82. Hoboken: Taylor and Francis.

McKenzie, Mandy & Kirkwood, Deborah & Tyson, Danielle & Naylor, Bronwyn. 2016. *Out of Character? Legal Responses to Intimate Partner Homicides by Men in Victoria 2005–2014.* Melbourne: Domestic Violence Resource Centre Victoria.

Mertens, Charlotte & Pardy, Maree. 2017. "Sexurity" and its effects in Eastern Democratic Republic of Congo. *Third World Quarterly* 38(4). 956–979.

Meyer, Silke. 2011. Seeking help for intimate partner violence: Victims' experiences when approaching the criminal justice system for IPV-related support and protection in an Australian jurisdiction. *Feminist Criminology* 6. 268–90.

Moon, Claire. 2008. *Narrating Political Reconciliation: South Africa's Truth and Reconciliation Commission.* Lanham: Lexington Books.

Muvingi, Ismael. 2009. Sitting on powder kegs: Socio-economic rights in transitional societies. *International Journal of Transitional Justice* 2. 266–91.

National Council to Reduce Violence against Women and their Children. 2009. *Time for Action: The National Council's Plan for Australia to Reduce Violence against Women and their Children 2009–21.* Department of Families, Housing, Community Services and Indigenous Affairs, Commonwealth of Australia.

Otto, Dianne. 2017. Beyond legal justice: Some personal reflections on people's tribunals, listening and responsibility. *London Review of International Law* 5(2). 225–49.

Owens, Larry. 2016. Reflections of a pracademic: A journey from social work practitioner to academic. *Reflections: Narratives of Professional Helping* 22(1). 37–43.

Pfitzner, Naomi & Fitz-Gibbon, Kate & True, Jacqui. 2020. *Responding to the 'Shadow Pandemic': Practitioner Views on the Nature of and Responses to Violence against Women in Victoria, Australia During the COVID-19 Restrictions.* Australia: Monash Gender and Family Violence Prevention Centre, Monash University.

Porter, Elizabeth. 2007. Women's truth narratives: The power of compassionate listening. *Critical Half* 4(2). 20–5.

Ramsay, Jean & Rutterford, Clare & Gregory, Alison & Dunne, Danielle & Eledridge, Sandra & Sharp, Debbie & Feder, Gene. 2012. Domestic violence:

Knowledge, attitudes and clinical practice of selected UK primary healthcare clinicians. *British Journal of General Practice* September. 647–55.

Rittel, Horst & Webber, Melvin. 1973. Dilemmas in a general theory of planning. *Policy Sciences* 4(2). 155–69.

Rose, Evelyn. 2015. Twenty years since democracy in South Africa: Reconsidering the contributions of the Truth and Reconciliation Commission. *Melbourne Journal of Politics* 37. 61–77.

Rose, Evelyn & Mertens, Charlotte & Balint, Jennifer. 2018. *Addressing Family Violence: Contemporary Best Practice and Community Legal Centres*. Report prepared by the University of Melbourne in collaboration with the Federation of Community Legal Centres.

Royal Commission into Family Violence. 2016. *Report and Recommendations*. State Government of Victoria.

Rudd, Kevin. 2008. *Apology to Australia's Indigenous Peoples*. (https://www.australia.gov.au/about-australia/our-country/our-people/apology-to-australias-indigenous-peoples)

Salter, Michael. 2016. Real men don't hit women: Constructing masculinity in the prevention of violence against women. *Australian and New Zealand Journal of Criminology* 49(4). 463–79.

Schaffer, Kay & Smith, Sidonie. 2004. *Human Rights and Narrated Lives: The Ethics of Recognition*. New York: Palgrave Macmillan.

Sifris, Ronli. 2014. *Reproductive Freedom, Torture, and International Human Rights: Challenging the Masculinisation of Torture*. Abingdon: Routledge.

Simm, Gabrielle. 2018. Peoples' tribunals, women's courts and international crimes of sexual violence. In Byrnes, Andrew & Simm, Gabrielle (eds.), *Peoples' Tribunals and International Law*, 61–83. Cambridge: Cambridge University Press.

South African Truth and Reconciliation Commission. 1998. *Truth and Reconciliation Commission Report*. (http://www.justice.gov.za/trc/report/)

Stanley, Elizabeth. 2014. The victimisation of children in state-run homes in New Zealand. In Rothe, Dawn & Kauzlarich, David (eds.), *Towards a Victimology of State Crime*, 46–65. London: Routledge.

Stark, Evan. 2007. *Coercive Control: How Men Entrap Women in Personal Life*. New York: Oxford University Press.

Stark, Evan & Flitcraft, Anne. 1996. *Women at Risk: Domestic Violence and Women's Health*. Thousand Oaks, CA: Sage.

State Government of Victoria. 2020. *Restorative Justice for Victim Survivors of Family Violence*. (https://www.justice.vic.gov.au/fvrjservice)

Tatz, Colin. 1985. Racism, responsibility, and reparation: South Africa, Germany, and Australia. *Australian Journal of Politics and History* 31(1). 162–72.

Taylor Mill, Harriet. 1869. Enfranchisement of women. In Rossi, Alice (ed.), *Essays on Sex Equality by John Stuart Mill and Harriet Taylor Mill*, 89–122. Chicago: University of Chicago Press.

Tower, Marion & Rowe, Jennifer & Wallis, Marianne. 2011. Normalising policies of inaction: The case of health care in Australia for women affected by domestic violence. *Health Care for Women International* 32. 855–68.

True, Jacqui. 2012. *The Political Economy of Violence against Women*. New York: Oxford University Press.

Tyson, Danielle. 2011. Victoria's new homicide laws: Provocative reforms or more stories of women 'asking for it'? *Current Issues in Criminal Justice* 23(2). 203–33.

Tyson, Danielle. 2013. *Sex, Culpability and the Defence of Provocation.* London: Routledge.

Ulbrick, Madeleine & Jago, Marianne. 2018. *"Officer She's Psychotic and I Need Protection": Police Misidentification of the Primary Aggressor in Family Violence Incidents in Victoria.* Women's Legal Service Victoria.

Victims of Crime Assistance Tribunal. 2016. *Determining an Application.* (https://www.vocat.vic.gov.au/determining-application/did-violent-crime-occur)

Ward, Tony & Green, Penny. 2016. Law, the state, and the dialectics of state crime. *Critical Criminology* 24(2). 217–30.

Women's Aid. 2020. *A Perfect Storm: The Impact of the Covid-19 Pandemic on Domestic Abuse Survivors and the Services Supporting Them.* Bristol: Women's Aid.

Women's Legal Service Victoria. 2015. *Economic Abuse and Economic Recovery of Family Violence Victims.* (Official Submission to the Royal Commission into Family Violence.)

Yates, Sophie. 2020. Gender, context and constraint: Framing family violence in Victoria. *Women's Studies International Forum* 78(102321).

Index